Digital Business Management

Swen Schneider • Lutz Anderie

Digital Business Management

Transforming to a Data-Driven Organization Using AI

Springer

Swen Schneider
Frankfurt University of Applied Sciences
Frankfurt, Germany

Lutz Anderie
Frankfurt University of Applied Sciences
Frankfurt, Germany

ISBN 978-3-031-83176-8 ISBN 978-3-031-83177-5 (eBook)
https://doi.org/10.1007/978-3-031-83177-5

This Springer imprint is published by the registered company Springer Nature Switzerland AG
The registered company address is: Gewerbestrasse 11, 6330 Cham, Switzerland

Preface

In today's rapidly evolving technological landscape, the ability to harness the power of artificial intelligence (AI) has become a cornerstone of success in both academia and the business world. *Digital Business Management* is more than just a textbook; it's a comprehensive guide designed to equip readers with the knowledge and skills necessary to thrive success in this dynamic environment.

By exploring the interplay between AI and digital business, this book offers a practical guide to navigating the complexities of the digital age. It demonstrates how companies can enhance efficiency, drive innovation, and achieve sustainable growth through effective AI implementation.

It bridges the gap between scholarly knowledge and actionable insights. It focuses besides Digitalization on the role of Artificial Intelligence (AI), particularly ChatGPT, in transforming business processes. More than just a tool, ChatGPT is critically examined, with special attention given to applied Prompt Engineering—the skill of crafting precise inputs for AI systems. By exploring these interactions, the book demonstrates how companies can enhance efficiency and drive innovation, offering readers a practical guide to successfully navigating the digital landscape.

In an era where technology has reshaped every facet of our lives, the ability to harness the power of artificial intelligence (AI) has become a paramount skill for both academic and professional success. *Digital Business Management* is a compass guiding you through the intricate landscape of the digital age and focusing on business success. Drawing upon our collective expertise in academia and industry, we have meticulously crafted this resource to provide a comprehensive understanding of digital business management. By leveraging the innovative capabilities of generative AI, we have created a dynamic and engaging learning experience that seamlessly blends theoretical concepts with real-world applications.

Solid foundation by exploring the *fundamental principles and strategies* that underpin successful digital enterprises is key to success in any business. Through the power of AI, we have been able to streamline the learning process, making complex ideas accessible and digestible.

The *Industry and Business Cases* delves into practical examples of how AI can be applied to drive innovation and achieve tangible results. By using Prompt

Engineering techniques, we have generated a diverse range of case studies that illustrate the potential of AI in various business domains.

Throughout this textbook, we have strived to make the content accessible and engaging, regardless of your background or experience level. Whether you are a seasoned professional or a budding entrepreneur, you will find valuable insights and practical guidance within these pages.

By understanding how to effectively leverage AI, you can position yourself at the forefront of the digital revolution. This book is more than just a tool; it's a catalyst for personal and professional growth. It's an invitation to embark on a journey of discovery, innovation, and unparalleled success.

We invite you to delve into the pages of *Digital Business Management* and unlock the boundless potential of AI in shaping your future.

Frankfurt, Germany

Swen Schneider
Lutz Anderie

About the Book

The textbook *Digital Business Management* is based on lectures by Swen Schneider and Lutz Anderie at Frankfurt University of Applied Sciences/Germany. Edited by Schneider and Anderie, the book stands out for its innovative use of generative AI. Content was developed from a lecture series in the Digital Business program, where lectures were recorded, transcribed, and enhanced through AI tools. The textbook provides concise explanations of key concepts in digital business, supported by graphics and case studies from companies like Uber, Airbnb, Microsoft Azure, Amazon, and Netflix.

By harnessing AI to summarize, analyze, and prepare complex business cases, Digital Business Management offers a forward-thinking and comprehensive approach to understanding digital transformation. This AI-driven approach not only transforms academic material but also showcases the real-world application of digital strategies in the evolving business landscape.

Further Reading notes: To ensure readers have access to the most current information, literature sources older than 5 years will be supplemented with the author's LinkedIn profile as a reference instead of the original source. Alternatively, the webpage of the university he is affiliated with or the company he works for.

Key Features

- *Three-part structure*: Divided into "How to Work with AI and Generate Success in Business," "From Digital to Data-Driven Organization," and "Industry and Business Case Prompt Engineering."
- *Generative AI-powered content*: Utilizes ChatGPT, Microsoft Bing, Copilot, and Google Gemini to create engaging and informative content.
- *Practical applications*: Real-world case studies and examples showcase successful AI implementations by leading companies.
- *Interactive elements*: Includes YouTube tutorials and a digital learning app (Digital Business Management Schneider Anderie) for enhanced learning.

Target Audience

- Students
- Entrepreneurs
- Executives
- Anyone interested in digital business strategies

Discover the Future of Digital Business

Digital Business Management is a guide to the future of business. By harnessing the power of AI, this book equips readers with the knowledge and tools necessary to thrive in the digital age.

Contents

Part III Industry and Business Cases Prompt Engineering

About the Authors

Prof. Dr. Swen Schneider is the Director of the Institute for Data-Driven Business and has been a professor of Information Systems at Frankfurt University of Applied Sciences since 2003. From 2013 to 2019, he was the Dean of the Faculty and part of the extended university management. His research focuses on Digital Business, E-Commerce, Business Process Management, Applied AI, Trust and Bots, as well as eFinance solutions. As the program director of the Master's in Digital Business Management (M.Sc.) and founder of the Institute for Data-Driven Business, he advises companies on digital transformation, Enterprise Architecture, and Robotic Process Automation (RPA). His research also explores the use of bots and trust-building in online environments. He regularly publishes in recognized academic journals and writes articles on applied AI in practice. He also runs a podcast titled Psycho Digitale, which explores philosophical reflections on AI and psychology. He has conducted research and taught in the UK, India, and the USA, where, during a research stay at the University of Wisconsin-La Crosse, he led a project on generative AI in higher education. Swen Schneider studied Business Administration with a major in Information Management and a minor in Psychology and Computational Linguistics at the University of Trier, and earned his Ph.D. in Information Systems at Goethe University Frankfurt/Germany. He has held leadership roles at Mastercard, IBM, and Commerzbank, working on projects related to payment systems, mobile internet, and ePayments.

Prof. Dr. Lutz Anderie is a #1 bestselling author of business books on games, digitalization, and artificial intelligence. He is a Professor of Information Systems at the Frankfurt University of Applied Sciences. He led and conducted the Frankfurt Game Studies© I-III, an academic research series focused on the monetization and value chain of the games industry. The games industry is a digital frontrunner, bridging technology and entertainment with rapid advancements in AI, VR, and AR. Anderie has extensive global operational and strategic management experience in digital business, sales, marketing, and e-commerce with leading companies such as Sony, Hasbro, Paramount, Atari, and Fujifilm. He has held senior leadership roles as CEO, Vice President, Managing Director, Sales Director, Marketing Director, and E-Commerce Director with major stock market-listed corporations and SMBs (Small and Medium-Sized Businesses). He has built a strong, practical network in the consumer goods industry (manufacturers and retailers). He works with the 100 largest FMCG companies, such as Coca-Cola, Danone, Ferrero, and Procter & Gamble, in strategy and management development. Prof. Dr. Anderie runs a YouTube channel (keyword: Anderie) and two websites (Anderie-Management.com and Anderie-Digital.com). He is a founding member of the German Games Industry Association (game) and a member of the Quality Association for Serious Games (RAL), a registered association. He is also a member of the Institute for Data-Driven Business.

Part I
How to Work with AI and Generate Success in Business

Chapter 1
Effective AI Prompting

1.1 What Is AI and How Can It Be Applied in Business?

Artificial intelligence (AI) encompasses various fields, including machine learning, natural language processing, computer vision, robotics, expert systems, and more. Each field focuses on specific tasks, such as learning from data, understanding language, interpreting images, building robots, and reasoning like experts. AI can be broadly categorized into two main types: narrow AI and general AI (artificial general intelligence). This book focuses on the application of large language models (LLMs), which are considered narrow AI.

Artificial intelligence (AI) is the ability of machines to automate human-like tasks such as learning, problem-solving, and decision-making. You could achieve business success by leveraging AI to optimize business processes, reduce costs, and implement innovative solutions like robotic process automation or data-driven customer management. Personally, it can help you make more efficient decisions, gain a knowledge advantage, or quickly adapt to new topics.

1.2 AI Prompting and Prompt Engineering

A **prompt** is an input or instruction given to an AI model to generate a specific response. In the context of large language models (LLMs), prompts are used to instruct the LLM on what kind of text to generate. We encourage you to evolve the prompts in this book to meet your specific contemporary needs.

Example for a basic prompt: "Describe On Demand Service Companies in 80 words"
Example for an advanced prompt: "Explain the actions taken to address the challenges or capitalize on the opportunities for On Demand Service Companies. This could involve strategies implemented, decisions made, or interventions undertaken. What happened recently? Limit your response to 200 words"

S. Schneider, L. Anderie, *Digital Business Management*,
https://doi.org/10.1007/978-3-031-83177-5_1

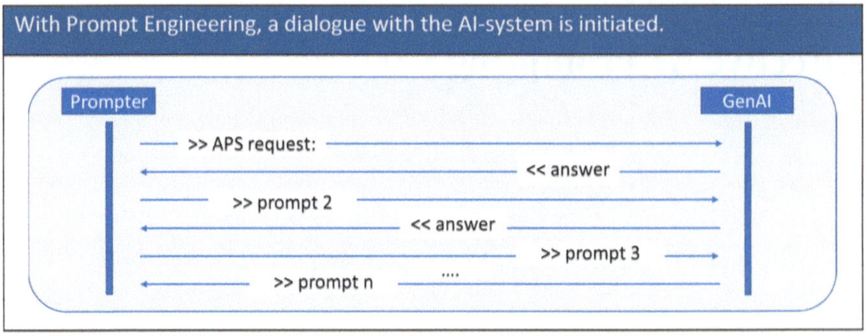

Fig. 1.1 Prompt Engineering

In most cases, you won't stop at just one question. Example application: as a leader in the technology sector, I want to find out whether/how/why the current AI trends are relevant for our company, because the background of the question is our future strategic direction, so that by the next meeting, the information can be concisely and clearly explained in 500 words and illustrated with real-life use cases. The output should be delivered in the form of a report.

This leads to an introduction to Prompt Engineering (iterative improvement of the prompts with interactive feedback), where questions are built interactively with the system and new questions are posed based on the answers received (Fig. 1.1).

Prompt Engineering is the process of crafting instructions, receiving responses, and iteratively refining your queries to guide a generative AI toward producing the desired text output. We recommend leveraging Prompt Engineering to address the "Essentials of Digital Business Management" outlined in the next part of the book and generate practical, real-life solutions.

Your benefits of Prompt Engineering: By leveraging AI and Prompt Engineering, you can unlock practical solutions, streamline Digital Business management, and enhance decision-making processes, ultimately driving innovation and efficiency:

- Increased Efficiency: AI can automate tasks like data analysis and initial content drafts, freeing up your time for critical thinking and in-depth analysis.
- Enhanced Creativity: AI can explore diverse perspectives and identify trends you might have missed, sparking new lines of inquiry.
- Improved Clarity: AI can help in structuring complex topics and presenting them in a concise and easy-to-understand manner.

Besides addressing the questions, you can also predefine your persona in the tool with specific needs or expectations in the settings. This ensures that all subsequent prompts are answered within that context, eliminating the need to repeatedly specify that information.

1.3 The AI Prompt Schema [AIPS]

But a prompt is more than just a simple question. The following AI Prompt Schema (Fig. 1.2) implies an organized template or set of guidelines for constructing prompts, typically including specific fields like target audience, desired output, tone, length, and context. It ensures consistency in prompt structure, allowing for customization based on task needs while optimizing for AI understanding and making the Prompt Engineering process user-friendly, even for nonexperts. This question structure provides the LLM with more background information as a prompt, leading to a better result.

WHO wants to understand [GOAL] with the purpose of the request because [CONTEXT], so that [PRIORITY/TIMEFRAME] can be explained in [TONE/LENGTH] using [EXAMPLES] in [TABLE/TEXT/IMAGE].

The AIPS (AI Prompt Schema) by Schneider/Anderie is based on seven questions **(who, what, why, when, how, wherein, where)** incorporating essential inputs for an excellent prompt. I [WHO, target audience] want to find out whether/how/why [WHAT, goal] applies, because the background of the question is [WHY, context], so that [WHEN, priority/timeframe] [HOW, tone/length] can be clearly explained and illustrated with [WHEREIN, examples]. The output should be delivered in the form of [WHERE, text/table/image].

Here's a roadmap to effectively work with OpenAI/ChatGPT, Google/Gemini, AI, and Prompt Engineering:

1. **Define Your Learning Objectives:** The foundation for any successful academic and business project lies in clear learning objectives. Ask yourself: What key takeaways do you want to gain from the case study? Understanding these goals will guide your approach to prompting the AI.
2. **Choose the Right AI and Large Language model:** Ensure that you work with the latest software version of a large language model, which is part of the so-called generative AI. Additionally, there are other large language models, such as Google Gemini. You can choose the one you prefer and access it via your computer or mobile phone.

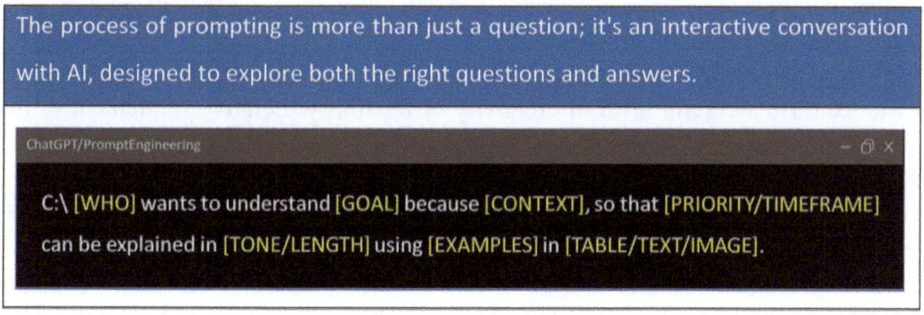

Fig. 1.2 The AI prompt schema

3. **Craft Compelling Prompts:** Here's where the magic happens! Your prompts will act as instructions for the AI, shaping the direction and content it generates. Effective prompts are:
   - Specific: Focus on a particular aspect of the case study, like analyzing a company's marketing strategy or its financial performance.
   - Clear: Use concise language and avoid ambiguity.
   - Informative: Provide context and relevant keywords to guide the AI toward the desired outcome.
4. **Refine and Iterate:** The initial AI output will likely require revision. Read through the generated content carefully, assessing its accuracy, relevance, and alignment with your learning objectives. Refine your prompts based on this evaluation and have the AI iterate until you achieve the desired level of detail and clarity.

As of the time of writing, the most popular LLMs are ChatGPT, developed by OpenAI and accessible through Microsoft Bing search engine, and Gemini, developed by Google Alphabet. It's advisable to verify the latest versions online, as product names, capabilities, and pricing models may change due to technical advancements and marketing strategies.

1.4 How to Work With the Industry and Business Cases

In today's academic landscape and business world, AI and Prompt Engineering offer exciting possibilities for generating content for industry analysis and business case studies. By harnessing AI's capabilities alongside your own expertise, you can streamline research, enhance clarity, and explore new avenues of analysis.

Start your research by using the basic prompts as a foundation. Then initiate a discussion with the AI system and engage in Prompt Engineering. Use the advanced questions as a starting point and apply the AI framework to guide the discussion.

Your key questions on the industry and business cases should be:
What industries thrive in the digital landscape, and who are the key players? How do they compete and generate revenue, and what challenges do they encounter, both generally and for specific players?

An optimal prompt balances detailed instructions with enough freedom for the AI to exercise a certain level of creativity or flexibility. Iterative refinement of the prompt can also help to continuously improve the results. It contains all relevant details to precisely guide the output but is not overloaded, leaving enough room for the AI to creatively interpret. Clarity and precision are crucial to obtaining consistent and useful results.

Through stepwise refinement, the AIPS can be divided into additional prompts that become increasingly detailed and better aligned with the desired outcome. This approach, known as chain-of-thought prompting, allows the AI not only to address specific needs but also to interactively generate new ideas with the user. It also enables a "learning by teaching" scenario, where the user explains what they have understood and the AI provides feedback.

Beyond the specified needs within the persona, the AI can be assigned specific roles (explain me on expert or a child level). Additionally, during this process, the AI can be asked for advice, enabling a more targeted and effective generation of results that better meet the requirements.

- Prompt 1: Create a model schema outlining data entity structures and relationships. Ensure clarity and consistency for effective integration and understanding.
- Prompt 2: Generate a visual model schema to illustrate data entity hierarchies and connections, improving stakeholder communication with a clear, engaging diagram.
- Prompt 3: Analyze the current model schema for optimization opportunities, enhancing efficiency, scalability, and data integrity through actionable improvements.
- Prompt 4: Compare different model schema designs to identify the best approach, evaluating pros and cons for informed, best-practice decisions.

Part II
From Digital Business to a Data-Driven Organization

Chapter 2
From E-Business to Digital Business

Abstract

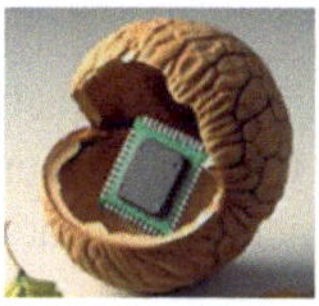

In a nutshell
The digital revolution has birthed the digital enterprise, where E-Commerce and E-Business distinctions are key. Network effects, disruption, and the shift from physical to digital products shape successful strategies. The ultimate goal is the full automation of primary processes, offering a seamless self-service experience for customers.

Keywords Digital business · E-Commerce · E-Business · Digitalization · Digital products · Commercial activities · Business operations · Network effects · Digital channels · Transactions · Digital era · Business models

Basic Prompts

- What is the fundamental difference between E-Commerce and E-Business?
- How do network effects contribute to the success of a Digital Business?
- What are the key characteristics of a Digital Business?
- How does the categorization of products (physical, semi-physical, semi-digital, digital) impact Digital Business strategies?

S. Schneider, L. Anderie, *Digital Business Management*,
https://doi.org/10.1007/978-3-031-83177-5_2

In the era of **digitalization**, nearly every task can be accomplished through online platforms. This phenomenon has spurred the emergence of digital enterprises, which are predominantly or entirely operated in the physical-virtual realm. But what precisely constitutes a Digital Business? It denotes the manner in which commercial activities are conducted in the contemporary digital era, encapsulating every facet of business operations, ranging from marketing and sales to product innovation and day-to-day functioning. The aim of the following discourse is to offer an introductory overview of Digital Business, shedding light on its fundamental principles and key components.

2.1 E-Business and E-Commerce

E-Commerce and E-Business are two aspects of Digital Business operations, each serving a distinct function within the modern business landscape. **E-Commerce**, or electronic commerce, is primarily focused on the facilitation of commercial transactions through digital channels.

Figure 2.1 provides an overview on the difference of E-Commerce and E-Business. In essence, while E-Business emphasizes **cost management**. E-Commerce prioritizes **revenue generation** through digital channels, thereby fostering efficient and profitable commercial engagements in the digital landscape. It is the activity of buying and selling goods and services over the Internet. It encompasses a wide range of commercial transactions conducted through various digital

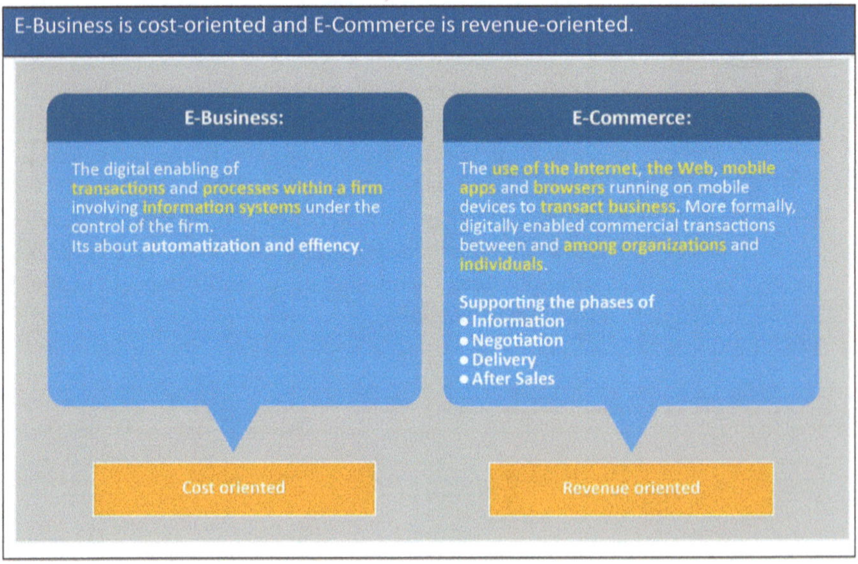

Fig. 2.1 The difference of E-Business and E-Commerce

platforms, from large online retailers like Amazon to smaller specialized shops. E-Commerce enables consumers to shop for products, compare prices, and make purchases from the comfort of their homes using computers or mobile devices. This digital marketplace operates 24/7 and offers a vast selection of products across global borders. It streamlines sales, marketing, and customer service processes, providing convenience for consumers and expanding market reach for businesses. E-Commerce embodies a focus on **maximizing revenue generation**. It leverages the Internet, web platforms, and mobile applications, enabling commercial transactions among entities and individuals. E-Commerce is covering various phases of a commercial transaction, including initial **information phase** comprising gathering and research, the **negotiation phase** (although this is often limited in platforms like Amazon where prices are fixed), **delivery phase** (which can be either digital, like downloading an MP3 file, or physical), and **after-sales support**. This model is designed to maximize revenue generation by streamlining the process of commercial transactions to enhance profitability and improve the customer experience. Conversely, **E-Business** enables companies to automate processes, manage E-Business operations more effectively, and facilitate communication between employees, suppliers, and customers. It supports operational processes within a company, utilizing information systems managed internally to enhance optimization and efficiency. **E-Business** leans toward **cost-efficiency** and **automatization** especially of business processes. It also tries to improve **interoperability and data flow by connecting systems** with each other.

E-Commerce encompasses various classifications based on the nature of transactions. The primary categories include **business-to-consumer (B2C), business-to-business (B2B),** and **consumer-to-consumer (C2C).** Figure 2.2 illustrates, in a self-explanatory manner, how E-Commerce can be categorized by placing "Demanding Business Activities" and the related "Offerings of Business Activities" in perspective.

In **B2B** transactions, companies engage in the exchange of services and goods among themselves. **B2C** involves businesses selling products or services directly to consumers, representing a conventional E-Commerce model. Of growing significance is the C2C model, wherein individuals interact on digital platforms to exchange services, information, or products. An example for consumer to administration (C2A) could be the electronic tax declaration. This dynamic platform-mediated exchange highlights the evolving nature of E-Commerce, emphasizing peer-to-peer interactions and leveraging IT and web platforms for seamless transactions.

Digital products or **intangible products** significantly shape the landscape of Digital Business by offering unique advantages and characteristics compared to traditional physical goods. Figure 2.3 depicts how products can be categorized into four types: physical products, semi-physical products, semi-digital products, and (purely) digital products. Each type varies in its degree of digital integration.

Physical products are tangible goods that exist in the real world and have no reliance on digital components for their core functionality or value. These products

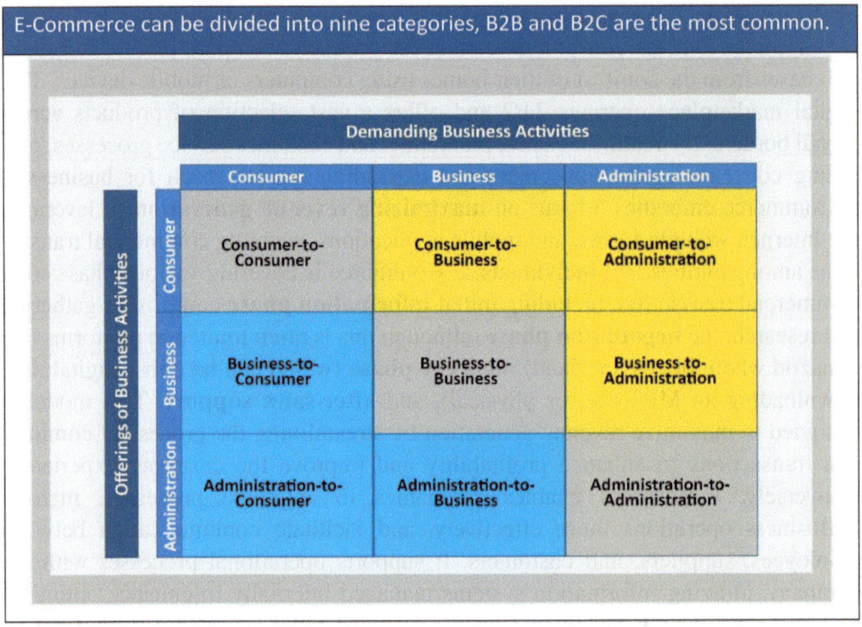

Fig. 2.2 Categorization of E-Commerce

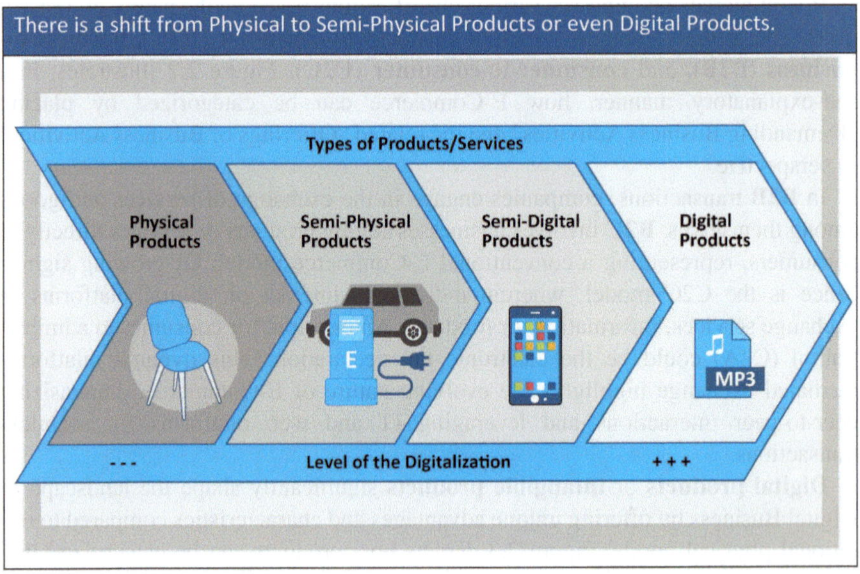

Fig. 2.3 Intangible products (from physical to digital products)

can be crafted from a variety of materials, such as wood, metal, plastic, fabric, or even food.

Semi-physical products primarily focus on a physical item but are enhanced by digital features. For example, a car equipped with a regularly updated navigation system represents a semi-physical product. The car remains the main product, yet it integrates digital technology to improve the user experience and functionality.

Semi-digital products are those that, while primarily digital, are linked to a physical element. A classic example is a music CD; the primary value is the music (digital content) stored on the disc, but it requires the physical medium of a CD for playback. This category blends physical presence with digital utility, providing a tangible aspect to digital data.

Pure digital products, such as MP3 files or virtual game items, exist entirely in a digital format with no physical component. Their value lies in their content and the convenience of instant accessibility. They are easily reproducible, and unlike physical products, they do not degrade over time, making them perpetually "new" in terms of quality. This permanence and ease of distribution allow for widespread sharing and potentially lower costs.

Semi-digital products are those that, while primarily digital, are linked to a physical element. A classic example is a music CD; the primary value is the music (digital content) stored on the disc, but it requires the physical medium of a CD for playback. This category blends physical presence with digital utility, providing a tangible aspect to digital data.

Transition from physical to digital is evident in many sectors, as seen with books evolving into e-books. This shift highlights a growing trend where traditional products are increasingly augmented or replaced by digital alternatives, offering greater convenience and updated features. Digital products also introduce challenges, such as issues related to copyright and the rapid pace of technological change, which can shorten product lifecycles. Nonetheless, they represent a pivotal element of modern commerce, increasingly blurring the lines between physical and digital realms and shaping consumer behavior. In many cases, this shift **transfers predominantly physical products into semi-physical products** to generate additional added value alongside the actual product.

E-Commerce can be categorized into different dimensions that revolve around the type of goods and the nature of the transaction process. The dimensions of electronic commerce, as presented by Turban (Fig. 2.4), can be differentiated into three aspects: **the virtualization of products, the virtualization of processes, and the virtualization of delivery agents**.

Products, agents, and the delivery process can be either digital or physical. In the case of a physical product with a physical agent and a physical process, we refer to it as traditional commerce or **brick-and-mortar business**. Conversely, if all elements are virtual—virtual processes, virtual agents, and digital products—then it is termed **pure electronic commerce or digital commerce.** However, most dimensions lie somewhere in between, **representing a blend of digitalization and physicality.** For example, traditional E-Commerce involves purchasing jeans at a physical store and paying with cash, whereas ordering an eBook online, downloading it, and

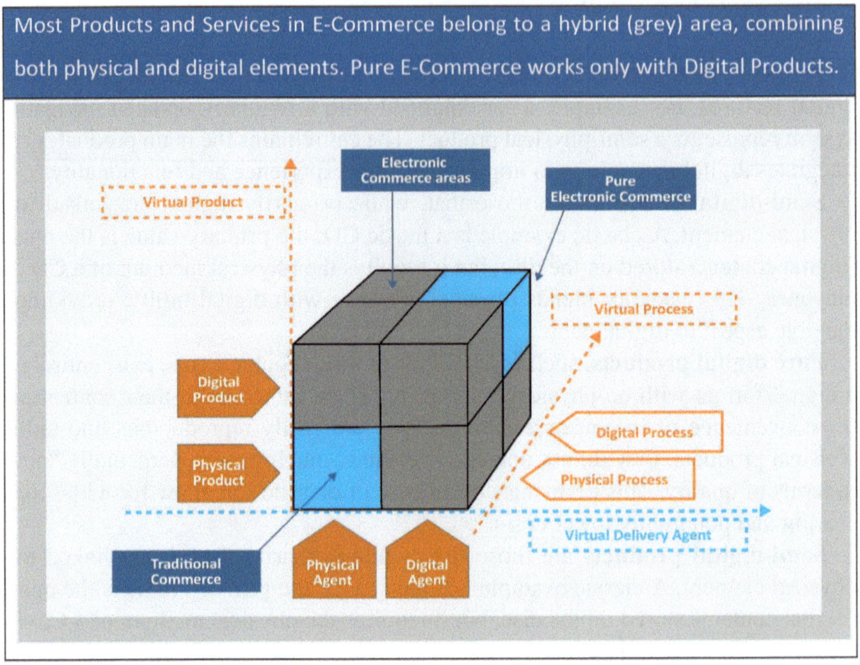

Fig. 2.4 Electronic commerce adapted from Turban

paying electronically represents a digital commerce transaction. Starting with the basics, E-Commerce primarily involves the buying and selling of goods and services over the Internet. This discussion using the dimensions has revolutionized traditional commerce by **moving the commercial engagement from physical stores to virtual platforms**. For example, instead of visiting a store to try on jeans and pay with cash (traditional E-Commerce), a consumer can now browse selections, make comparisons, and purchase products and download directly online (pure E-Commerce).

2.2 Digital Business

Digital Business encompasses Digital Business models, **services and products**, **processes**, and **technologies**, all in dependence on the associated **digital value**. Furthermore, methods of customer interaction that provide companies with a competitive edge (Fig. 2.5).

The **grade of digitalization** starts with **digitization**, which involves converting current documents into digital formats. This transition leads to **digitalization**, which introduces new business processes and approaches to managing digital

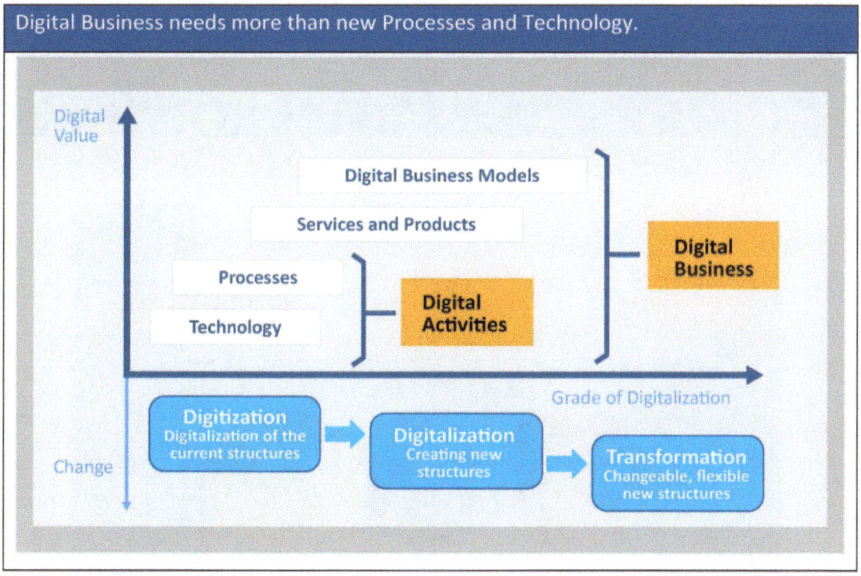

Fig. 2.5 Characteristics of a Digital Business

content additionally. Ultimately, it comes to a (digital) **transformation**, characterized by adaptable, flexible, and innovative structures.

Digital Business extends beyond mere engagement in digital activities. While digital activities are driven only by innovative processes and technologies, Digital Business involves the development of new services, products, and business models, as well as customer interaction. Figure 2.6 is visualizing the characteristics of a Digital Business comprises E-Business and E-Commerce.

It leverages **digital technologies to overhaul traditional business processes, operations, and models,** thereby enhancing efficiency, fostering innovation, **improving the customer experience**, and bolstering competitiveness in the digital economy.

A company can be considered a Digital Business if its E-Business activities are automated and its IT systems are interconnected, enabling data exchange. Figure 2.6 is visualizing the Digital Business framework. Additionally, various software systems, such as supply chain management (SCM), enterprise resource planning (ERP), and customer relationship management (CRM) programs, operate within E-Business. Middleware, or so-called enterprise application integration (EAI), facilitates the interconnection of these systems within the company. Through the interfaces of Digital Business, companies engage with suppliers and customers. When these interactions occur over the Internet, it's termed E-Commerce. While E-Commerce systems connect with customers and suppliers over the Internet, E-Business systems focus on supporting business processes and data exchange between internal systems. Businesses utilize portals and websites to connect with customers, either through their own or other B2C marketplaces. On the supplier

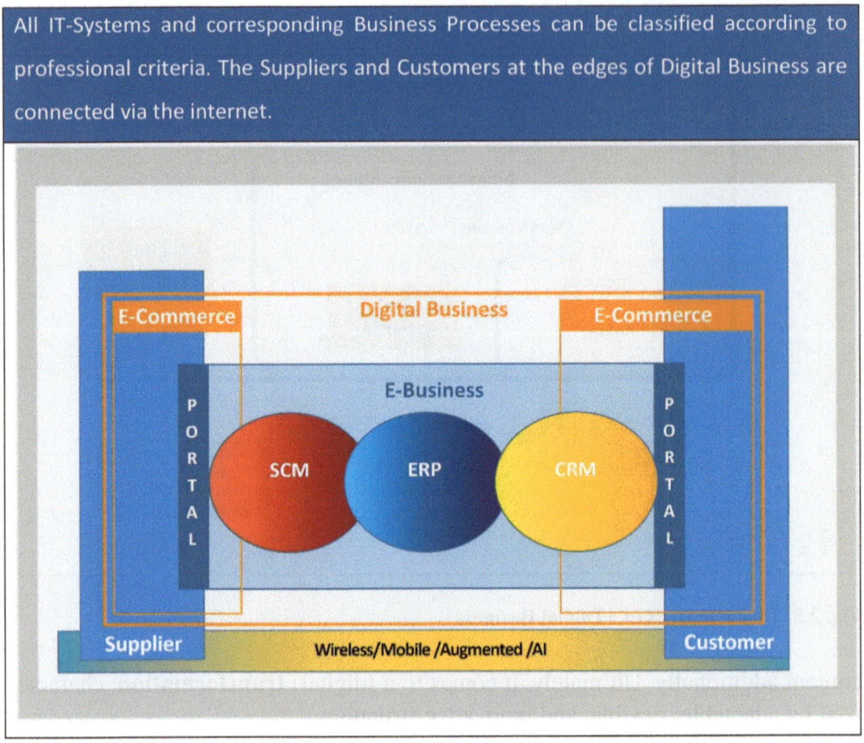

Fig. 2.6 The Digital Business framework (overview I)

side, they may employ e-procurement tools, B2B eMarketplaces, or integrate supply chain management software with vendor systems. This integration leads to extended and streamlined business to business processes without or at least less human interaction (Fig. 2.7).

2.3 Network Effects and Digital Leadership

Digital network effects are a crucial phenomenon in E-Commerce. They arise when the value of a digital product or service grows as more users engage with it, thereby improving user experience, engagement, and the overall utility for all participants. The key differences lie in scale and speed, as well as in cost structure. Digital products typically have low marginal costs for additional users, unlike traditional products, which may face higher costs as they scale. Additionally, digital products can leverage data utilization more effectively.

Network effects, as visualized in Fig. 2.8, also known as **network externalities or Metcalfe's law**, describe a phenomenon where the value of a product or service increases with the number of users. This concept holds particular significance in

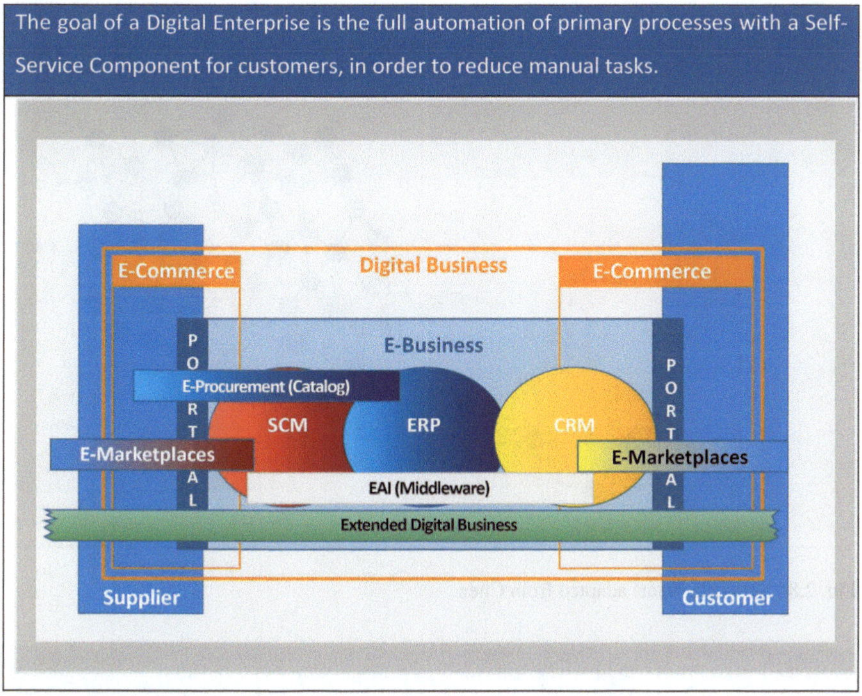

Fig. 2.7 The Digital Business framework (detail view II)

sectors such as technology, social media, telecommunications, and others where connectivity and user participation are pivotal. Consequently, the value for an individual user augments as more users engage with the product or service.

This dynamic stands in contrast to traditional market dynamics. For instance, **the greater the number of individuals joining a social network, the more advantageous it becomes for each participant** (compare the social marketing). Conversely, in conventional markets, commodities like gold become more valuable when they are less widespread among consumers.

Digital leadership involves guiding an organization through digital transformation by fostering innovation, leveraging technology, driving data-driven decisions, managing change, prioritizing customer needs, and empowering employees for agility and growth (see chapter below). Another interpretation of digital leadership can be understood as **personnel management in the digital age**. Fig. 2.9 explores different scenarios of how leadership roles might evolve in the digital age. It examines how digital transformation and technological advancements could reshape the functions and significance of leaders within organizations. Each scenario presents a distinct vision of leadership, ranging from diminished roles with automated decision-making to enhanced roles where leaders manage complex human-machine interactions and protect valuable data.

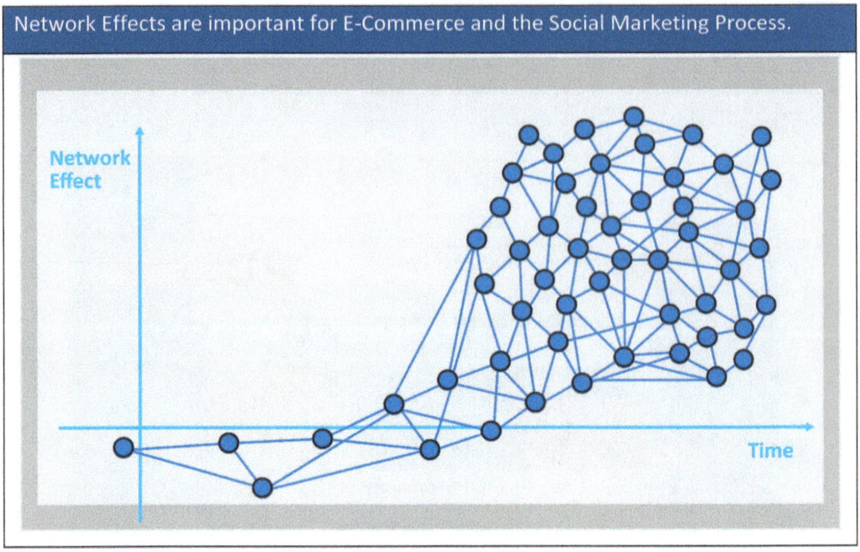

Fig. 2.8 Network effects adapted from Chen

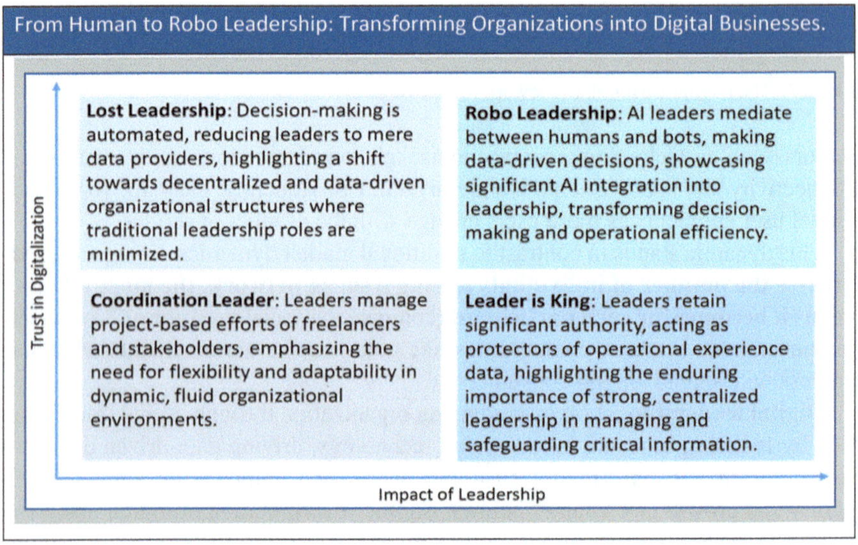

Fig. 2.9 Robo leadership

From human to robo leadership to transform organizations signifies the transition from traditional human-led management to **AI-driven leadership.** The core of this transformation lies in leveraging artificial intelligence to enhance decision-making, optimize processes, and improve efficiency.

2.4 Innovation, Disruption, and Transformation

Innovation is the process of creating new ideas, products, or methods that provide value. **Types include product, process, organizational, marketing, and technological innovation**. Innovation often leads to disruption by introducing groundbreaking changes that significantly alter or replace existing markets, products, or processes (Fig. 2.10).

Disruption stands as a powerful force reshaping industries and markets. It can be referred to a book by Clayton Christensen, *The Innovator's Dilemma*. Disruption represents a significant shift or interruption that change the usual course of operations within an industry, market, or system. *The Innovator's Dilemma* exposes a surprising reason successful companies fail: disruptive innovation. These innovations aren't head-to-head competitors; **they're simpler, less powerful technologies that initially target new or underserved markets.** Here's the problem: established companies keep improving products for their happy, high-value customers. Meanwhile, the disruptive technology slowly gets better, eventually becoming good enough to threaten the entire market. The trap lies in the "dilemma zone"—the sweet spot where the new technology seems irrelevant to the core business but holds the potential for massive disruption. Christensen argues that focusing solely on

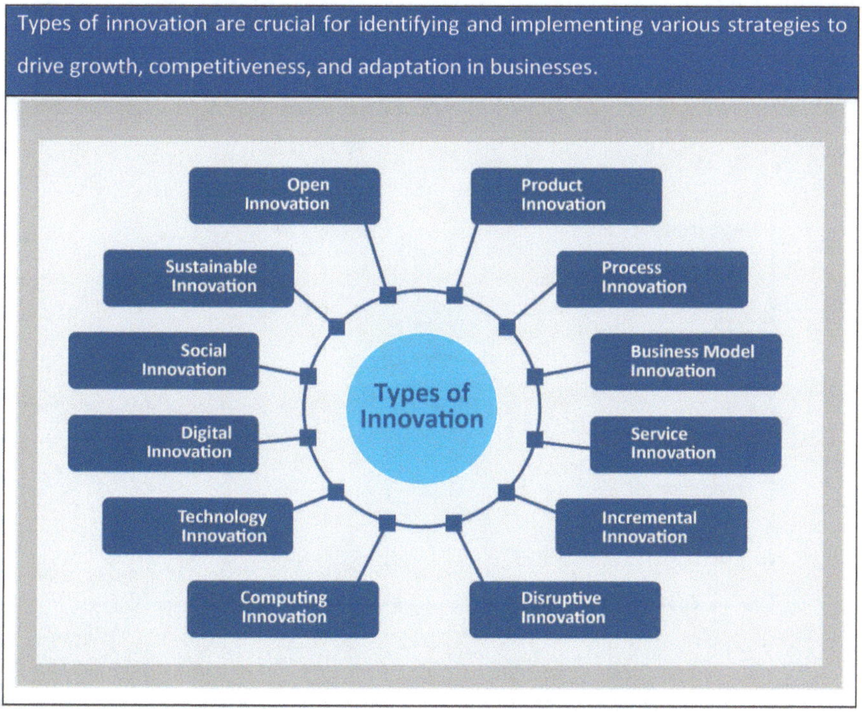

Fig. 2.10 Types of innovation. Adapted from https://ideascale.com/blog/what-is-innovation/

what core customers want can leave companies blindsided by innovation happening on the periphery. The key takeaway? Recognizing and adapting to disruptive forces before they become an existential threat.

Figure 2.11 illustrates the dilemma zone: the disruptive tech is initially unattractive to the leader's core business, but holds the potential to become a major threat. It's a tough call to invest in something that might cannibalize your own success!

In the realm of business, disruption often involves the introduction of disruptive innovations that challenge prevailing norms, practices, and established industry players. These **innovations have the potential to displace traditional methods or companies and even give rise to entirely new markets or industries.** In many instances, disruptive products may initially offer lower quality or utilize simpler technologies compared to market leaders. Despite this, market leaders may struggle to acknowledge or adapt to these disruptive technologies, often due to concerns about cannibalizing their existing products or customer base. This **hesitation may lead to a loss of market share or revenue,** and by the time they consider transitioning to these new products or services, it may be too late. (Digital) Transformation can be understood in two ways: as a degree of digitalization and as a process of internal disruption. Digital transformation can be viewed from two perspectives.

Level of digitalization: this perspective sees digital transformation as a continuous process of integrating digital technologies, processes, and models into a business. This increases the level of digitalization within the company. Internal triggered disruption: this perspective focuses on digital transformation as a strategic process

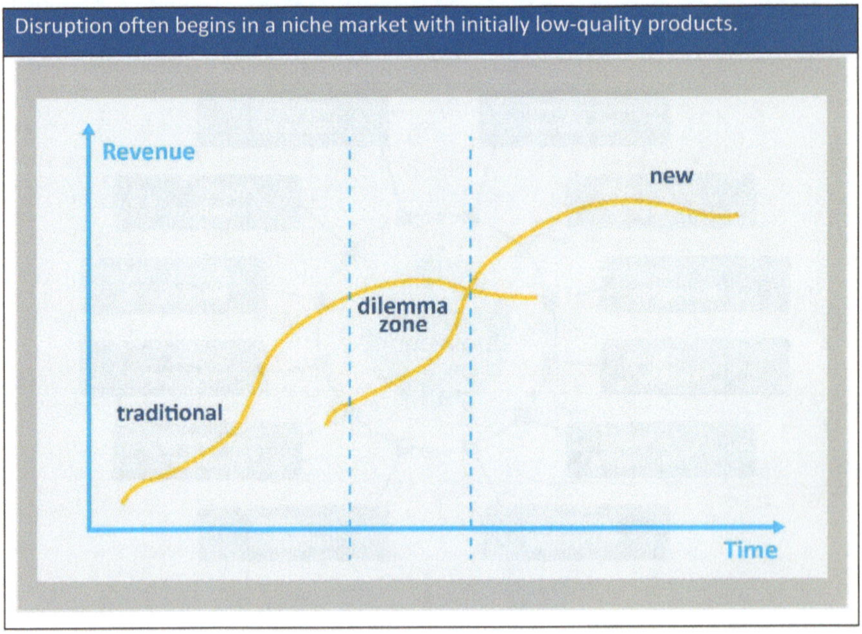

Fig. 2.11 Disruption adapted from Christensen

where an organization leverages digital tools and innovation to disrupt its own business model or market, creating new value propositions for customers.

Review Questions

1. What are the differences between E-Commerce and E-Business, and how do digital products relate to these differences?
2. How can industry-leading firms prevent disruption, and what is the significance behind the term "Innovator's dilemma"?
3. What is the goal of a digital enterprise, and how can it be achieved?
4. Why do network effects become increasingly important in Digital Business?

Your Advanced Questions for Starting Prompt Engineering

- How can organizations foster a culture of innovation and experimentation to thrive in a rapidly changing digital landscape?
- More and more activities will be data driven. How will digital Business adapt AI?

Business Case

Please work on business Case no. 1: "Self-driving Cars—when the disruptor gets disrupted" with WAYMO and TESLA.

Further Readings

Chen A (2023) The cold start problem: how to start and scale network effects
Christensen C (2024) The innovator's dilemma. https://www.christenseninstitute.org/
Hanlon A (2024) Digital business: strategy, management and transformation
Turban E et al (2024) Electronic commerce. https://www.linkedin.com/in/efraim-turban-7a682912/

Chapter 3
Digital Business Strategies

Abstract

In a nutshell

The chapter covers platforms, sharing, and crowd economy models, emphasizing their role in the digital landscape. The importance of eStrategies and business models is highlighted, including the business model canvas as a strategic tool. Revenue models in e-commerce are explored, along with the impact of e-commerce on industry structure and value chains. Finally, Porter's generic business strategies and the five forces model are introduced as frameworks for understanding competitive advantage in the digital world.

Keywords Platform economy · Sharing economy · Crowd economy · Revenue model · Digitalization · Value chain · Disruption · eStrategy · Business model canvas

Basic Prompts

Compare platform and sharing economy.
Explain the concept of the platform economy and provide examples.
How do business models and revenue models differ in the digital landscape?
Discuss the impact of digitalization on traditional business models.

S. Schneider, L. Anderie, *Digital Business Management*,
https://doi.org/10.1007/978-3-031-83177-5_3

3.1 Platform and Sharing Economy and Crowd Strategies

A **platform economy** is a digital system where value is exchanged through online platforms, connecting producers and consumers, often leveraging network effects and data-driven insights to facilitate transactions and interactions. In most cases, the platform is only the **intermediary** and is just connecting customers and suppliers by delivering a value added to the user (Fig. 3.1).

Digitalization supports the expansion of the **sharing economy** and drives the establishment of large platforms. This value addition may include enhanced overview, improved offers, or features like rankings, ratings, and recommendations. In many instances, the platform economy engenders temporary monopolies, leading to what is known as the **winner-takes-all economy**, where a single solution dominates the market, making it challenging for competitors to enter. An electronic marketplace connects multiple sellers and buyers for transactions, while an electronic platform offers broader digital services and functions. Another notable phenomenon is the **attention economy,** where users "pay" with their attention rather than data or money. Examples include platforms like Facebook or YouTube, where users either subscribe to premium services or watch advertisements in exchange for access to content.

The **sharing economy** involves companies that specialize in providing goods temporarily via web-based platforms, often accompanied by services. The concept revolves around customers not owning particular products; instead, they rent them and pay solely for their usage. But renting typically involved formal agreements and limited access. The sharing economy involves peer-to-peer exchanges in the B2B,

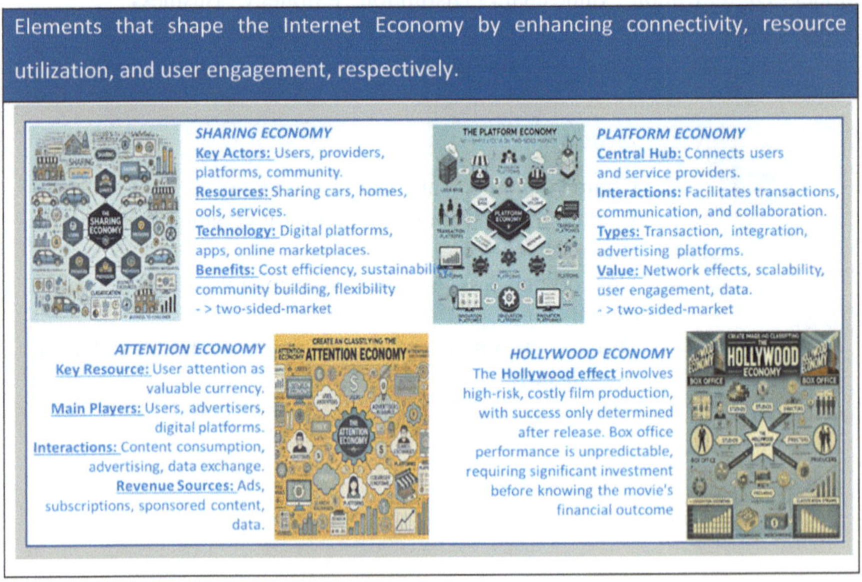

Fig. 3.1 Elements of the Internet economy

B2C, and C2C area, often facilitated by digital platforms, promoting broader access and temporary usage.

Crowd strategies involve harnessing the collective intelligence, creativity, or resources of a group to achieve a common goal, often through collaboration, idea-sharing, crowdfunding, or collective problem-solving.

3.2 eStrategy and Business Models

An **eStrategy**, short for electronic strategy, outlines a company's plan for using digital technologies within their **business model** to achieve their overall business goals. This plan goes beyond simply creating a website and considers how digital tools can impact all aspects of the organization to generate profits within the marketplace. Therefore, a **business plan** has to be created—a document that describes a firm's business model. While closely related, a business model may differ from a business strategy, though they sometimes overlap, particularly when the business model considers the competitive landscape. The business model occupies a central position within the business plan. A **business model** is a set of **planned activities** designed to **result in profit** within a marketplace, often based on a **value proposition** that defines how a company's product or service fulfills the needs of customers. In the process of creating a business model and prior to writing a business plan, it's worth generating the business model canvas.

The **business model canvas,** which is visualized in Fig. 3.2, is a strategic management tool that provides a visual chart that helps businesses innovate and systematically analyze, design, and implement new business models. **Key partnerships** define the network of suppliers and partners that make the business model work. **Customer segments** define the different groups of people or organizations a business aims to reach and serve. **Key activities** describe the most important things a company must do to make its business model work. **Key resources** identify the most important assets required to make a business model work. The **value propositions** describe the bundle of products and services that create value for a specific customer segment. **Customer relationships** describe the types of relationships a company establishes with specific customer segments. **Sales channels** outline how a company communicates with and reaches its customer segments to deliver its value proposition. **Key resources** identify the most important assets required to make a business model work. **Key activities** describe the most important things a company must do to make its business model work. **Key partnerships** define the network of suppliers and partners that make the business model work. **Cost structure** describes all costs incurred to operate a business model. **Revenue streams** represents the cash a company generates from each **customer segment**.

A **business model** outlines how a company creates value, delivers products or services, and sustains a competitive advantage. In contrast, a **revenue model** specifies how the firm generates revenue, achieves profitability, and ensures a superior return on invested capital (ROI).

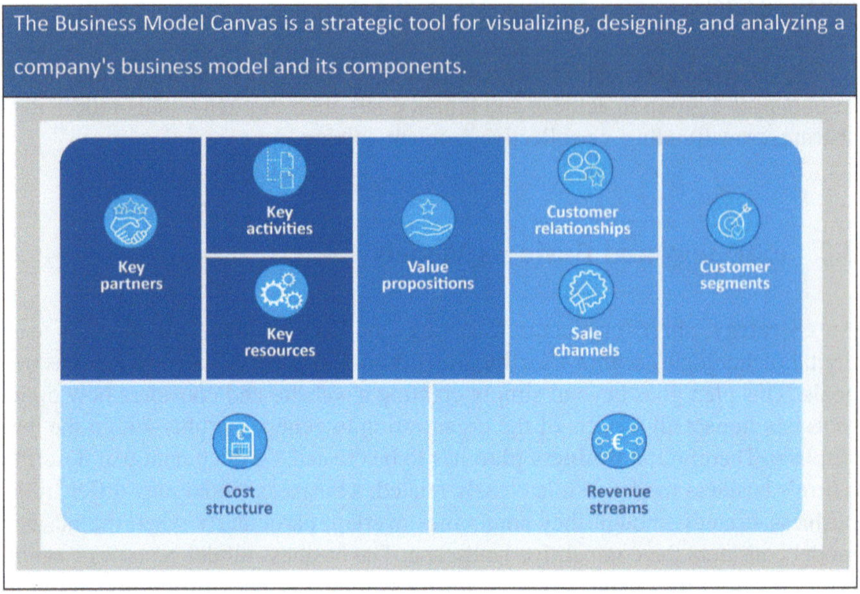

Fig. 3.2 Business model canvas

In the E-Commerce area, a business model is a kind of business model that aims to use and leverage the unique qualities of the Internet, the Web, and the mobile platform. One example of an eStrategy is the **freemium strategy** which involves companies offering a basic level of their product or service for free, for a certain time or with the option to access additional premium features or levels through a subscription. To craft a successful business model across various domains, not limited to E-Commerce, it's essential to ensure that the model adequately encompasses the eight critical elements:

- The **value proposition** is the unique offering that prompts customers to choose your business over others. A key question for this is: "Why should the customer buy from you?"
- The **revenue model** defines how the E-Business will earn income. An essential inquiry here is: "How will you earn money?"
- **Market opportunity** refers to the specific market segment the business aims to serve and its potential size. The question to consider is: "What marketspace do you intend to serve, and what is its size?"
- **The competitive environment** encompasses the other businesses operating in the same space. It prompts the question: "Who else occupies your intended marketspace?"
- **A competitive advantage** is what makes the firm stand out in the competitive landscape. The corresponding question is: "What special advantages does your firm bring to the marketspace?"

- **The market strategy** is the plan for promoting products or services to attract the target audience. The key question is: "How do you plan to promote your products or services to attract your target audience?"
- **Organizational development** involves the structure of the company necessary to execute the E-Business plan. A vital question is: "What types of organizational structures within the firm are necessary to carry out the Business plan?"
- **The management team** component revolves around the leadership and their qualifications. The question to address here is: "What kinds of experiences and background are important for the company's leaders to have?

An eStrategy, or electronic strategy (as a part of the corporate Strategy), outlines a plan for leveraging digital technologies to achieve business goals. It encompasses aspects like online presence, digital marketing, E-Commerce, and data analytics. It aligns technological capabilities with organizational objectives, ensuring efficient use of digital resources to drive growth and competitiveness in the digital landscape.

3.3 Revenue Models in E-Commerce

The **revenue model of a company delineates its approach to generating income**, achieving profitability, and yielding a competitive return on invested capital. The terms "revenue model" and "financial model" are often used interchangeably in this context. Business entities are tasked not only with earning profits but also with delivering returns on invested capital that surpass those of alternative investments. Merely attaining profits is insufficient for defining success according to Porter; instead, success hinges on a company's ability to generate returns that outstrip those offered by alternative investment opportunities. Companies that fall short of meeting this criterion face the risk of ceasing operations. These models are fundamental ways in which companies can generate income, each with its unique approach to capitalizing on the company's assets and market position. There are five primary revenue models in Digital Business:

- A company utilizing a **subscription revenue model** (e.g., Netflix) offers its users various content or services and, in turn, charges a subscription fee which grants access to some or all of its offerings. In B2B, the most common subscription model is called SaaS (software as a service).
- In the **advertising revenue model** (e.g., Google), a company creates a platform for advertisers to showcase their advertisements and generates income by charging these advertisers fees for the service.
- When operating under an **affiliate revenue model** (e.g., Shopify Affiliate Program), a company directs business toward an affiliate partner and earns a commission, either a referral fee or a percentage, from the sales generated through this redirection.
- The **transaction fee revenue model** (e.g., Uber) is one where a company earns its revenue by collecting fees for facilitating or carrying out transactions.

- Lastly, the **sales revenue model** (e.g., Amazon) is where a company's income is derived from the direct sale of goods, information, or services to consumers.

3.4 Value Chains and Porter Strategies

The **industry structure** configures industries, particularly in terms of competition between companies, and has been significantly influenced by E-Commerce technologies across various sectors. Broadly speaking, E-Commerce, because of **more transparency, has intensified price competition across almost all markets.** Adopting E-Commerce technology has been relatively straightforward for established firms, enabling them to strive for a competitive edge against their competitors. Additionally, disruption can occur as a result of the introduction of substitutes.

While analyzing industry structure provides insights into the influence of E-Commerce technology on the broader business landscape within an industry, a **more detailed examination of industry value chains** can offer a clearer understanding of how E-Commerce might alter business processes at the industry level.

The **value chain**, as shown in Fig. 3.3, serves as a fundamental tool for understanding the impact of information technology on both **industry** and **firm** operations. Its premise is straightforward: by lowering information costs, E-Commerce presents each participant in an industry value chain with fresh opportunities to optimize their positions by reducing costs and/or increasing prices. For example, manufacturers can diminish procurement expenses by establishing automated Internet-based B2B exchanges with suppliers. Moreover, manufacturers can cultivate direct relationships with customers, circumventing the expenses associated with distributors and retailers. A **value** chain for a **firm** is a concept used in business management and strategy that describes the full range of activities involved in the creation of a product or service, from its conception to its delivery to the end consumer, and beyond. These activities are categorized into primary and support activities. Primary activities are:

- Inbound Logistics: The receiving and storing of raw materials or components.
- Operations: The processes of transforming raw materials or components into finished products or services.
- Outbound Logistics: The distribution and delivery of finished products to customers.
- Marketing and Sales: Activities related to promoting and selling the product or service.
- Service: Providing customer support, maintenance, and other after-sales services.

Support activities are:

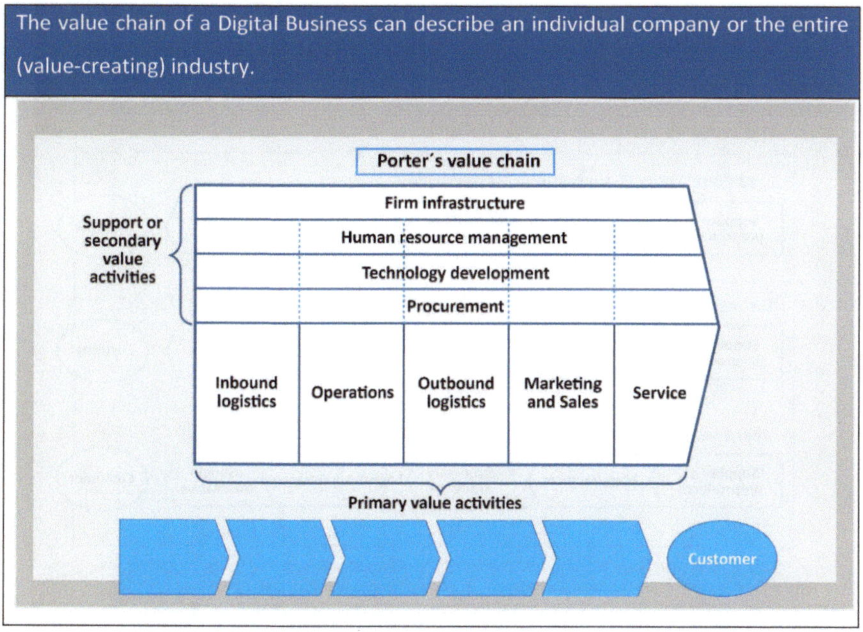

Fig. 3.3 Value chain of a digital business

- Firm Infrastructure: The support systems and structures needed to carry out value chain activities, such as information technology, facilities, and organizational structure.
- Human Resource Management: Activities related to recruiting, training, and managing employees.
- Technology Development: Research and development activities aimed at improving products, processes, or services.
- Procurement: The process of sourcing and acquiring raw materials, components, or services needed for the value chain.

Building on the concept of the value chain, Fig. 3.4 depicts the **industry**-wide **value chain**. Especially through the Internet, a distinction can be made between **disintermediation**, which involves the elimination of value-added stages or intermediaries between sellers and buyers, and **intermediation**, which involves the creation of new intermediary roles, new value-adding stages in the value chain.

Overall, Porter's value chain analysis provides insights into how companies can optimize their operations, enhance competitiveness, and create value for customers.

While Porter has developed a range of strategies, his framework (Fig. 3.5) focuses on four generic business strategies for achieving **competitive advantage**:

- Cost Leadership: This strategy focuses on becoming the most efficient producer in the industry. Companies achieve this through economies of scale, efficient

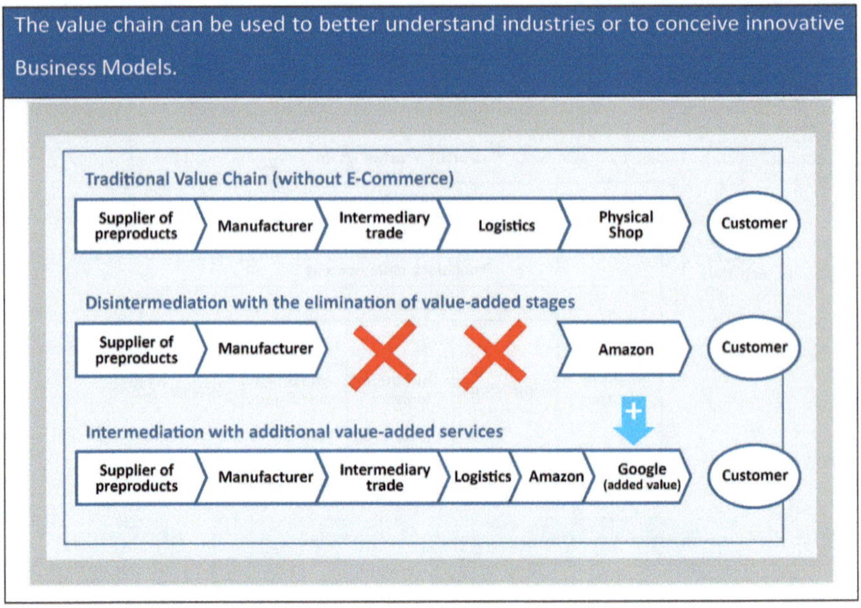

Fig. 3.4 Value chains to analyze industries

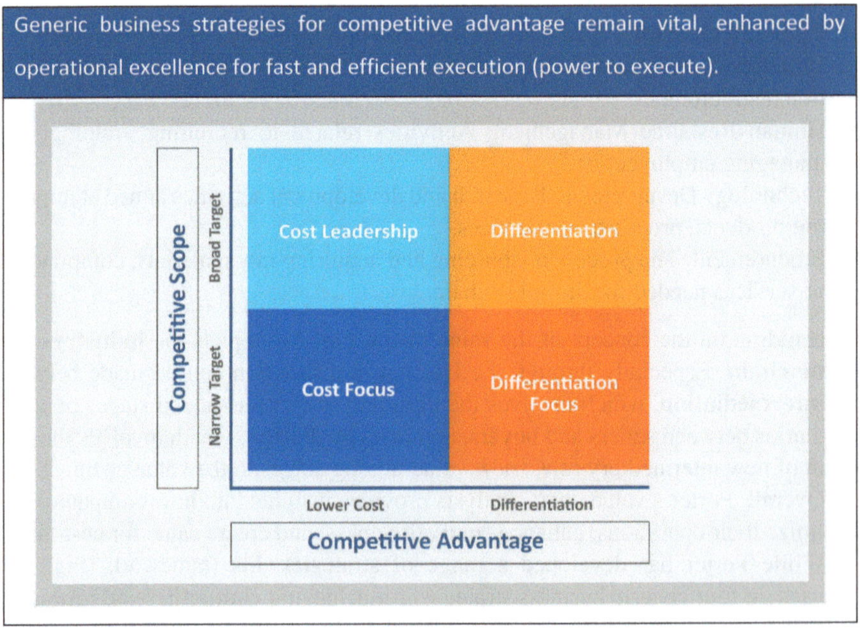

Fig. 3.5 Generic eStrategies

operations, and strong supplier relationships. They aim to offer the lowest prices in the market.

- Differentiation: This strategy focuses on creating a product or service that is unique and valuable to customers. This can be achieved through innovation, branding, or superior customer service. Companies with this strategy aim to charge a premium price for their offerings.
- Focus: This strategy focuses on serving a narrow market niche. Companies with this strategy tailor their products and services to the specific needs of a particular customer segment. There are two subcategories of focus strategies:
  - Cost Focus: This strategy combines a focus on a narrow market niche with a cost leadership approach.
  - Differentiation Focus: This strategy combines a focus on a narrow market niche with a differentiation approach.

Those firms capable of delivering superior products at the most competitive prices on a global scale hold a distinct advantage.

Michael **Porter's five forces model** (Fig. 3.6) is a widely used tool; it evaluates the **bargaining power** of **buyers** and **suppliers**, **threat of new entrants**, **threat of substitutes**, and **competitive rivalry**. This helps assess industry attractiveness and formulate strategies to mitigate threats, capitalize on opportunities, and maintain a competitive advantage.

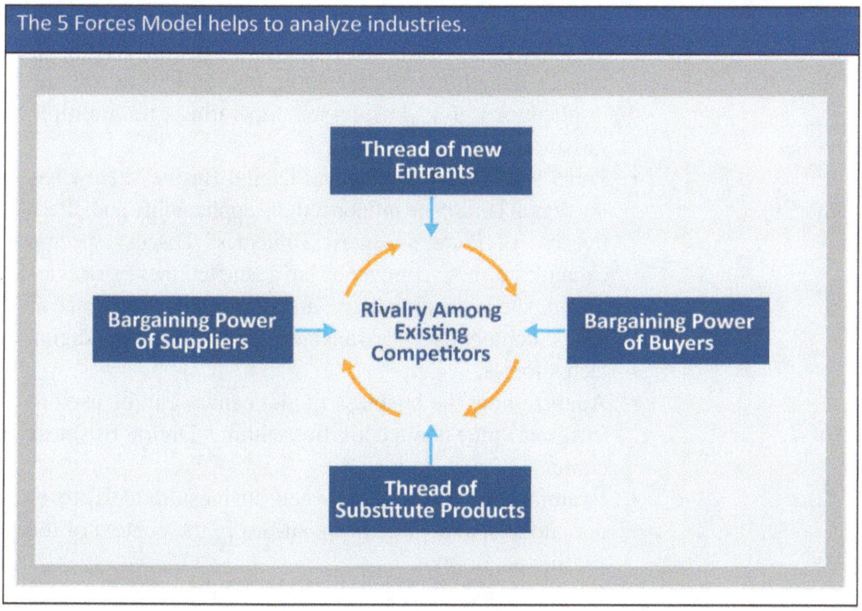

Fig. 3.6 Five forces model to analyze Digital Business industries

Review Questions

1. Is there a relation between a platform business and the shared economy?
2. When is a business model canvas most helpful?
3. What are the primary revenue models?
4. In what way do Porter's value chain and industry analysis help companies choose from his generic strategies (cost leadership, differentiation, or focus)?
5. Choose an industry/sector (e.g., movie streaming) and create its value chain.

Your Advanced Questions for Starting Prompt Engineering

- How can businesses effectively leverage platform strategies to create sustainable competitive advantage in the digital economy?
- What are the key challenges and opportunities associated with managing digital ecosystems, and how can firms optimize their participation in these networks?
- How can organizations balance the need for data-driven decision-making with ethical considerations related to data privacy and security?
- To what extent does the concept of digital sovereignty impact the global digital economy, and what are the implications for businesses operating in multiple jurisdictions?
- Porter's generic strategies and Digital Business: How has the digital landscape influenced the applicability and effectiveness of Porter's generic strategies? Discuss specific examples of how companies have adapted these strategies to compete in the digital age, and explore the emergence of new competitive advantages enabled by digital technologies.
- Analyze how the business model canvas can be used to integrate value chain activities within a Digital Business context.
- Examine the interplay between business models, revenue models, and value propositions in the context of the sharing economy.
- Compare and contrast the competitive advantages of cost leadership, differentiation, and focus strategies in the digital age.

Business Case

Please read Business Case No. 2, "Shared Economy and On-Demand Service Companies," featuring AIRBNB and UBER. What are the challenges these companies face?

Further Readings

Hohpe G et al (2024) Platform strategy: innovation through harmonization

Porter M (2024) Competitive advantage: creating and sustaining superior performance. https://www.hbs.edu/faculty/Pages/profile.aspx?facId=6532

Chapter 4
Digital Infrastructure

Abstract

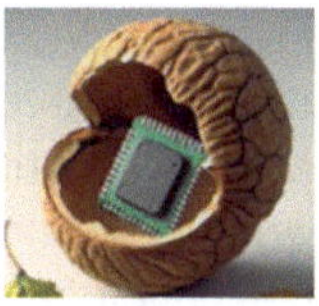

In a nutshell
The chapter covers digital communication foundations, Internet architecture, and protocols. It examines mobile Internet evolution, including 5G. RFID and QR codes' role in connecting physical and digital worlds is highlighted. Cloud computing concepts are explained. The chapter concludes with ePayments, blockchain, and cryptography, focusing on secure digital transactions.

Keywords Internet · TCP/IP · Mobile internet · Electromagnetic spectrum · 5G · Cloud computing · Blockchain · ePayments · Cryptography · IoT · Algorithms

Basic Prompts

- Explain the difference between TCP and IP protocols.
- What is the role of cloud computing in Digital Business?
- How does 5G technology differ from previous generations of mobile networks?
- Describe the concept of blockchain and its potential applications.

S. Schneider, L. Anderie, *Digital Business Management*,
https://doi.org/10.1007/978-3-031-83177-5_4

4.1 Internet and Mobile Infrastructures

The **Internet**, a global network, operates on a decentralized architecture using TCP/IP protocols, enhancing robustness and resilience. This **decentralization** ensures the network remains operational even if parts fail, as data can reroute through other paths. The Internet links countless devices, allowing them to communicate. It operates using standardized communication protocols, notably TCP/IP (Transmission Control Protocol/Internet Protocol). TCP manages the direct connections between devices, ensuring reliable, ordered, and error-checked delivery of data across the network. IP handles the routing and addressing, determining the paths that data packets take from sender to receiver. Together, these protocols facilitate the seamless exchange of data and support services like the World Wide Web, email, file sharing, and streaming media.

Since the Internet is the foundation of Digital Business, it continues to expand into a global network of interconnected computers. As a result, more and more devices will utilize mobile Internet access. The **mobile Internet enables access to the Internet through mobile devices**. It allows users to browse websites, stream videos, use apps, and connect to social media on-the-go, leveraging technologies like 3G, 4G, and 5G for **connectivity anywhere** cellular service is available. Increasingly, businesses are utilizing the mobile Internet, which comprises various frequencies **divided into bands**, with each technology operating on a specific band. Figure 4.1 features the visual representation of the **electromagnetic spectrum** and its applications in various technologies. It's organized by frequency, which is measured in hertz (Hz), and depicts how different frequencies are used in our everyday technology. If more data is to be transmitted over a radio channel, it competes with others. One solution is the so-called **multiplexing**, where algorithms are used to transmit compressed data.

On the far left, starting at low frequencies, we have illustrations representing railway electricity and rotating current, which usually operate at low frequencies, such as 50 or 60 Hz in common power systems. As we move to the right, the frequencies increase, and we encounter the traditional bands used in radio broadcasting: longwave (LW), medium wave (MW), shortwave (KW), and the bands for FM radio and TV. Further to the right, we have ultra-high frequency (UHF) bands, commonly used for digital TV, followed by mobile phone frequencies around 1–2 GHz (Gigahertz) in the mobile communications band. The microwave section is next, which is used for radar systems, satellite communication, and microwave ovens, operating typically in the GHz range. Then we see infrared (IR), which is used for remote controls, some types of heaters, and other devices that utilize IR for communication. The visible light spectrum follows, illustrating that this is a very small part of the overall electromagnetic spectrum. Next, we see ultraviolet (UV) light, which is beyond the visible spectrum and has applications in medical treatment and sterilization. Finally, at the high-frequency end of the spectrum, we have X-rays and gamma rays, used in medical imaging and treatments, as well as in scientific research. **Humans can perceive visible light, which ranges from about 380 to**

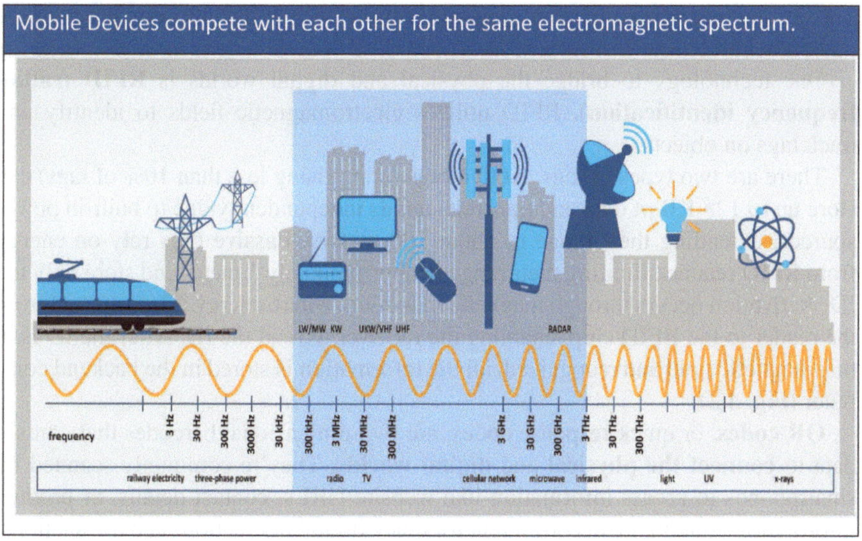

Fig. 4.1 The electromagnetic spectrum and technologies

750 nanometers on the electromagnetic spectrum. A nanometer (nm) is a unit used to measure incredibly small things, like atoms and molecules. It's one-billionth of a meter, written as 0.000000001 meters. This range includes all the colors we can see, from violet at the shortest wavelength to red at the longest.

The wave illustrations at the bottom of the image demonstrate the change in wavelength as the frequency increases: long wavelengths for low frequencies and short wavelengths for high frequencies. Smartphones, 5G, WLAN, and RFID are also using a part of this spectrum**. 5G stands for "fifth generation**" and it's the latest standard for cellular network technology. It's the successor to 4G, which is what most mobile phones use today. 5G has the potential to be much faster than 4G, with theoretical peak speeds of up to 20 gigabits per second (Gbps). It offers **lower latency**, which refers to the time it takes for data to travel between two points. **5G's significantly lower latency** and **higher bandwidth** compared to 4G unlock real-time responsiveness, making it ideal for applications like online gaming, virtual reality, and self-driving cars. Targeted for 2030, 6G promises a leap in performance, enabling real-time data analysis and even more efficient network management. This represents a significant advancement beyond the current discussions surrounding net neutrality.

Although **mobile Internet** has been around for a long time, the challenges remain the same: **battery capacity**, **bandwidth**, and **latency**. Despite significant advancements in all areas, they still fall short of expectations. While bandwidth has been expanded with current 5G technology, users no longer just want to exchange emails, view pictures, or watch videos; they want to video call in real time without delays between sender and receiver (latency). The widespread introduction of sensors and machine-to-machine communication (IoT) will continue to put pressure on bandwidth.

One technology to bridge the physical and digital worlds is **RFID (radio-frequency identification).** RFID utilizes electromagnetic fields to identify and track tags on objects.

There are two types of tags. **Active tags** (comprising less than 10% of tags) can store up to 128 KB of data and transmit signals independently due to built-in power sources, extending their range to about 100 meters. **Passive tags** rely on energy from RFID readers, limiting their range to approximately 1 meter and store only the ID. Activation occurs through magnetic induction, where energy is transmitted from the reader to the RFID chip, enabling the receiver to read the ID. After the ID is in this magnetic field and recognized, all the information is stored in the backend computer (Fig. 4.2).

QR codes, or quick response codes, are two-dimensional barcodes that contain data to **connect the physical** and **digital worlds.** They're commonly scanned by smartphones to access information like website URLs, contact details, or product information, making them convenient for quick digital interactions and transactions.

4.2 Cloud Computing

With cloud computing, one can differentiate between **on-premise** and **cloud** setups. On-premise entails utilizing computing resources within a company owned data center. In contrast, **cloud computing provides external computing power**, accessed via the Internet. Cloud services encompass **on-demand self-service and** need to have powerful **network accessibility, resource pooling, scalability**, and **elasticity.** Businesses can leverage cloud computing through three main service models: infrastructure as a service (IaaS), platform as a service (PaaS), and software as a service (SaaS). These models are illustrated in Fig. 4.3. **Infrastructure as a service (IaaS)** provides the foundation—computing power, storage, and networking. **Platform as a service (PaaS)** offers a ready-to-use platform for building and deploying applications. Finally, **software as a service (SaaS)** delivers applications accessible via the Internet, such as collaboration tools and CRM solutions. Cloud services can further be categorized into private, community, hybrid, and public options, each with distinct features and deployment models. **Private cloud** involves dedicated hardware usage, while **public cloud** ensures logical isolation from other users on shared hardware. Hybrid cloud combines public and private resources. Community cloud involves shared hardware among collaborating companies.

Load balancing in cloud computing involves distributing incoming network traffic or computational tasks across multiple servers or resources to ensure **optimal performance, reliability, and resource utilization**.

Big cloud providers, sometimes called **hyperscalers**, offer cloud computing services at a massive scale. These services encompass **storage**, **computing power**, and **networking**. To achieve this immense capacity, they utilize a strategy called

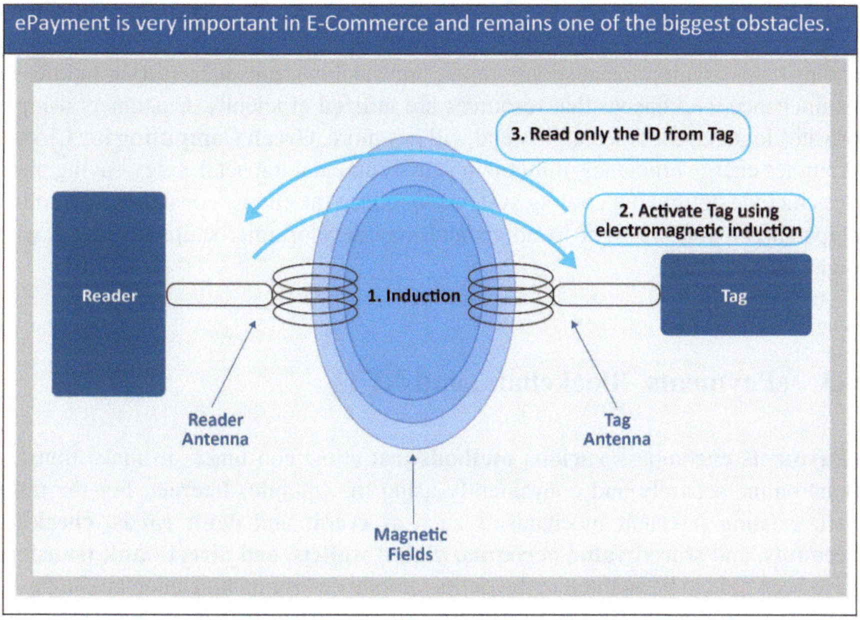

Fig. 4.2 RFID (radio-frequency identification)

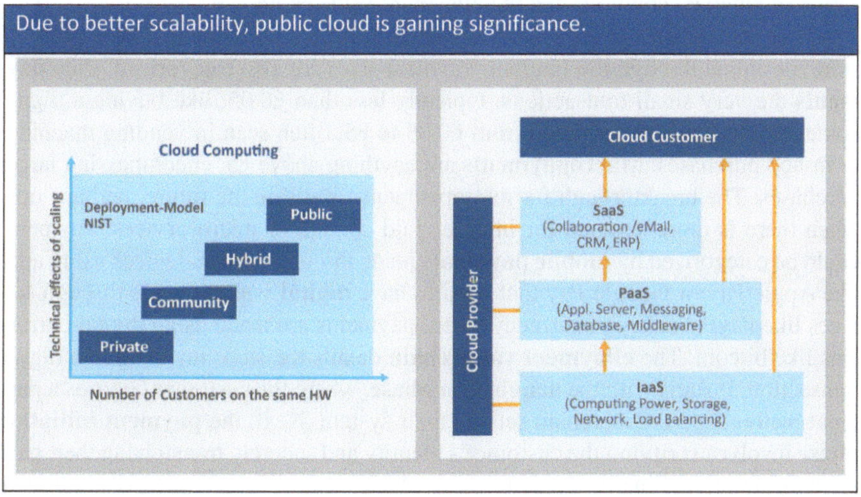

Fig. 4.3 Cloud computing

geographically distributed cloud storage. This means your data isn't confined to a single location; it's spread strategically across different data centers, potentially even in various countries. **Cloud load balancers** typically monitor the health and capacity of servers or resources in real time, directing incoming requests to the most suitable server based on various **factors** such as **server load**, **response time**, **geographic location**, and **availability**. By evenly distributing the workload, load balancing helps to minimize response times, prevent downtime due to server failures or maintenance, and ensure that resources are utilized efficiently. Customers using a private cloud have less scalability and will pay more. **Green Computing for Clouds** promotes energy efficiency, minimizing environmental impact. Energy-saving practices include optimizing cooling systems to reduce the energy consumed by cooling chips and/or find the right locations and may develop microchips operating with higher temperature.

4.3 ePayments, Blockchain, and NFTs

ePayments encompass **various methods** that allow consumers to make transactions online securely and conveniently using the (mobile) Internet. For the most part, existing payment mechanisms such as **credit** and **debit cards, checking accounts**, and **stored value accounts, digital wallets**, and **direct bank transfers** have been able to be adapted to the online/mobile environment. Understanding payment options requires considering both how and when customers pay. User can prepay for goods or services upfront, pay for them at the time of purchase (pay now), or defer payment to a later date (pay later). Figure 4.4 illustrates the categorization of payment solutions and the ePayment value chain.

These transactions can occur in either an offline environment, like a physical store, or online through the Internet. Payment sizes are also categorized. **Pico payments** are very small transactions, typically less than €0.05, like buying a digital content. **Micropayments** range from €0.05 to €5, often seen in vending machines or in-app purchases. **Macropayments** are anything above €5, encompassing larger purchases. The breakthrough for micropayments is still in the future, perhaps only when there is more demand for Internet paid content or microservices. Payments could be categorized by **mobile payments** made through mobile devices using apps like Apple Pay or Google Pay that need to have **digital wallets** made through services like PayPal or cryptocurrency where payments are made using digital currencies like bitcoin. The **ePayment value chain** details the steps involved in a digital transaction. It starts with the **acquisition phase**, where the customer chooses a payment method and the merchant sets up their system. Next, the **payment initiation phase** involves verifying the customer's identity and securely transferring their payment information. Finally, the **processing phase** ensures the payment is authorized, checks for fraud, and settles the transaction between the customer's bank and the merchant. The image below categorizes key considerations for payment systems from the perspectives of the customer and the merchant, with an intersecting set representing shared priorities. **Customers** value acceptability, charge fees (cost), reliability, anonymity, currency convertibility, ease of use, and transparency.

Merchants focus on usage frequency, pricing, payment delays, payment deficits, integration with back-end systems like SAP, support services, and customer loyalty.

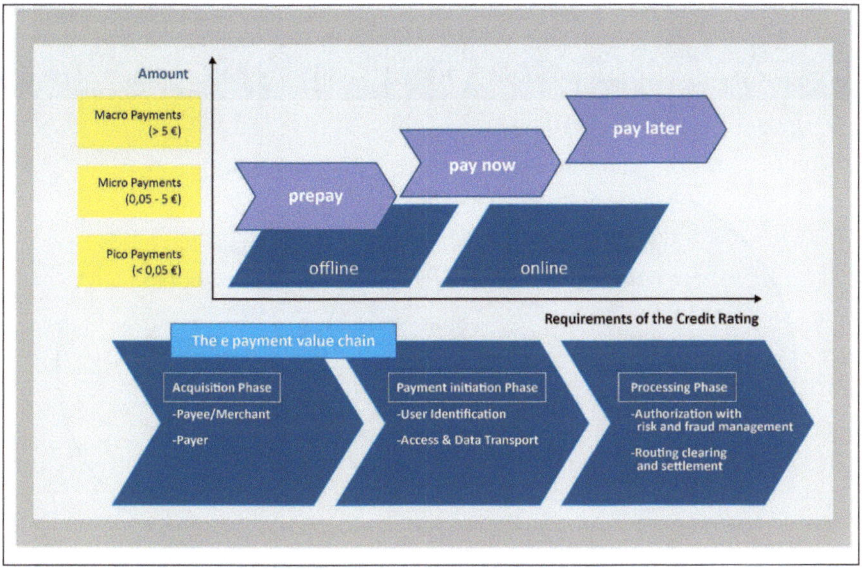

Fig. 4.4 Categorization of payment solutions and ePayment value chain

Figure 4.5 illustrates the categorization of payment solutions and shows the intersection of customers and merchants. Both parties share concerns about atomicity and consistency (ensuring transactions are completed fully or not at all), reputation, security, and efficiency/time (minimizing the time taken to complete transactions). **Mobile payment** systems, prevalent in Europe and Asia, are surging in the United States with necessary infrastructure now emerging. Near-field communication (NFC), a short-range wireless tech, facilitates these transactions within 5 cm.

The concept of **distributed ledger technology** is gaining popularity, with **blockchain** being a prominent example. Interest in distributed ledgers is rising, particularly for blockchains—software-based, decentralized platforms enabling secure trading of digital assets. Distributed ledger technology, which can be explained as a decentralized cash ledger, general ledger, or account ledger, is also synonymously referred to as a transaction database. It's more secure than other concepts because all participants of the network must approve the transaction, which makes counterfeiting more difficult.

Figure 4.6 outlines how distributed ledger technology (blockchain) works.

Bitcoin is a decentralized digital currency that operates on a peer-to-peer network. Transactions are recorded on a public ledger called the blockchain. Users send and receive bitcoins using **wallet software on a personal computer**, mobile device, or a web application. Bitcoin transactions are verified by network nodes through cryptography and recorded in the blockchain. Miners process transactions and secure the network using specialized hardware to solve complex mathematical problems, earning bitcoins as a reward for adding a block of transactions to the Blockchain (**proof of work**). This process is known as **mining**. Bitcoin's

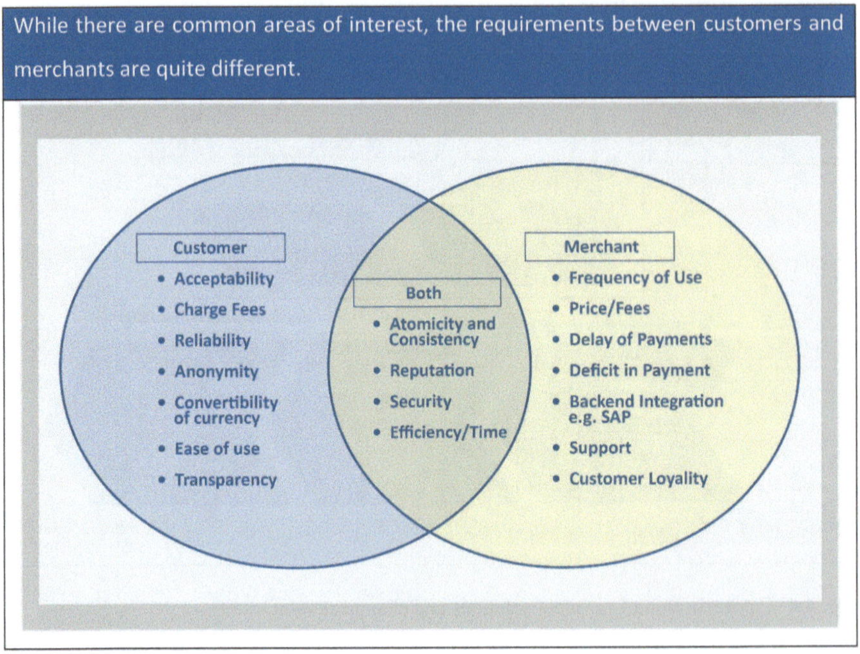

Fig. 4.5 Categorization of payment solutions

decentralized nature ensures it operates without a central authority. Because of low performance and high energy consumption, there are additions. The **Lightning Network** is an off-chain solution. No transactions take place on the blockchain via the Lightning Network. Instead, transactions take place in a layer above the blockchain. **NFTs, or non-fungible tokens,** are a type of digital assets that represents ownership or proof of authenticity of a unique item or piece of content using blockchain technology. Unlike cryptocurrencies such as bitcoin or Ethereum, which are fungible and can be exchanged on a one-to-one basis, NFTs are:

- Unique and cannot be exchanged on a like-for-like basis. The key characteristics are uniqueness. Each NFT is distinct and cannot be replicated or replaced with another token.
- Ownership: NFTs are often used to represent ownership of digital or physical assets, such as digital art, collectibles, music, videos, virtual real estate, in-game items, and more.
- Blockchain-based: NFTs are typically built on blockchain platforms like Ethereum, which provide transparency, security, and immutability.
- Indivisibility: NFTs cannot be divided into smaller units like cryptocurrencies can. They exist as whole tokens.
- Interoperability: NFTs can be bought, sold, and traded on various online marketplaces and platforms.

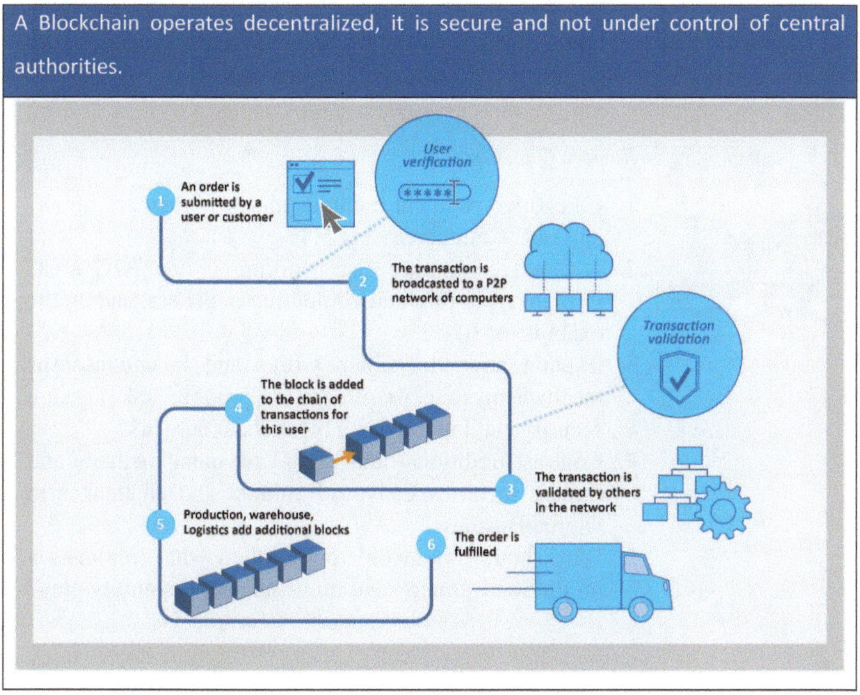

Fig. 4.6 Distributed ledger—blockchain. (Adapted from Laudon/Traver)

4.4 Algorithms, Security, and Cryptography

In Digital Business, algorithms, security, and cryptography are fundamental for safeguarding data integrity, ensuring transactional security, and maintaining user trust. An **algorithm** is a recipe-like set of instructions for solving a problem, breaking it down into clear steps. A computer algorithm takes this concept and translates it into a specific programming language. **Cryptography** uses mathematical algorithms to encrypt data, turning it into an unreadable format that can only be decrypted with the correct key. This ensures that sensitive information such as credit card numbers, personal data, and corporate information remains confidential during transmission and storage. Security measures, strengthened by cryptographic techniques, protect against unauthorized access, data breaches, and cyberattacks. They enable **secure communication channels** over the Internet, allowing for the safe exchange of information between parties in a Digital Business ecosystem. Authentication, a subset of security, uses cryptographic methods to verify the identity of users and devices, assuring that only authorized individuals can access certain data or perform certain actions. Digital signatures, another application of cryptography, ensure the authenticity and integrity of digital documents, providing a non-repudiable proof of agreement or transaction. Cryptography also underpins various other security protocols crucial for Digital Business operations, including

Secure Sockets Layer (SSL)/Transport Layer Security (TLS) for secure web browsing, and blockchain technology for secure and transparent record-keeping in activities like supply chain management and financial transactions.

Review Questions

1. Categorize payment methods and why they are important in E-Commerce?
2. Is cloud computing also working in the B2C area? Explain types of cloud computing in general and on the example of B2C?
3. Explain how blockchain works and how consensus mechanisms (e.g., proof of work, proof of stake) ensure security and integrity in a blockchain network.
4. Contrast traditional and digital payment methods and discuss their respective advantages and challenges in Digital Business.
5. Why should one avoid lock-in, and what role does a multi-cloud strategy and multi-tenancy capability play?

Your Advanced Questions for Starting Prompt Engineering

- Analyze the potential impact of quantum computing on the security and infrastructure of the Internet, particularly in relation to cryptography and Blockchain technology.
- Evaluate the economic implications of spectrum scarcity in the context of 5G and future mobile network development, considering factors such as auctioning, licensing, and technological innovation.
- Examine the challenges and opportunities presented by the convergence of IoT, cloud computing, and artificial intelligence, focusing on data privacy, security, and ethical considerations.
- Discuss the role of government regulation in fostering innovation and competition within the digital payments ecosystem, considering factors such as consumer protection, financial stability, and market structure.

Business Case

Please work on Business Case No. 3, “The Scaling Effects of Cloud Service Business” featuring Amazon Web Services (AWS) and Microsoft Azure. Why are these hyperscalers so successful, and will this continue?

Further Readings

Clarke E (2023) Cryptocurrency trading for complete beginners: navigate the world of crypto investment for massive profits with bitcoin, altcoins, non-fungible tokens, and crypto-art

Goldberg S (2022) The field guide to global payments

Mishra N (2023) Mastering IT infrastructure management: concepts, techniques, and applications

Ruparelia N (2023) Cloud computing

Chapter 5
E-Commerce Shops and Web Presence

Abstract

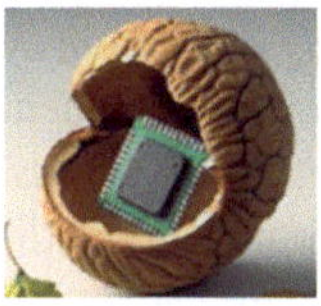

In a nutshell
Building a successful E-Commerce shop requires a solid foundation centered around platform selection, user experience, SEO, and social media marketing. Understanding the customer journey and lifetime value is crucial for long-term success. Mass customization offers a competitive advantage by combining scalability with personalization. eMarketplaces provide additional sales channels, while Web design and mobile optimization are essential for reaching customers.

Keywords E-Commerce platform · User experience (UX) · SEO · Social media marketing · Mass customization · eMarketplace · Webshops · Customer lifetime value (CLTV) · Customer journey · Web design · Supply chain management and eProcurement

Basic Prompts

- What are the key components of a successful E-Commerce platform?
- How can businesses leverage mass customization to gain a competitive advantage?
- What is the importance of SEO and social media marketing in E-Commerce?
- Explain the concept of customer lifetime value and its significance for businesses.
- Describe the difference between native apps and Web apps.

S. Schneider, L. Anderie, *Digital Business Management*,
https://doi.org/10.1007/978-3-031-83177-5_5

5.1 Web Shops and eMarketplaces with Mass Customization

When building your **E-Commerce shop** and Web presence, a strong foundation is crucial. This rests on five key pillars. The first is choosing the right E-Commerce platform (e.g., Shopify, WooCommerce, or Magento (also known as Adobe Commerce)) depending on the size and needs of your business. This platform will be the engine that powers your online store. The next pillar is crafting a user-centric website. This digital storefront should prioritize a seamless user experience to keep visitors engaged and ultimately convert them into loyal customers. A strong SEO strategy and social media marketing are essential to attract customers. By optimizing your website for organic search and leveraging social media platforms, you can connect with your target audience and promote your products.

Finally, nurturing a robust customer base requires a two-pronged approach: **search engine optimization (SEO)** and strategic social media marketing. By meticulously optimizing your website for organic search, your online store can achieve a prominent position in search engine results pages, enhancing its visibility to potential customers. This increased visibility acts as a springboard for connecting with your target audience. Social media platforms provide a dynamic environment to cultivate brand awareness, engage with potential customers, and ultimately promote your products.

Mass customization (Fig. 5.1) presents a strategic opportunity to gain a **competitive advantage**. This innovative approach allows customers to personalize specific features of a product while maintaining production costs near those of mass-produced goods. Mass customization blends the **scalability of mass production with the personal touch of hand-crafted goods.**

It leverages advanced manufacturing techniques, like modular designs and automated assembly lines, to produce large quantities efficiently. Simultaneously, it incorporates customer input to tailor features, style, or functionality, offering a bespoke end product. This approach sits between the uniformity of mass-produced items, which benefit from **economies of scale,** and the distinctive, artisan quality of handmade goods, which are often more costly and time-consuming to create. Mass customization aims to deliver the best of both worlds: affordability and personalized value.

In addition to eShops and a custom-built Web presence, eMarketplaces are an important interface for E-Commerce. An **eMarketplace or electronic market(place)** is a digital platform enabling buying and selling of goods, services, or financial assets. Examples include E-Commerce platforms (like Amazon), financial markets (such as stock exchanges), cryptocurrency exchanges (like Coinbase), and freelance platforms (like Upwork).

They offer accessibility, efficiency, and global reach for transactions. Pivitol questions for entering the electronic marketplace are presented in Fig. 5.2.

In B2B digital commerce, auctions offer a noteworthy alternative to traditional methods like requesting proposals, tenders, or quotes. Many auctions take place in electronic markets, where the English and Dutch auctions are the most famous ones.

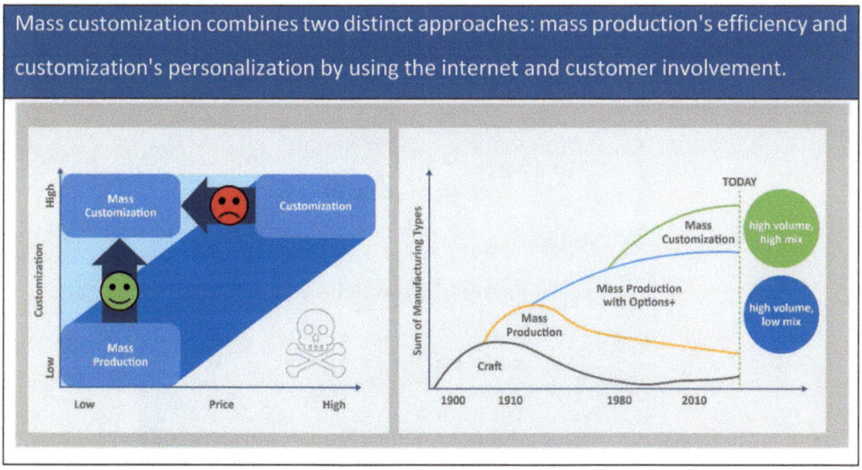

Fig. 5.1 Mass customization

In an **English auction**, the price starts low, and participants bid higher until no one is willing to bid higher. The item is then sold to the highest bidder at the final price. It's commonly used in traditional auction houses and online platforms like eBay. In a **Dutch auction**, the seller starts with a high price, which is gradually lowered until a buyer accepts the price or the reserve price is reached. It's often used in financial markets for initial public offerings (IPOs) and in some online auctions.

5.2 Webshops and Catalogs

Webshops are online retail stores where customers can browse and purchase goods. They use digital catalogs, which are collections of product images and descriptions, to showcase items, enabling customers to conveniently view and select products for purchase from any location with Internet access. Webshops must be ready for native apps and Web apps. **Native apps** are smartphone applications developed specifically for a mobile operating system, like iOS or Android, utilizing platform-specific programming languages. They are installed directly onto the device, often delivering high performance and a user experience that aligns with the platform's conventions. Conversely, **Web apps** are not installed locally but accessed through a mobile browser, using web technologies such as HTML5, CSS, and JavaScript. They are platform-independent and easier to maintain and do not require app store approval. Native apps can access device features like GPS and cameras more seamlessly, while web apps are more limited in functionality and hardware integration but are universally accessible.

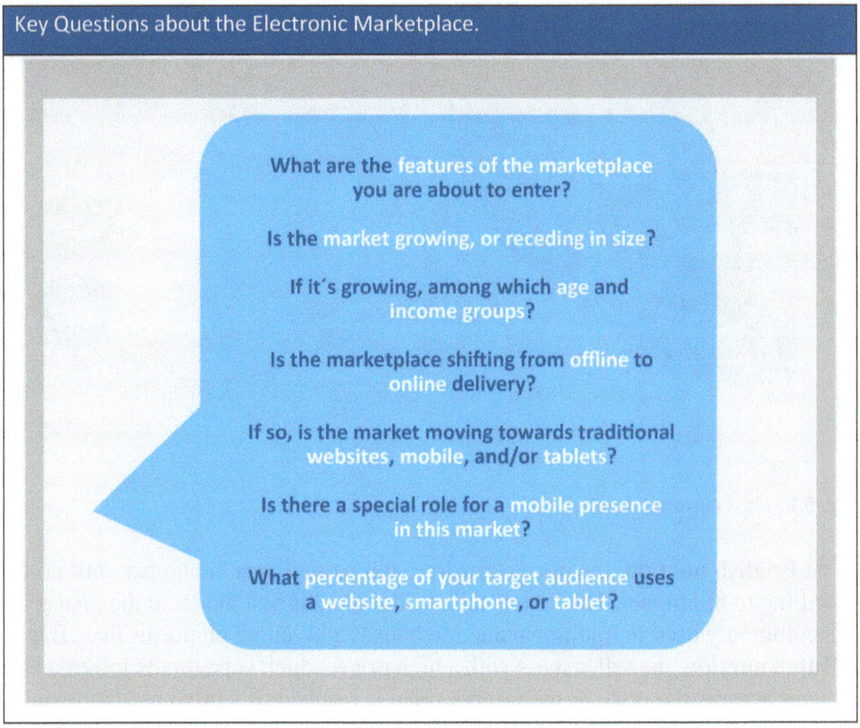

Fig. 5.2 Electronic marketplace

5.3 Customer Lifetime Value and Customer Journey

Customer lifetime value is the expected revenue generated from a single customer over the anticipated lifetime of that customer's relationship with you. The **customer lifetime value (CLV) is a metric that predicts the total revenue a customer will generate over their entire relationship** with a business.

The most common formula for customer lifetime value (CLTV) is:

$$\text{CLTV} = \text{Customer value} \times \text{Average customer lifespan}$$

The customer journey, as outlined in Fig. 5.3, details the various phases a customer goes through during its lifetime.

It helps businesses understand the long-term value of acquiring and retaining customers, guiding strategic decision-making and resource allocation.

The **customer journey** outlines the series of interactions a customer has with a business, from initial awareness to post-purchase support. **It encompasses touchpoints across various channels and stages**, such as awareness, consideration, purchase, retention, and advocacy. Understanding and optimizing this journey is **crucial** for **delivering a seamless** and satisfying **customer experience.**

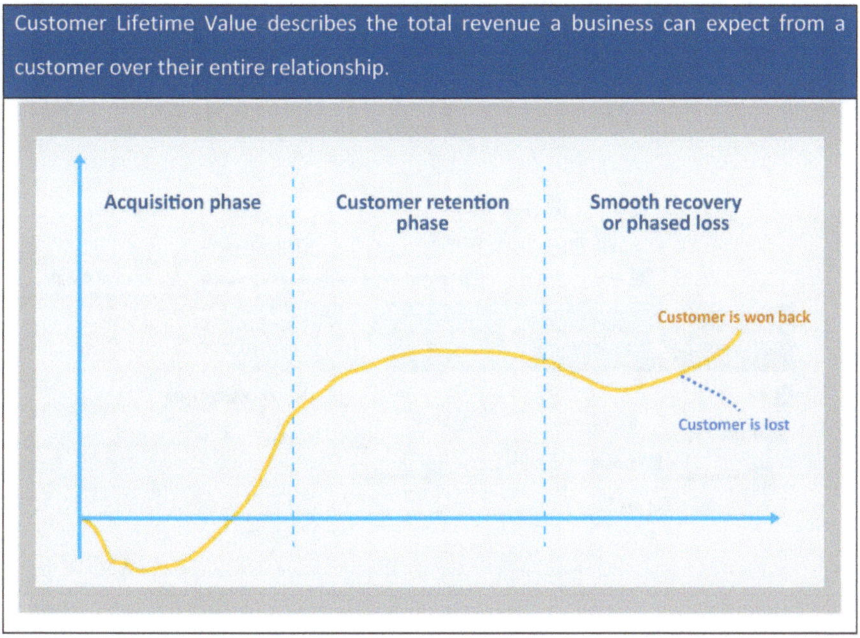

Fig. 5.3 Customer lifetime value

Figure 5.4 is depicting a progression through **five stages: awareness, consideration, purchase, retention, and advocacy.** It links these phases, suggesting a dynamic flow. Alongside, colored dots correspond to different marketing channels and customer touchpoints, such as public relations, reviews, social media, and direct mail, which are strategically aligned with each stage. The map underscores the multifaceted approach businesses take to guide potential customers from initial awareness of a product or service to the point where they not only become repeat buyers but also brand advocates.

5.4 Web Design and Analysis of Internet Usage

Web design is the creation of visually appealing and user-friendly websites using elements like **layout, colors, graphics, and content, aiming for functionality, usability, and positive user experience**. System analysis for building a mobile presence has to respect E-Business objectives, the functionality, and the information requirements.

Figure 5.5 illustrates how a custom-built web presence can be created. Success hinges on utilizing a variety of tools, including programming languages like Python or HTML5, and specialized web content management systems (website-builder) like WordPress. The criteria for a good Web design are:

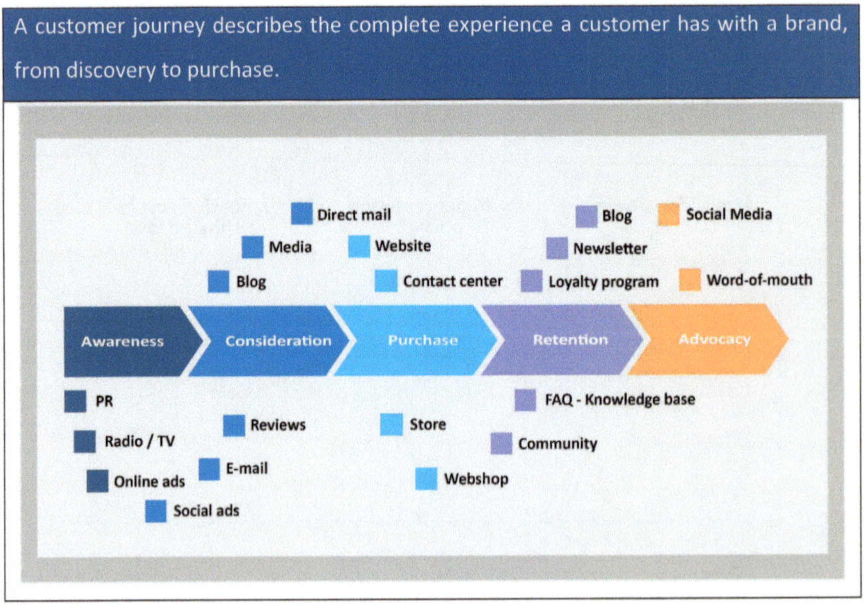

Fig. 5.4 Customer journey

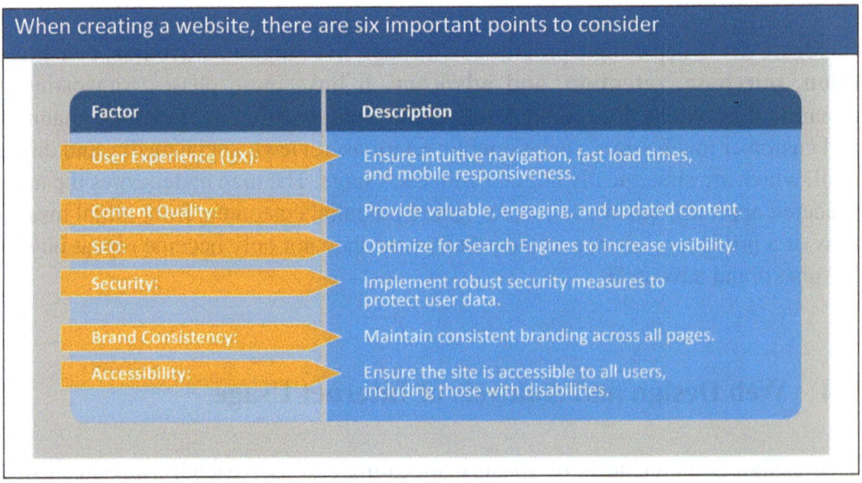

Fig. 5.5 Creating a Web presence

- User Experience (UX) and Human Computer Interface: Prioritize intuitive navigation, clear information architecture, and user-friendly, etc.
- Visual Appeal: Use a visually appealing layout, color scheme, typography, and imagery that align with your brand identity.

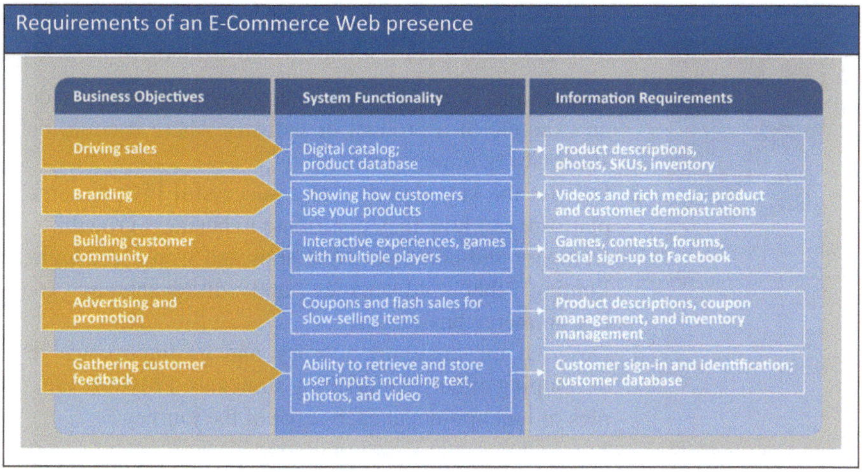

Fig. 5.6 Requirements of an E-Commerce Web presence. (Adapted from Laudon/Traver)

- Responsiveness: Ensure the website is optimized for various devices and screen sizes, providing a seamless experience across desktops, mobile.
- Loading Speed: Optimize page loading times to minimize bounce rates and improve user retention compare conversion rate.
- Accessibility: Design with accessibility in mind to ensure that people with disabilities can perceive, understand, navigate, and interact.
- Content Quality: Deliver high-quality, relevant, and engaging content that meets the needs of your target audience. Use clear and concise language.
- Search engine optimization (SEO) and SEM:
- Consistency: Maintain consistency in design elements, such as colors, fonts, and layout, throughout the website to reinforce brand.
- Security: Prioritize website security to protect user data and maintain trust. Utilize HTTPS protocol; implement robust authentication mechanism.
- Feedback and Iteration: Gather user feedback through analytics, surveys, and usability testing to identify areas for improvement.

A web presence must also support the buying and selling of goods and services through mobile devices and apps, which is called mobile commerce. Important are fast loading, intuitive design, easy navigation, mobile payment options, security, responsive customer service, personalized experience, and clear calls-to-action. Figure 5.6 indicates the requirements of a successful E-Commerce Web presence.

Review Questions

1. Explain the concept of mass customization and provide an example of a product or industry where it could be successfully implemented.
2. Discuss the key elements of a successful E-Commerce platform and how they contribute to business growth.
3. Compare and contrast native apps and web apps, highlighting their advantages and disadvantages for E-Commerce businesses.
4. Describe the customer journey and its importance in developing effective marketing strategies. Provide examples of touchpoints at each stage of the journey.

Your Advanced Questions for Starting Prompt Engineering

- How can businesses effectively leverage a combination of mass customization and eMarketplaces to enhance customer satisfaction and increase revenue?
- Discuss the role of data analytics in optimizing the customer journey and improving customer lifetime value in an E-Commerce context.
- Examine the challenges and opportunities presented by the increasing use of mobile commerce and its impact on traditional retail businesses.

Business Case

Please read Business Case No. 4, "Competitive Landscape of the E-Commerce Industry" featuring the companies Temu, Amazon, Shein, Otto, and Alibaba. Discuss the competitive situation in the industry and its impact on brick-and-mortar retail.

Further Readings

Aichner T, Salvador F (2024) Mass customization and customer centricity: In Honor of the contributions of cipriano forzaber
Sixolisiwe D (2024) E-Commerce hustle: mastering success in the digital marketplace
Yablonski J (2024) Laws of UX: using psychology to design better products and services

Further Reading

[illegible]

Chapter 6
Digital Marketing and Advertising

Abstract

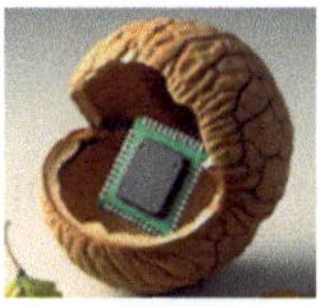

In a nutshell

This chapter provides an overview of eMarketing, emphasizing its role in modern business. It explores the consumer decision-making process in the digital realm and discusses key eMarketing strategies. Search engine optimization (SEO) and Search engine marketing (SEM) are presented as essential tools for online visibility. The concept of dynamic pricing and affiliate marketing is introduced, along with the significance of the long tail in E-Commerce. By understanding these elements, businesses can develop effective eMarketing strategies to reach and engage target audiences.

Keywords eMarketing · Digital marketing · Online marketing · Consumer behavior · Search engine optimization (SEO) · Search engine marketing (SEM) · Dynamic pricing · Affiliate marketing · Long tail

S. Schneider, L. Anderie, *Digital Business Management*,
https://doi.org/10.1007/978-3-031-83177-5_6

Basic Prompts

- How does understanding consumer behavior influence the development of effective eMarketing strategies?
- What are the key differences between SEO and SEM, and how do they contribute to a successful online marketing campaign?
- Explain the concept of the long tail and its implications for E-Commerce businesses.
- How can businesses leverage dynamic pricing to optimize revenue in the digital marketplace?
- Discuss the role of social media in the consumer purchase decision process and its impact on eMarketing.

6.1 Types of eMarketing

Marketing (see Fig. 6.1) is a customer-centric approach to business management, encompassing all the activities listed below:

- Product development.
- Pricing strategy.

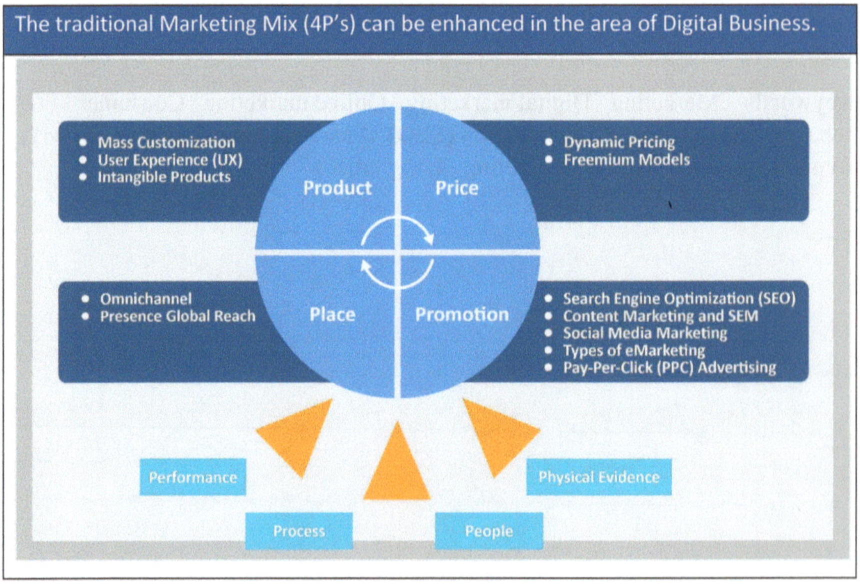

Fig. 6.1 Marketing mix in the area of Digital Business

- Place (distribution channels).
- Promotion.

The traditional marketing mix (4Ps) is often supplemented today by four additional Ps, especially in the context of service marketing and modern business environments (8 Ps of marketing):

- People: All individuals involved in the service delivery and consumption, including employees and customers.
- Process: The procedures, mechanisms, and flow of activities that lead to the delivery of the product or service.
- Physical Evidence: The tangible elements that help customers evaluate the service before purchase, such as facilities, brochures, and online reviews.
- Performance: "This is about the performance as well as the usability of the website."

Online marketing is promoting products or services over the Internet using tools like social media, email, search engines, and websites to reach a targeted audience, engage with them, and drive sales or other desired actions. The objective of online marketing—as in all marketing—is to build customer relationships so that the firm can achieve above-average returns (both by offering superior products or services and by communicating the brand's features to the consumer).

Online marketing, distinct from traditional channels, is **characterized by its personalized, participatory, peer-to-peer, and community-building features.** It allows for tailored communication, catering to individual preferences. It fosters engagement, enabling interaction between brands and consumers. Moreover, it facilitates peer recommendations and reviews, influencing purchasing decisions. Community-building aspects create a sense of belonging and loyalty among consumers, enhancing brand advocacy and long-term relationships in the digital realm. To measure this, there are several scales available, like click-through rates. **Click-through rates** in E-Commerce typically range from 1% to 5%, varying by industry and strategy. Click-through rates reflect the percentage of users clicking on links or ads, crucial for gauging campaign effectiveness. Optimization through targeted content, advertising, and user experience enhances CTR, driving engagement and potential sales. Other metrics include the **conversion rate** or the **bounce rate** (percentage of visitors who leave the website after viewing only one page). Conversion rate is the percentage of website visitors who complete a desired action, such as making a purchase or signing up for a newsletter. It measures the effectiveness of a website in converting visitors into customers or leads. Figure 6.2 shows various marketing methods and indicates their effectiveness.

Marketing methods and their effectiveness vary significantly.

Marketing Methods	Typical Click-through Rates
Banner ads	.05% - .25%
Google enhanced search ads (Product Listing Ads)	2.8% - 3.6%
Google ads search listing	2.09% - 6.05% (3.7% average)
Video	.34% - .85%
Rich media	.13% - .35%
Sponsorships	1.5% - 3.0%
Native ads	.80% - 1.8%
Content marketing	.19% - .29%
Affiliate relationships	.20% - .40%
E-mail marketing in-house list	3.0% - 5.0%
E-mail marketing purchased list	.01% - 1.5%
Social network display ads	.15% - .25%
Mobile display ads	.09% - 1.25%

Fig. 6.2 Marketing methods. (Adapted from Laudon/Traver)

6.2 Consumer Purchase Decision Process/Consumer Behavior

Understanding **online consumer behavior** is important for firms once they identify their audience. This involves delving into the interdisciplinary study of consumer behavior, drawing from sociology, psychology, and economics. The **consumer purchase decision process** is the journey a customer takes from recognizing a need to evaluating options, making a purchase, and reflecting on their experience. Models in this field aim to **predict purchasing patterns,** considering factors like timing, location, and motivation. By comprehending the decision-making process, businesses can tailor marketing strategies effectively. This holistic approach not only enhances product sales but also fosters a deeper connection with consumers, ultimately leading to long-term success in the marketplace.

The **research online, purchase offline (ROPO)** effect describes the phenomenon where consumers research products or services online but make their purchase through offline channels, such as in-store. This trend underscores the importance of online presence even for brick-and-mortar businesses. Consumers use online platforms to gather information, compare prices, and read reviews before making

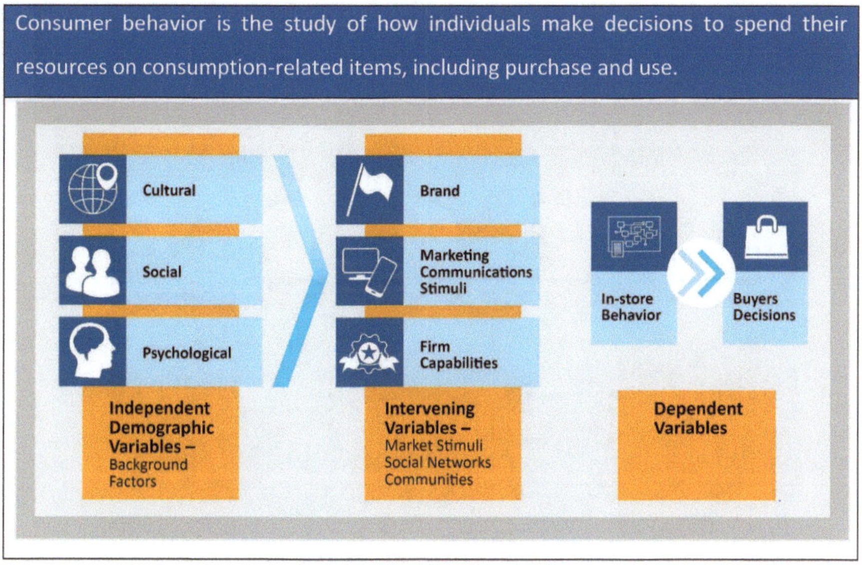

Fig. 6.3 Consumer behavior. (Adapted from Laudon/Traver)

informed purchasing decisions offline. **Research offline, purchase online (ROPO)** effect also exists, where consumers research products or services through offline channels, such as visiting physical stores or seeking recommendations from friends, and then make their purchase online.

The online purchasing decision follows a structured process comprising five stages. It begins with the consumer becoming aware of a need, prompting them to seek more information online. Subsequently, they evaluate various alternatives available, weighing factors like price, quality, and reviews. Figure 6.3 shows how consumer behavior is influencing the consumer purchase decision.

Upon thorough consideration, the consumer makes the actual purchase decision online. Following the purchase, there may be post-purchase contact with the firm, which could involve feedback, inquiries, or support. Understanding and optimizing each stage of this process is crucial for businesses to effectively engage consumers and drive successful online transactions while fostering long-term customer satisfaction and loyalty.

The **consumer decision-making process** encompasses five stages (see Fig. 6.4): Awareness of need prompts information search, where consumers gather details online. Evaluation of alternatives involves comparing options based on price, quality, and reviews.

Consumers then make the purchase decision, often online. Post-purchase, they may engage with the firm for feedback or support. Understanding these stages helps businesses tailor marketing strategies to guide consumers seamlessly through the purchasing journey, enhancing satisfaction and fostering loyalty.

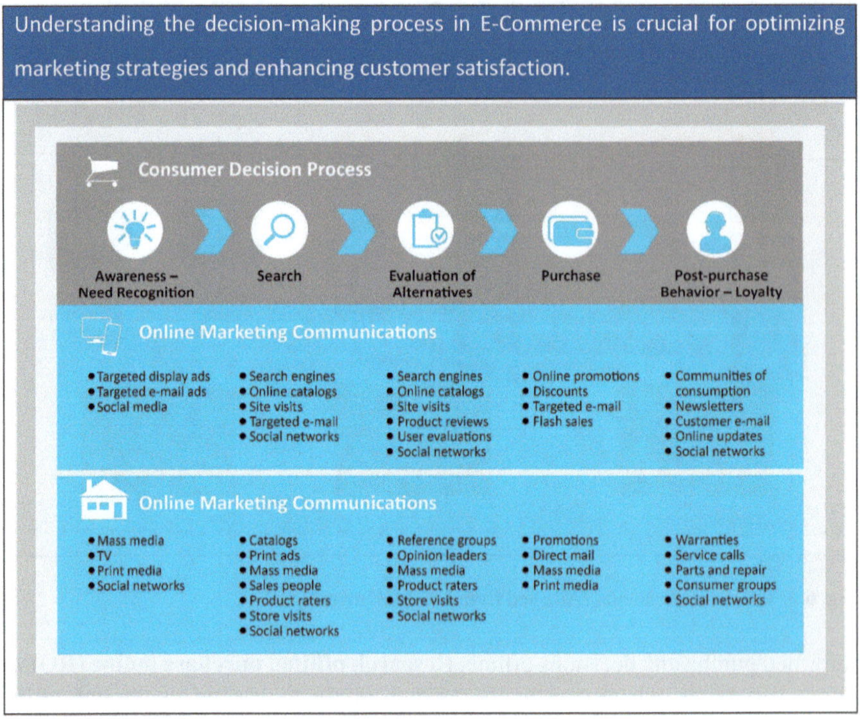

Fig. 6.4 Decision-making process. (Adapted from Laudon/Traver)

6.3 Digital Advertising and Search Engine Marketing (SEM/SEO)

Digital advertising is promoting products, services, or brands through online channels like display ads, social media, and search engines. It leverages the Internet to target specific audiences, track performance, and optimize campaigns. This dynamic approach enables businesses to reach consumers effectively in the digital landscape.

A **search engine** is an online tool that allows users to search and retrieve information from the Internet by entering keywords or phrases, displaying relevant results ranked by relevance.

Google search operates by deploying complex algorithms to crawl and index web pages across the Internet. When a user enters keywords or phrases into the search bar, Google's algorithms analyze these queries and match them with indexed web pages. The search engine then ranks these pages based on numerous factors, including relevance, quality, and authority. **Google's PageRank Algorithm**, among others, plays a crucial role in determining the order of search results. Additionally, factors like user location, search history, and device type may influence result rankings. Google's continuous updates and improvements, such as the BERT algorithm for natural language processing, enhance search accuracy and relevance. Overall,

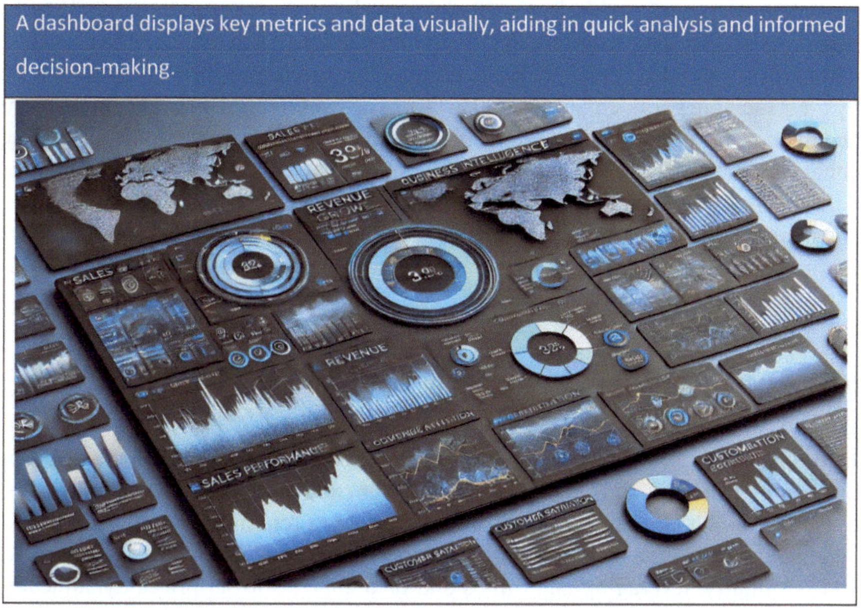

Fig. 6.5 Monitoring of E-Commerce KPI's

Google search aims to deliver the most useful and relevant information to users based on their search queries.

SEO (search engine optimization) and **SEM (search engine marketing)** are both digital marketing strategies aimed at improving a website's visibility on **search engine results pages (SERPs)**. SEO and SEM are now often referred to together as **SEA (search engine advertising)**. Their performance can be monitored with business intelligence tools such as Google Analytics or Microsoft Power BI. As shown in Fig. 6.5, a dashboard visualizes key performance indicators (KPIs).

SEO involves optimizing website content, structure, and off-page factors to increase organic (unpaid) search traffic. It focuses on improving rankings through techniques like keyword research, content optimization, and link building. SEM, on the other hand, involves paid advertising campaigns, such as Google Ads, where E-Businesses bid on keywords to display ads in search results. The key difference is that SEO focuses on organic methods for improving visibility, while **SEM** involves paid advertising to gain immediate visibility on SERPs. SERP stands for search engine results page. It refers to the page that appears after a user enters a search query into a search engine like Google, Bing, or Yahoo. The SERP displays a list of relevant websites, ads, and other content related to the search query. Google Ads is an online advertising platform developed by Google. It allows businesses to create and display ads on Google's search engine results pages and across the Google Display Network. Advertisers bid on keywords relevant to their products or services to have their ads displayed to users when they search for related terms **(Google Ads)**. Google Ads operates on a pay-per-click (PPC) model, where advertisers only pay when users click on their ads. **Social search** involves leveraging social media platforms to discover information, recommendations, and trends. Users search within these platforms to find content, products, or services shared or recommended by their social network connections. This form of search relies on social interactions and user-generated content to inform decision-making and facilitate discovery, enhancing the user experience within social media environments. Next functionality will integrate AI. This artificial intelligence technologies such as machine learning and natural language processing enhance search engine capabilities, providing more accurate, relevant, and personalized search results to users.

6.4 Dynamic Pricing and Long Tail

Dynamic pricing is a strategy where prices for products or services fluctuate based on various factors such as demand, competition, and supply. Unlike fixed pricing, dynamic pricing allows businesses to adjust prices in real time to optimize revenue and maximize profits. It's commonly used in E-Commerce and industries like travel and hospitality, leveraging algorithms and data analysis to set prices dynamically. Another more Internet-specific pricing strategy is **freemium pricing** which offers basic services or products for free while charging a premium for advanced features or functionalities. This model allows customers to access a basic version at no cost, enticing them to upgrade to a paid version for additional benefits or enhanced services.

Affiliate marketing is a performance-based marketing strategy where firms pay commissions, typically 4% to 20%, to other websites for driving traffic or sales to their site. Affiliates promote products or services through links and earn a commission for each click or purchase generated. This model accounts for approximately 10% of online retail sales, with top retailers having an average of 2000 affiliates in their program.

The **long tail concept** (see Fig. 6.6), popularized by Chris Anderson, illustrates the phenomenon where niche products collectively make up a significant portion of total sales, alongside mainstream items.

In E-Commerce, platforms like Amazon or Netflix can offer a vast array of niche products or content due to low distribution costs and unlimited virtual shelf space. While individual niche products may have lower sales volumes, their cumulative demand in the "long tail"can rival or even surpass that of popular items, highlighting the importance of catering to diverse interests and preferences in today's digital marketplace for sustained profitability and customer satisfaction.

The long tail concept (Fig. 6.6) is a pivotal economic theory that reshapes our understanding of market demand and sales strategy, particularly in the digital era. Coined by Chris Anderson, it challenges the traditional 80/20 rule that prioritized the best-selling items—often 20% of products generating 80% of sales. The long tail suggests that our focus should not be limited to the "hits" but should also include the multitude of niche products that represent a vast market. In the context of

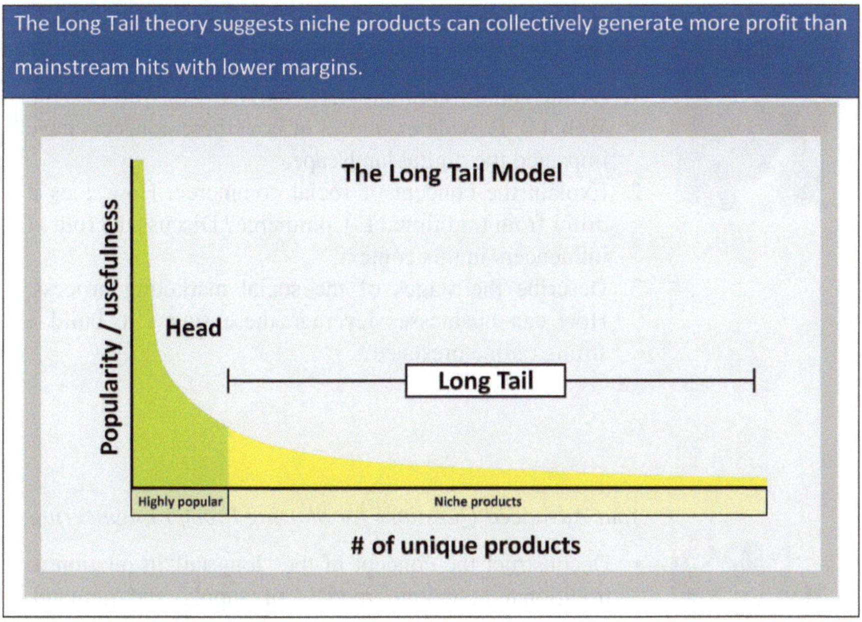

Fig. 6.6 The long tail. (Adapted from Anderson)

E-Commerce, companies such as Amazon exemplify the long tail strategy by offering an immense variety of products. Unlike brick-and-mortar stores limited by physical shelf space, online platforms can virtually stock an endless range of items, from bestsellers to the most obscure. Similarly, streaming services like Netflix take advantage of the long tail by providing not just blockbuster movies and TV shows but also independent films, documentaries, and foreign content that cater to all tastes and preferences. The **Long tail** thrives on the dynamics of online consumer behavior. Consumers' diverse interests can now be met with the vast inventory made available through E-Commerce and digital content platforms. This variety, combined with powerful search capabilities and recommendation algorithms, enables customers to discover and purchase niche products that they might never have found in a traditional retail setting. While each niche product might sell infrequently, the aggregate sales of these countless items can be substantial, often equaling or surpassing the sales of the few hot-selling products. This reflects a shift from a mass market to a vast number of mini-markets. The long tail has significant implications for producers and retailers. It suggests that by catering to niche markets, businesses can attract and retain customers with specific interests, leading to increased overall sales, customer satisfaction, and loyalty. It underlines the importance of an inventory strategy that, rather than focusing solely on high-demand items, also includes diverse, less popular ones to cover a wider spectrum of consumer demand in the expansive online marketplace. This approach not only fulfills the varied preferences of a fragmented audience but also secures a competitive advantage in a marketplace that values diversity and individuality.

Review Questions

1. Define and differentiate between Web 2.0, Web 3.0, and Web 4.0. Provide examples of how these concepts have impacted the digital landscape.
2. Explain the concept of social commerce. How does it differ from traditional E-Commerce? Discuss the role of influencers in this context.
3. Describe the stages of the social marketing process. How can businesses leverage these stages to build a strong online presence?

Your Advanced Questions for Starting Prompt Engineering

- Deconstruct the concept of the "long tail"in relation to traditional economic models of supply and demand. How does it challenge or reinforce existing theories about consumer behavior and market structure?
- Develop a digital marketing strategy for a luxury brand seeking to expand its market reach while preserving brand exclusivity. How can the brand leverage both the "head" and the "tail" of the market to achieve this?
- Discuss the role of social media in the consumer purchase decision process and its impact on eMarketing.

Business Case

Please read Business Case No. 5, "The Search Engine Market" featuring Google, Bing, METAGER, and STARTPAGE. Why are search engines essential for advertising?

Further Readings

Adha Akbari D (2024) Branding and eMarketing: maximizing brand potential through E-marketing

Anderson C (2024) The long tail: how endless choice is creating unlimited demand. https://www.linkedin.com/in/chrisanderson6/

Cutler K (2023) Search marketing: a strategic approach to SEO and SEM

Kotler P, Kartajaya H, Setiawan I (2024) Marketing 4.0: moving from traditional to digital. Wiley. https://emeriti.northwestern.edu/philip-kotler/

Chapter 7
Social and Mobile Commerce with Location-Based Services

Abstract

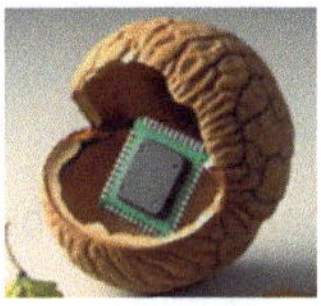

In a nutshell
The chapter explores the evolution of the Internet, from the static Web 1.0 to the interactive Web 2.0 and the emerging Web 3.0 and 4.0. It highlights the rise of social media and its impact on business, focusing on social marketing and its stages. The importance of mobile devices is emphasized with a focus on mobile commerce and location-based services. Finally, the text introduces social commerce and influencer marketing as key strategies in the digital landscape. The smartphone as we know and use it today was launched by Steve Jobs in 2007.

Keywords Mobile commerce (M-Commerce) · Social media · Social networks · Web 2.0 · Web 3.0 · Location-based services (LBS) · Mobile business · Social commerce · Influencer marketing · User-generated content

The terms **social media** and **social networks** are often used interchangeably, but they complement each other. Social media are platforms for content creation and sharing, while social networks are the connections and relationships formed between users on those platforms.

S. Schneider, L. Anderie, *Digital Business Management*,
https://doi.org/10.1007/978-3-031-83177-5_7

Basic Prompts

- What are the main differences between Web 1.0, 2.0, 3.0, and 4.0?
- How has social media transformed the way businesses interact with customers?
- What is the significance of mobile commerce and location-based services in today's digital landscape?
- Explain the concept of social commerce and how it differs from traditional E-Commerce.
- What is the role of influencer marketing in promoting products and services?

7.1 Social Media and Online Communities

The evolution of the World Wide Web in terms of interaction patterns can be described in four phases.

Web 1.0: Often referred to as the "static Web," it was the first stage of the World Wide Web where content was predominantly read-only and users could not interact with the content. Information flowed only one way—from the computer (web server) to the person (user). **Web 2.0:** Known as the "social Web," it transformed the Internet into an interactive and social space where users could interact with each other and contribute content. Information flow became bidirectional between person and person, facilitated by the computer (Internet platforms).

Web 3.0: Sometimes called the "semantic Web," this is about computers being able to understand and interpret information like humans do, to deliver a more personalized Web experience. The information flow here is between computers (M2M, **machine-to-machine communication**) where they use data to learn, adapt, and potentially operate autonomously, especially in the **Internet of Things** (IoT) area.

While the concept of Web 3.0 is gaining traction and there are various projects and technologies being developed to bring it to fruition, a fully realized Web 3.0 is not yet a reality.

Web 3.0 is not synonymous with Web3, which, in conjunction with blockchain technology, proposes a fundamentally new way of interacting with and experiencing the Internet.

Web 4.0: Often referred to as the "symbiotic Web," it is an emerging concept where the interaction between computers and humans becomes more interconnected, possibly indicating a future where AI systems work in tandem with humans, anticipating needs and functioning as a part of human intelligence.

Figure 7.1 is visualizing the development of the Web (top) and the blockchain technology (bottom). Web1, Web2, and Web3 represent separate phases in the evolution of the World Wide Web, each characterized by unique features and functionalities. Key distinctions among these phases include the level of interactivity, the degree of decentralization, and the role of user-generated content and usage of artificial intelligence. Superintelligence is an advanced form of artificial intelligence surpassing human intelligence, capable of solving complex problems and potentially transforming society.

Social media encompasses online platforms and tools utilized by individuals to exchange opinions, experiences, insights, perceptions, and diverse media formats, such as photos, videos, and music. It serves as a digital space where people connect and interact, sharing their thoughts and content with one another (Fig. 7.2).

These platforms enable users to communicate and engage with each other in real time, using various formats such as text, images, videos, and audio. A central concept is **user-generated content,** as social media heavily depends on content created and shared by users. This interactivity is further enhanced through features like likes, comments, shares, and direct messaging, fostering real-time connections among people globally. This facilitates the creation of virtual communities based on shared interests, professions, or other criteria. Another significant aspect is network building, where users can follow or connect with other users and businesses, thereby expanding their networks.

Social networks are an online community with a virtual space where individuals with shared interests, goals, or identities come together to communicate, exchange information, and build relationships. Figure 7.3 presents a comparison of functions in social network analysis and social media analysis.

Social networks can range from general social media sites like Facebook and X to professional networks like LinkedIn, visual content platforms like Instagram and Pinterest, video sharing sites like YouTube and TikTok, and specialized forums like Reddit.

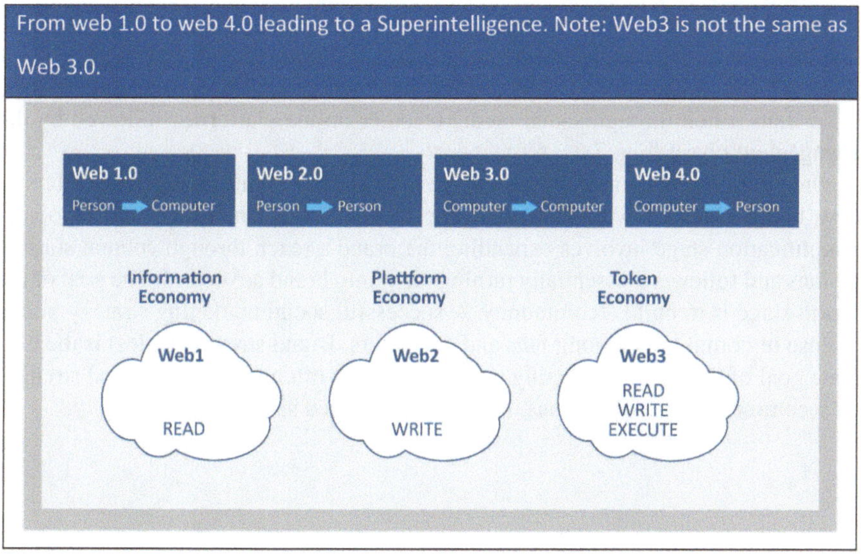

Fig. 7.1 From Web 1.0 to Web 4.0

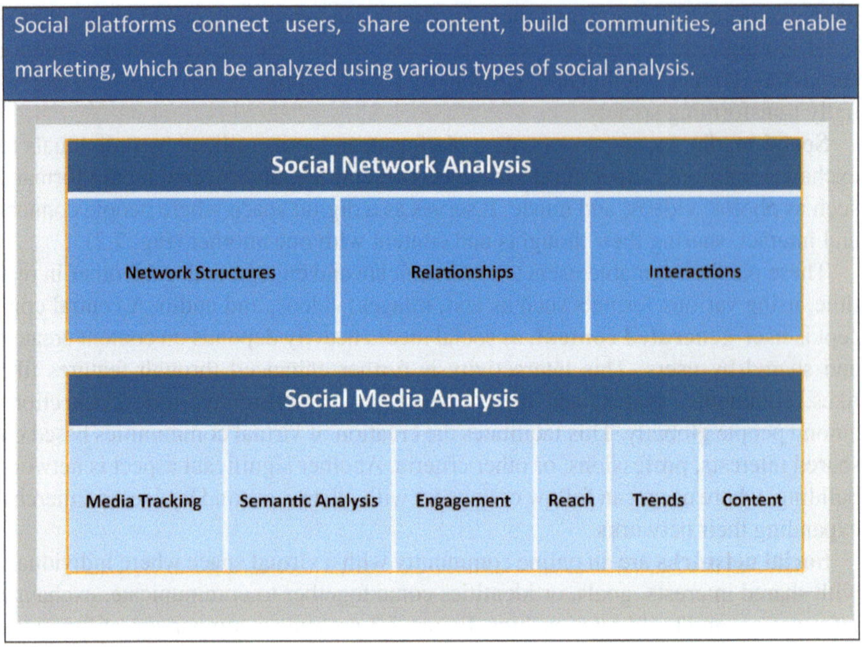

Fig. 7.2 Social platforms and types of social analysis

Each network caters to different interests and communication styles, from text and image sharing to blogging and live streaming. Figure 7.4 provides examples of services and functions offered by social media platforms.

Social Marketing Process.

The model of the social marketing process is broken down into five stages. It starts with fan acquisition. This is the first stage where a brand aims to gain followers or fans, often through social media or other online platforms, followed by the engagement phase (Fig. 7.5).

Once fans are acquired, the next stage is to engage them. Engagement refers to how brands interact with their audience to keep them interested and involved. Amplification stage involves expanding the brand's reach through content sharing by fans and followers, essentially turning them into brand advocates. The goal of the fourth stage is to build a community. A successful social marketing strategy builds a sense of community among fans and customers. Brand strength (sales) is the ultimate goal of the social marketing process which is often to enhance brand strength by recommendations of the fans, leading to increased sales.

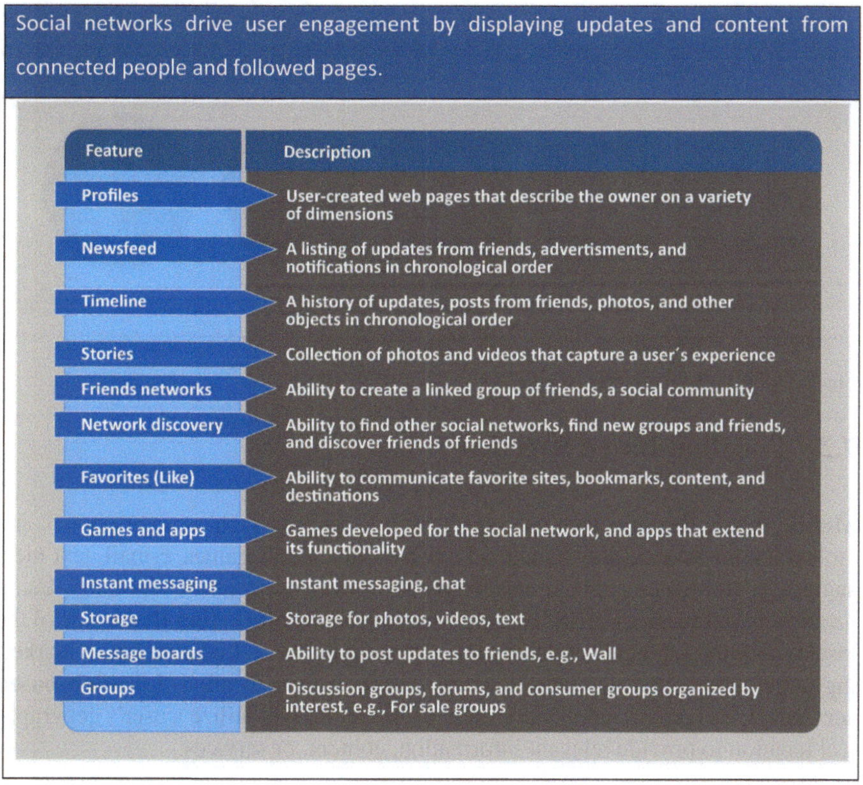

Fig. 7.3 Features of social networks. (Adapted from Laudon/Traver)

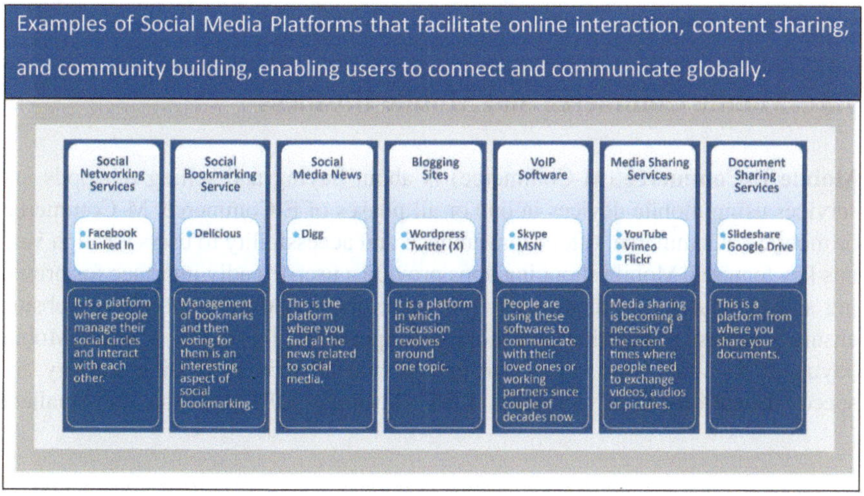

Fig. 7.4 Social media platforms

Fig. 7.5 The social marketing process

7.2 Location-Based Services

Mobile marketing involves the use of mobile devices such as smartphones and tablet computers to display banner ads, rich media, video, games, e-mail, text messaging, in-store messaging, quick response (QR) codes, and couponing. Using location-based services (LBS) leads to **location-based marketing that** is one of the fastest-growing segments of the digital marketing universe. Location-based marketing targets marketing messages to users based on their location. **Location-based services (LBS)** refer to applications and technologies that utilize a user's geographical location to provide relevant information, content, or services.

- Navigation and mapping.
- Location-based marketing.
- Location-based social networking.

7.3 Mobile Commerce and Mobile Business

Mobile E-Commerce (M-Commerce) is about buying and selling of goods and services using mobile devices in one or all phases of E-Commerce. M-Commerce, or mobile E-Commerce, offers convenience and accessibility to users through various key features. Mobile shopping apps provide a user-friendly interface for browsing and purchasing goods directly from smartphones. Mobile-optimized websites ensure **seamless navigation** and shopping experiences on smaller screens. Mobile payments facilitate transactions through mobile devices, enhancing security and speed. **Location-based services** (LBS) leverage GPS to offer personalized recommendations and targeted promotions based on users' geographic locations. Mobile marketing utilizes SMS, push notifications, and in-app ads to reach consumers effectively. In-app purchases allow users to buy additional features or content within applications, enhancing user experience and revenue for developers. Mobile ticketing and booking enable users to purchase tickets, make reservations, and access services conveniently through their mobile devices, revolutionizing industries like travel and entertainment. Together, these features propel the growth and convenience of M-Commerce, shaping the future of digital commerce. It should also be noted that in M-Commerce, people conduct their transactions not only with technical different devices but also in various situations (rushed on the way or waiting for the train), which impacts the design of the user interface, consumer behavior, and the transaction process. **Mobile E-Business** encompasses all internal business activities (and may also connect external business partner to cross business process in the supply chain) conducted over mobile devices, including communication, marketing, and operations management. Mobile E-Commerce refers to buying and selling goods and services via mobile devices. In contrast, mobile E-Business focuses on supporting all business processes and transactions within a company through mobile technology.

Social commerce refers to the integration of social media and E-Commerce platforms to facilitate online shopping experiences. It combines elements of social networking and online shopping to create a seamless buying process within social media platforms or through social interactions. Social commerce and collaborative filtering leverage social media and user preferences to recommend products and personalize shopping experiences, fostering community engagement and customer satisfaction. Social commerce is not like the traditional search for products on platforms using Google. Instead, users ask for **recommendations** from other people in their network and may not conduct a search at all. Such recommendations are not only made by people from one's own network but increasingly also by influencers. **Influencer marketing** involves brands partnering with online influencers to promote products, leveraging their credibility and reach to influence purchasing decisions. To evaluate the success of an influencer, the engagement rate is a crucial metric. It measures the ratio of interactions (comments, likes, shares) to the total number of followers or the number of people reached. Additionally, impressions and views are important metrics to consider (Fig. 7.6).

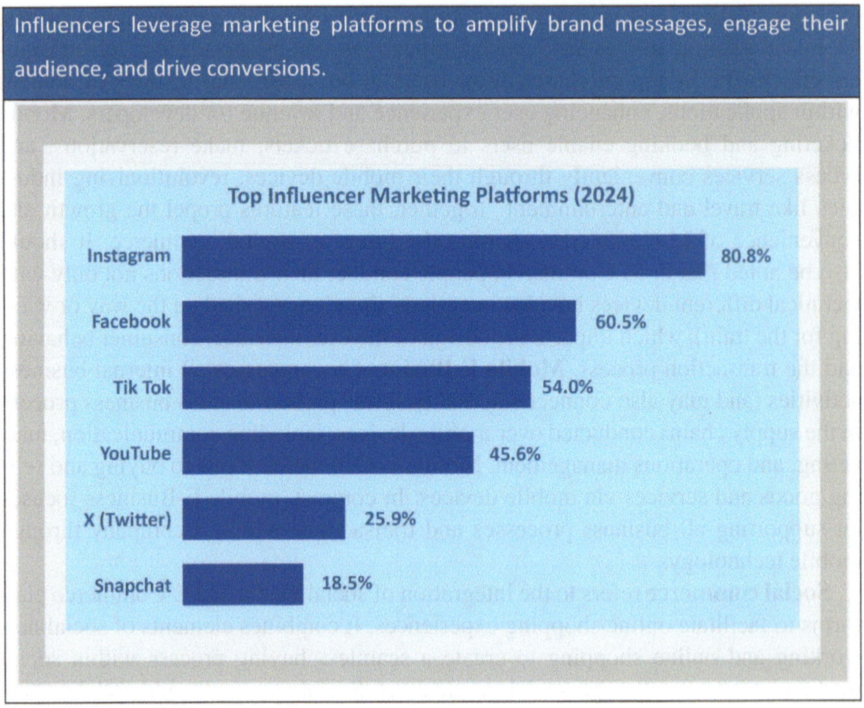

Fig. 7.6 Influencer marketing platforms. (Source: eMarketer)

The number of impressions or views indicates how often the influencer's content has been seen. The conversion rate reflects the percentage of viewers who have taken a desired action, such as making a purchase, after viewing the content.

Review Questions

1. Define and differentiate between Web 2.0, Web 3.0, and Web 4.0. Provide examples of how these concepts have impacted the digital landscape.
2. Explain the concept of social commerce. How does it differ from traditional E-Commerce? Discuss the role of influencers in this context.
3. Describe the stages of the social marketing process. How can businesses leverage these stages to build a strong online presence?
4. What is the significance of location-based services (LBS) in mobile marketing? Provide examples of how businesses can utilize LBS to their advantage.

Your Advanced Questions for Starting Prompt Engineering

- How has the evolution of technology, particularly mobile devices and AI, transformed the consumer decision-making process?
- What are the implications for marketers in understanding and influencing consumer behavior?
- Develop a comprehensive digital marketing strategy for a sustainable fashion brand targeting a niche market. How can the brand leverage long-tail marketing, influencer partnerships, and data analytics to build a loyal customer base?
- Discuss the ethical challenges posed by personalized advertising and data privacy in the context of E-Commerce. How can businesses balance the need for targeted marketing with consumer trust and data protection regulations?

Business Case

Please study Business Case No. 6, What are Social Networks"featuring FACEBOOK (Meta), LINKEDIN (Microsoft), and X/Twitter. Why do social networks have such power, and what significance do they have for democracies?

Further Readings

Harris-Lipschultz J (2024) Social media measurement and management: entrepreneurial digital analytics

eMarketer (2024) https://www.emarketer.com/

Sanchith G (2024) Internet marketing: key to success

Turban E et al (2024) Electronic commerce – a managerial and social networks perspective. https://www.linkedin.com/in/efraim-turban-7a682912/

Chapter 8
Content Management, Online Media, Ethics, and Fake News

Abstract

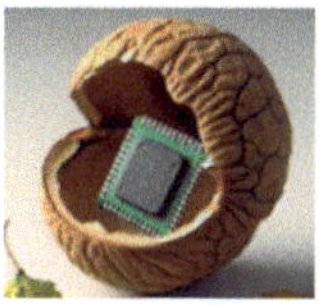

In a nutshell

The chapter explores the multifaceted landscape of digital information, from its creation and management to its ethical implications. It delves into the transformative potential of generative AI, highlighting its applications in content creation and customer interaction. The ethical dimensions of AI are examined, including concerns about fake news, deepfakes, and automated decision-making. The text further emphasizes the importance of trust management in the digital realm, addressing issues of transparency, accountability, and the evolving relationship between humans and technology.

Keywords Digital information lifecycle · Generative AI · Natural language processing (NLP) · Ethics · Fake news · Deepfakes · Automated decision-making · Whistleblowing · Net neutrality · Trust management

Basic Prompts

- What is generative AI and how does it work?
- What are the pros and cons of using AI to create content?
- What are some ethical concerns about using AI?
- How can businesses use AI to improve customer service?
- What is the difference between a bot and an avatar?

S. Schneider, L. Anderie, *Digital Business Management*,
https://doi.org/10.1007/978-3-031-83177-5_8

8.1 Content Management

A **content management system** (CMS) is an IT solution that supports the evolutionary lifecycle of digital information, regardless of whether it is structured or unstructured data. It separates the IT and web management duties typically overseen by IT departments from the content management responsibilities typically handled by business departments.

Figure 8.1 depicts the digital information lifecycle, encompassing the stages of creation, deployment, storage, and deletion for various digital documents. Management is required for digital documents such as text, images, audio, and video files that follow a content lifecycle. A CMS primarily focuses on managing content for websites, while an **Enterprise CMS** extends its scope to encompass all digital assets within a company, including documents, media files, and other digital resources, facilitating comprehensive management and collaboration across various departments and teams. That's why it is sometimes called a **Web CMS** when websites are managed.

8.2 Automated Content Production (Generative AI/ChatGPT)

Natural language processing (NLP) is a subset of generative AI that enables computers to generate new content, such as text, images, and music, based on provided training data. In E-Commerce, generative AI can personalize shopping experiences by creating tailored product descriptions, recommend products based on consumer behavior, and even design virtual merchandise displays. It enhances customer interaction by providing unique content that engages potential buyers. Automated content production, including the creation of text, video, music, and images, uses AI methods, particularly generative AI, which leverages deep learning techniques like transformers to understand and generate language (see Fig. 8.2).

Moreover, it can **simulate customer service** through chatbots that not only respond to queries but also initiate conversation, driving sales and improving customer satisfaction by offering instant, 24/7 assistance with a human-like touch. Large language models (LLMs), such as GPTs, operate by analyzing vast amounts of text data to understand language patterns, structure, and context. These models learn from the data they process, enabling them to generate coherent and contextually relevant text.

They use deep learning techniques, especially a form of neural networks called **transformers, to generate predictions about what word or phrase comes next**. LLMs can understand and generate human-like text because they've been trained on a diverse range of sources, learning nuances and complexities of language over time. When prompted with text, they process this input, compare it to learned patterns, and produce relevant and coherent output based on probabilities learned during training.

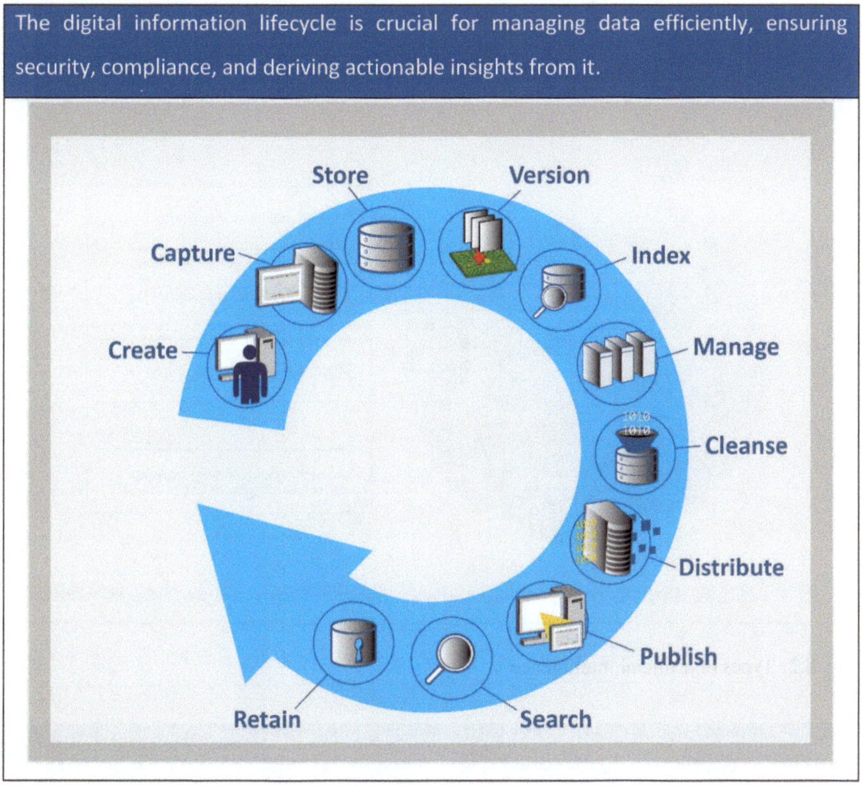

Fig. 8.1 Digital information lifecycle

Generative AI is a complex process that involves training a model on vast amounts of data to generate new content. Figure 8.3 provides a visual overview of this process, breaking it down into seven key steps. Initially, data is collected from various sources such as the Internet, sensors, and social media. This raw data is then processed and transformed into a format suitable for machine learning through a process known as **tokenization.** Subsequently, powerful algorithms, including machine learning and neural networks, are employed to identify patterns and relationships within the data. A crucial component is the generative pre-trained transformer, a type of neural network architecture that excels at processing sequential data. By feeding this model with vast quantities of text and code, it learns to generate human-like text, translate languages, write different kinds of creative content, and answer your questions in an informative way.

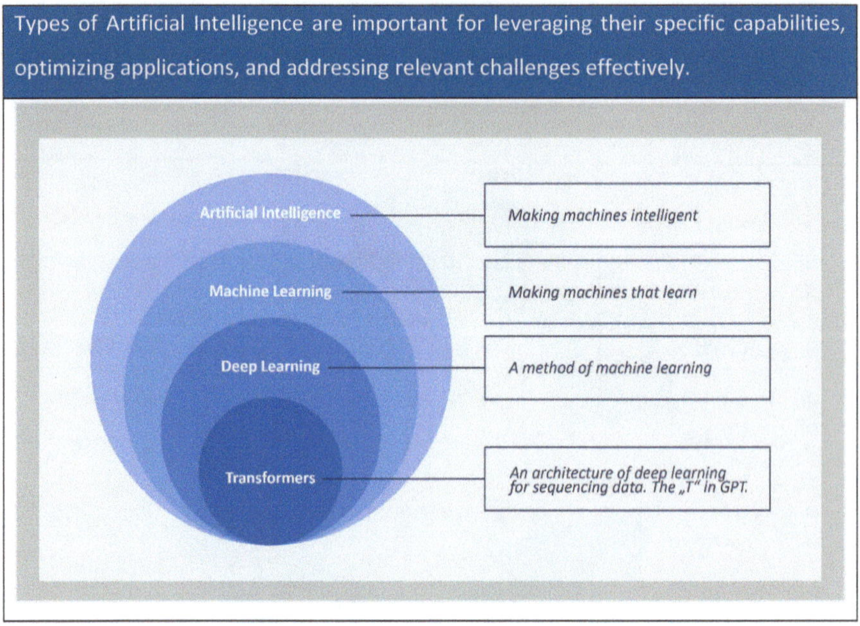

Fig. 8.2 Types of artificial intelligence

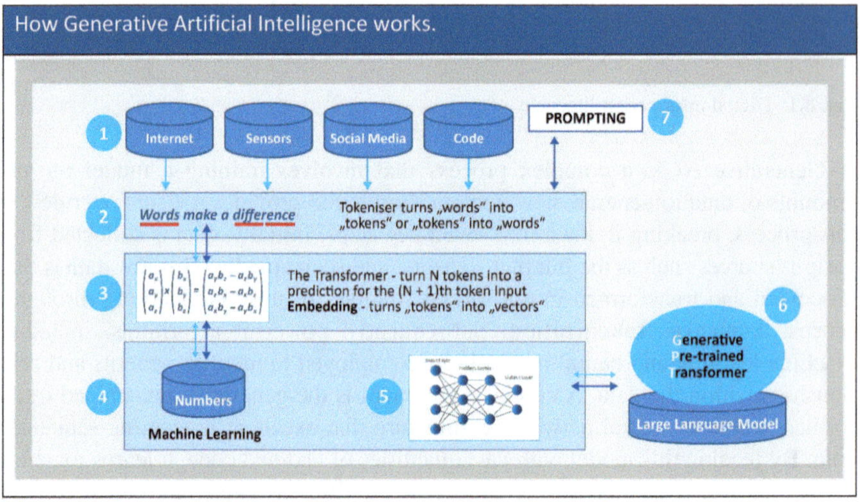

Fig. 8.3 Generative artificial intelligence

8.3 Ethics, Law, and Fake News

Ethics refers to the moral principles and values that govern individual or collective behavior and decision-making. It involves distinguishing between right and wrong, good and bad, and determining what actions are morally acceptable or unacceptable in various contexts. Key aspects are values and principles, morality and ethical decision-making, as well as social responsibility.

The **AI Act**, the **Digital Services Act (DSA)** and the **Digital Markets Act (DMA)** of the European Union along with the **German General Data Protection Regulation** establish the first Governance Frameworks in the area of AI and Digital Business. In Europe and Germany, AI legislation focuses on ethical standards, privacy, data protection, and the responsible development and deployment of AI technologies. The EU's proposed Artificial Intelligence Act, aiming to be the first comprehensive legal framework for AI, classifies AI systems according to their risk levels and imposes stricter requirements on high-risk applications. Germany complements this with its national strategies to foster AI innovation while ensuring transparency, security, and compliance with the General Data Protection Regulation (GDPR). These efforts reflect a balanced approach to harnessing AI's benefits, mitigating risks, and protecting individuals' rights in the digital age. In Europe and Germany, AI legislation focuses on ethical standards, privacy, data protection, and the responsible development and deployment of AI technologies. The EU's proposed Artificial Intelligence Act, aiming to be the first comprehensive legal framework for AI, classifies AI systems according to their risk levels and imposes stricter requirements on high-risk applications. Germany complements this with its national strategies to foster AI innovation while ensuring transparency, security, and compliance with the General Data Protection Regulation (GDPR). These efforts reflect a balanced approach to harnessing AI's benefits, mitigating risks, and protecting individuals' rights in the digital age.

Fake news are false or misleading information presented as legitimate news. It often involves deliberate misinformation or disinformation spread through various media channels, including traditional news outlets, social media platforms, websites, and online forums. Fake news can take many forms, including fabricated stories, hoaxes, conspiracy theories, manipulated images or videos, and misleading headlines. Key characteristics of fake news include:

- False Information: contains inaccurate or entirely fabricated information that is intentionally designed to deceive readers or viewers.
- Misleading Content: may include partial truths, distorted facts, or misleading framing to manipulate the audience's perception of events or issues.
- Virality: often spreads rapidly and widely through social media platforms.
- Agenda-Driven: may be created and circulated to advance specific agendas, promote particular viewpoints, or undermine trust in institutions, individuals, or groups.

- Confirmation Bias: can exploit people's preexisting beliefs, biases, and emotions, leading them to uncritically accept and share false information that aligns with their perspectives or reinforces their existing beliefs.
- Impact: Fake news can have significant social, political, and economic consequences, including undermining trust in the media, influencing public opinion, shaping political discourse, and fueling social tensions or conflicts.

A **deepfake** is a manipulated video or audio recording that uses advanced artificial intelligence techniques, particularly deep learning algorithms, to replace a person's likeness in the original content with someone else's likeness, often resulting in highly convincing but fabricated media. These creations can be used for various purposes, including entertainment, political misinformation, and fraud.

Three key ethical questions emerge in the digital age. Firstly, automated decision-making presents complex moral dilemmas, exemplified by the classic trolley problem adapted to autonomous driving scenarios. For instance, a critical question arises: should an individual be permitted to switch a lever to divert a train, thereby saving five people but causing the death of one? This issue becomes more complex if the one person at risk is the child of the person controlling the switch. Such scenarios highlight the ethical challenges inherent in designing autonomous systems capable of making life-or-death decisions. Figure 8.4 outlines the ethical dilemmas in automated decision-making. Secondly, the concept of whistleblowing and transparency becomes crucial in addressing illegal or unethical organizational behaviors. Platforms like WikiLeaks underscore the importance of exposing such activities to ensure accountability. Figure 8.5 indicates pros and cons of whistleblowing and transparency.

Lastly, the digital divide and the principle of net neutrality underscore the ethical imperative of equitable internet access. Net neutrality guarantees equal treatment of all Internet traffic, preventing discriminatory practices by Internet service providers. Figure 8.6 shows aspects of net neutrality.

Additional ethical questions arise in areas such as **content moderation and free speech** (censorship, hate speech, misinformation, and the balance between free expression and harmful content), **ethical marketing and consumer protection** (including misleading advertisements, consumer manipulation, and data exploitation), and **data privacy and security** (covering consent, data breaches, surveillance, and the balance between data utility and privacy rights).

8.4 Trust Management Using Bots and Avatars

Bots are software applications programmed to perform automated tasks, often repetitive, at a much faster rate than humans. They operate over the Internet for various purposes, including customer service (chatbots), content management, and data analysis, enhancing efficiency and scalability in digital operations or automatization

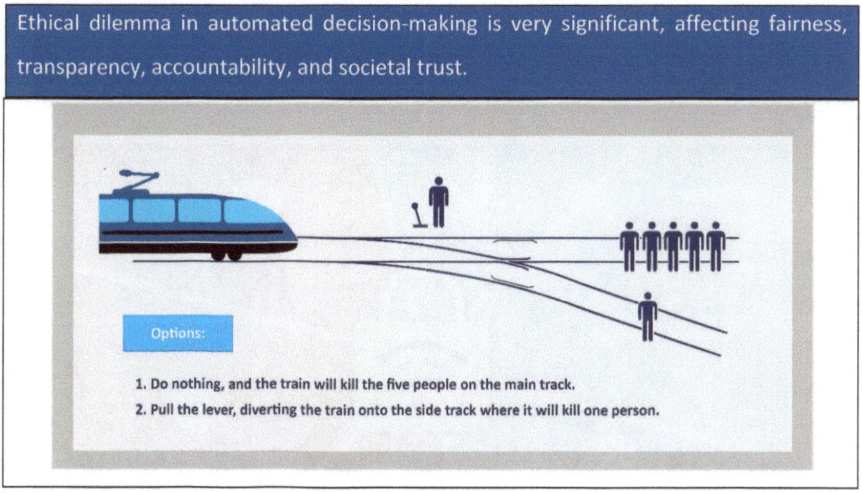

Fig. 8.4 Ethical dilemma in automated decision-making

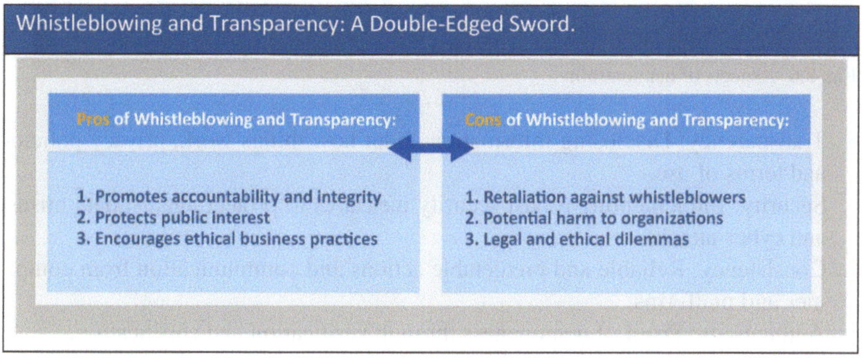

Fig. 8.5 Whistleblowing and transparency

(RPA robotic process automation). Avatars, while sharing similarities, serve a distinct purpose.

Avatars are graphical representations or digital personas of users in virtual spaces or online platforms. They can range from simple static images to complex 3D models, allowing individuals to express their identity, preferences, or fictional characters in video games, social media, and virtual reality environments.

Trust involves willingly offering services or engaging in actions that have inherent risks, without protective measures or mechanisms to oversee opportunistic conduct, while anticipating that the other party will act similarly in good faith. Trust is the sense of security and confidence in the reliability, integrity, and capability of a person or system. Trust can be built on the Internet in several ways:

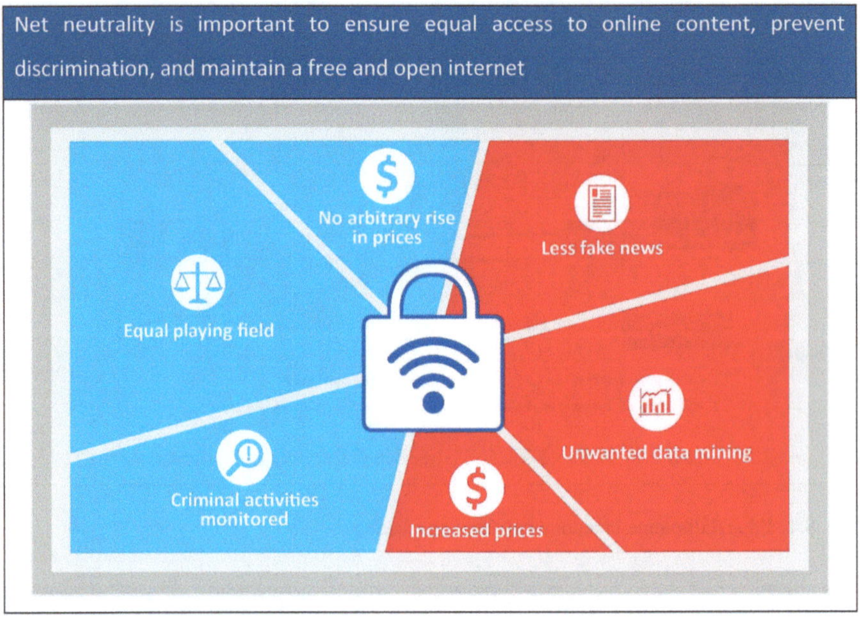

Fig. 8.6 Aspects of net neutrality

- Transparency: Disclosing information about how things work, privacy policies, and terms of use.
- Security: Implementing robust security measures to protect against data misuse and cyber-attacks.
- Consistency: Reliable and predictable actions and communication from companies and platforms.
- Authenticity: Proof of genuineness through verification and certification.
- User reviews and feedback: Positive testimonials and ratings from other users.
- Privacy: Respecting and protecting users' personal data.
- Responsible behavior: Ethics and social responsibility in business practices.
- Through these measures, users can develop trust in digital offerings, which is crucial for a positive and secure online experience.

Figure 8.7 indicates aspects and levels of trust management on the left-hand side and trust mechanisms with their related characteristics on the right-hand side.

In a world where people increasingly struggle to differentiate between human and machine, real or fake information, or even attempts at influencing (nudging) them, trust becomes ever more crucial.

As the digital landscape evolves, **bots** and **avatars** will increasingly assist users in a **multitude of tasks**, from information retrieval to complex negotiations. A critical function for these digital agents will be the assessment of information reliability. In an era marked by the proliferation of misinformation and influence attempts, discerning fact from fiction becomes paramount. People are increasingly unable to

Trust management on the internet is important because it ensures secure interactions, protects user data, fosters user confidence, and promotes reliable online transactions.

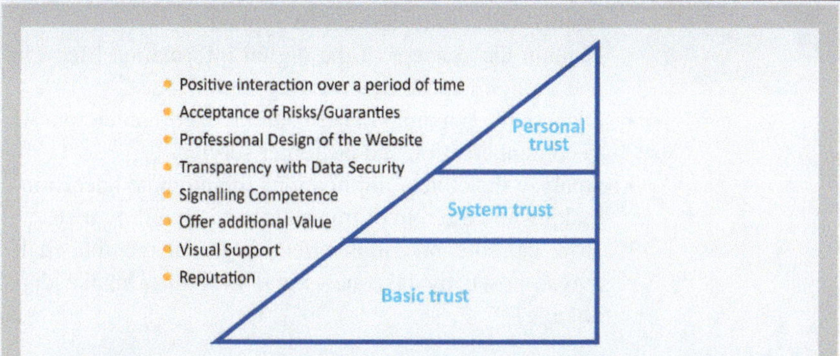

Trust Mechanism	Characteristics
Blockchain	Private Blockchain ← – – – Permissioned Blockchain – – – → Public Blockchain
Identity Management	Identification → Verification → Authentification → Trusting Interactions
Reputation	Ratings/Rankings Brands Recommendations Scores
Content Moderation Tools	Automated deletion of „bad" content by intelligent rules
Trust Transfer	Transfer trust from one trustworthy website/content to another
Swift Trust	Building Trust → because special need → disadvantages would be high
Tit-for-Tat Strategies	Continuous trustworthy interactions lead to ever higher levels of trust

Fig. 8.7 Trust management

distinguish between (deep) fake news and the truth. Therefore, trusted bots could take over the interfaces between humans and the Internet, using AI and other algorithms to verify the content.

Review Questions

1. What is AI and how does AI create fake news?
2. What are the benefits of using AI in business?
3. What is the difference between a chatbot and a human?
4. What are some concerns about using AI?

Your Advanced Questions for Starting Prompt Engineering

- Explore the concept of trust management in the digital realm. What strategies can be applied.
- Explain the concept of the digital information lifecycle and its significance in managing digital assets.
- Discuss the potential benefits and risks of generative AI in content creation and customer service.
- Analyze the ethical implications of automated decision-making and the role of transparency in building trust.
- How can organizations effectively manage the challenges posed by fake news and deepfakes in the digital age?

Business Case

Please read Case No. 7, “Generative AI and its Impact,” featuring ChatGPT and Google Gemini. Why are generative AI service companies and their bots so successful, and what future scenarios do they envision?

Further Readings

Carlton D (2024) More of everything you wanted to know about AI but don’t have time to read

Gobaw B (2024) Mastering ChatGPT 4.0: everyday ai at your fingertips

Strengholt P (2023) Data management at scale: modern data architecture with data mesh and data fabric

Chapter 9
Digital Business-to-Business Integration

Abstract

In a nutshell

The chapter explores the complexities of modern supply chain management. It highlights the integration of digital technologies, from eMarketplaces and eProcurement to robotics and Industry 4.0. The importance of efficient inventory management and the shift toward omnichannel retailing is emphasized. The text also underscores the role of technology in transforming traditional business operations and creating new opportunities.

Keywords Supply chain management (SCM) · eMarketplace · eProcurement · Omnichannel · Robotics · Industry 4.0 · Internet of Things (IoT) · Cyber-physical systems (CPS) · Computer-aided manufacturing (CAM) · Robotic process automation (RPA) · Supply chain management and eProcurement

Basic Prompts

- What is supply chain management?
- How does E-Commerce impact supply chain management?
- What are the benefits of using eProcurement?
- What is the difference between multichannel and omnichannel retailing?
- How does Industry 4.0 change the way products are made?

S. Schneider, L. Anderie, *Digital Business Management*,
https://doi.org/10.1007/978-3-031-83177-5_9

9.1 Supply Chain Management and B2B

Supply chain management (SCM) is the oversight of materials, information, and finances as they move from supplier to manufacturer to wholesaler to retailer to consumer. SCM involves coordinating and integrating these flows both within and among companies. Figure 9.1 visualizes the process chain of supply chain management.

SCM can connect directly to suppliers or via an **eMarketplace**. An eMarketplace is an online platform that facilitates the buying and selling of goods and services between businesses (B2B), businesses and consumers (B2C), or between consumers (C2C). It operates on the Internet, providing a virtual space where multiple vendors can present their products or services and customers can browse, compare, and purchase them. Figure 9.2 presents the historical development of eMarketplaces.

The ultimate goal of SCM is to reduce inventory (with the assumption that products are available when needed) and to offer a good connection for **collaborative planning**. It's a complex balancing act that involves managing supply and demand, sourcing raw materials, manufacturing, assembly, warehousing, tracking inventory levels, order entry and order management, distribution across all channels, and delivery to the customer. Effective SCM can lower costs, improve efficiency, and boost customer satisfaction. Supply chain management systems continuously link the activities of buying, making, and moving products from suppliers to purchasing

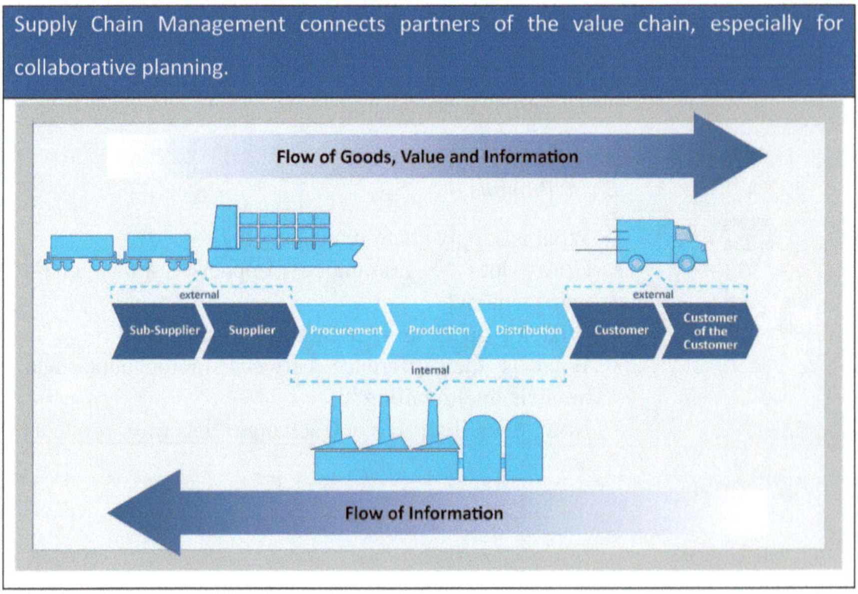

Fig. 9.1 Supply chain management

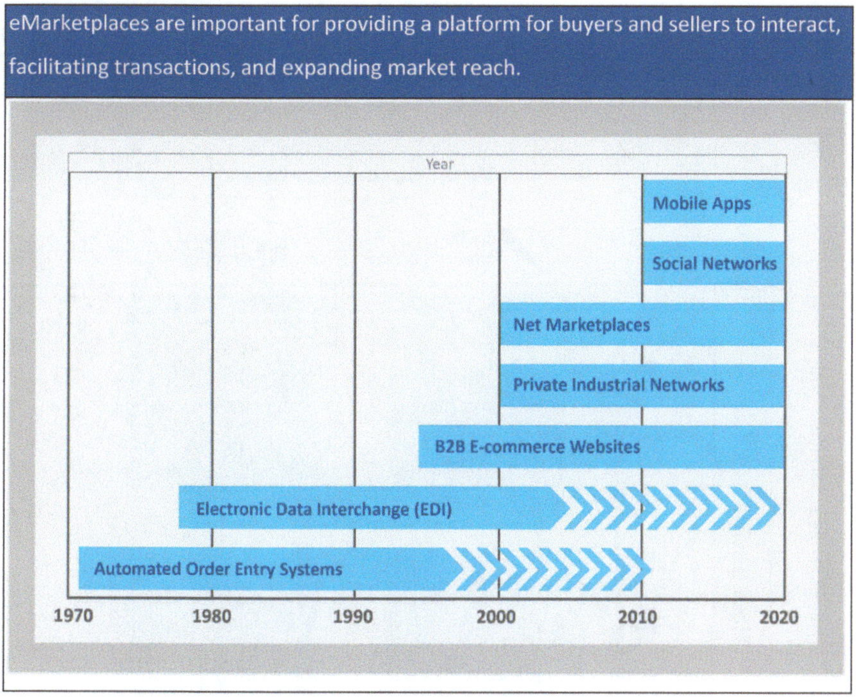

Fig. 9.2 eMarketplaces. (Adapted from Laudon/Traver)

firms, as well as integrating the demand side of the E-Business equation by including the order entry system in the process.

eProcurement revolutionizes procurement by digitizing processes. Cataloging allows easy access to goods and services. Workflow and approval streamline transactions, ensuring adherence to policies. This transformation redefines the procurement department's role, shifting from transactional to strategic. It empowers professionals to focus on sourcing, supplier relations, and value optimization. Automation reduces paperwork, errors, and time spent on routine tasks. Overall, eProcurement enhances efficiency, compliance, and strategic impact within organizations, driving innovation and cost savings. A and B items are essential for production and are managed through supply chain management (SCM). In contrast, C goods are less critical, used by employees (e.g., office supplies), and not directly linked to production. eProcurement focuses on acquiring C goods.

eDistributor provides an online catalog that represents the products of thousands of direct manufacturers. **eProcurement net marketplace** independently owned intermediary that connects hundreds of online suppliers offering millions of maintenance and repair parts to business firms who pay fees to join the market. Figure 9.3 categorizes eMarketplaces.

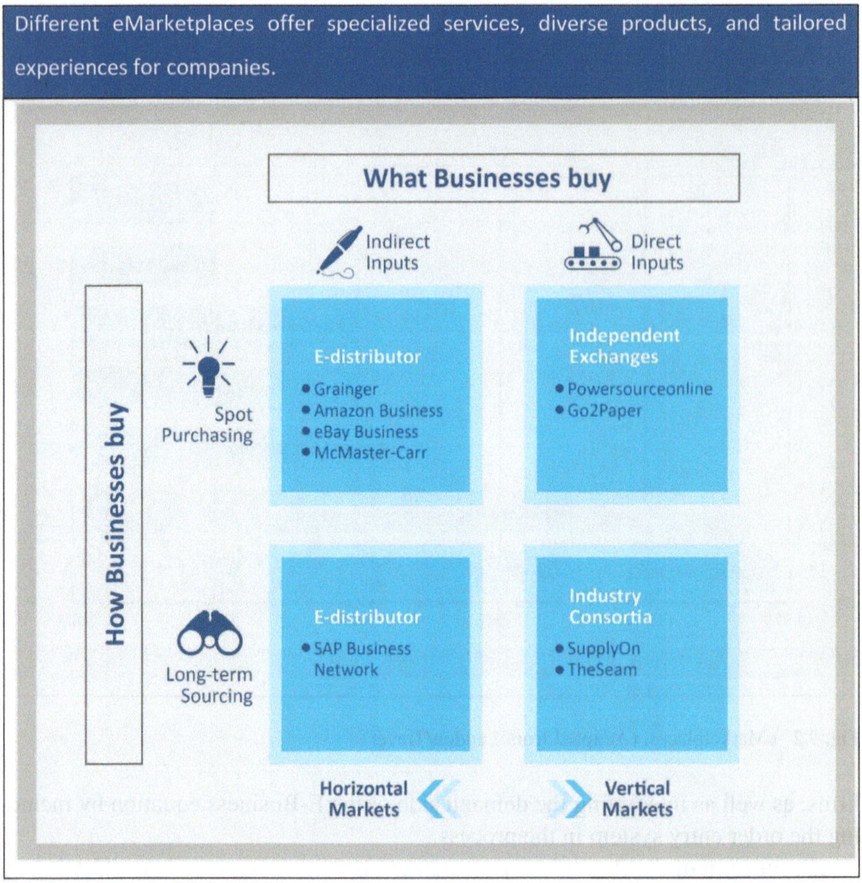

Fig. 9.3 Categorization of eMarketplaces. (Adapted from Laudon/Traver)

9.2 Omnichannel

Retail business is the sale of goods or services to consumers for personal or household use, carried out in stores, online, or through other channels. **Omnichannel** refers to a multichannel approach to sales that seeks to provide customers with a **seamless** shopping experience whether the client is shopping online from a mobile device, a laptop, or in a brick-and-mortar store. It integrates various communication and sales channels to work together, ensuring consistency and coherence in customer experience across the platforms. This strategy allows customers to engage with a company in a physical store, on an online website or mobile app, through a catalog, or through social media, and receive a unified experience.

Multichannel refers to offering products or services through various independent channels. Omnichannel integrates these channels seamlessly, providing a unified and consistent experience across all touchpoints, enabling customers to transition between channels effortlessly for a cohesive shopping journey.

9.3 Automatization and Robotics

Robotics plays a significant role in enhancing Digital Business operations. It enables automation of repetitive tasks, increases efficiency, and reduces errors. In Digital Business, robotics can be utilized in various areas such as manufacturing, logistics, customer service, and even data analysis, contributing to overall productivity and competitiveness. A good example is **robotic process automation (RPA).** RPA involves using software roBots or "Bots"to automate repetitive, rule-based tasks previously performed by humans. It streamlines workflows, enhances accuracy, and frees up human employees to focus on more complex or value-added activities, thus improving overall efficiency in Digital Business operations. Automatization is important for digital business; it boosts E-Business by increasing efficiency, reducing costs, ensuring consistency, and enhancing customer experience. It enables scalability and accurate data management and provides a competitive advantage by streamlining operations and minimizing human errors. Especially robotic process automation (RPA) (Fig. 9.4) uses software roBots to automate repetitive, rule-based tasks. It increases efficiency, reduces errors, and allows employees to focus on value-added activities.

9.4 Industry 4.0 and Internet of Things (IoT)

Industry 4.0, also known as the fourth industrial revolution, is the ongoing transformation of traditional manufacturing and industrial practices through the integration of digital technologies, data analytics, and automation. It represents a paradigm shift in supply chain management and the way goods are produced, impacting various industries especially manufacturing and logistics. Industry 4.0 builds upon the

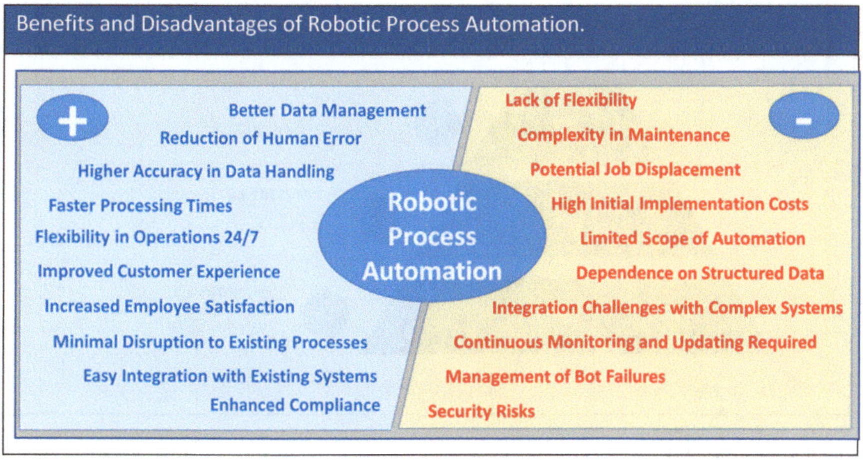

Fig. 9.4 Robotic process automation (RPA)

previous industrial revolutions mechanization (1st), mass production (2nd), and automation (3rd)—but is characterized by the convergence of physical, digital, and biological systems (Fig. 9.5).

The **Internet of Things (IoT)** refers to a network of interconnected devices, objects, and systems that communicate with each other and exchange data over the Internet. IoT is simply the network of interconnected things/devices which are embedded with sensors, software, network connectivity, and necessary electronics that enables them to collect and exchange data making them responsive. These "smart" devices are embedded with sensors, actuators, software, and connectivity capabilities that enable them to collect, transmit, and receive data, as well as interact with their environment or other devices autonomously or under human control. **Cyber-physical systems (CPS)** are integrated systems of computational algorithms and physical components, tightly coupled and interacting with each other. These systems combine digital processing capabilities with physical processes to monitor, control, and coordinate the behavior of physical entities. Production, which has long utilized an integrated solution with computer-aided manufacturing (CAM), is now being further enhanced with AI functionalities. **Computer-aided manufacturing (CAM)** refers to the use of computer software and automation to control manufacturing processes, such as machining, milling, and 3D printing. CAM software generates instructions (G-codes) for machine tools to produce precise parts based on digital designs (CAD models).

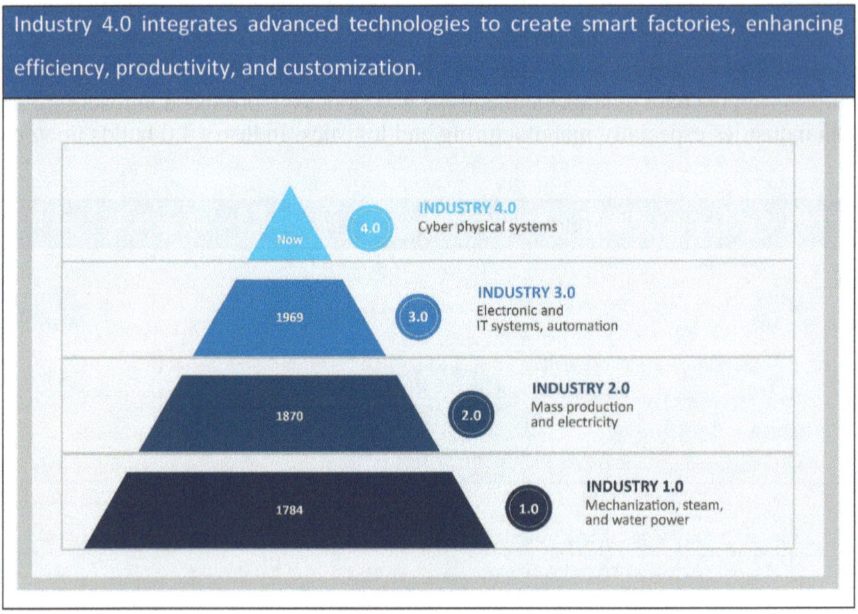

Fig. 9.5 Industry 4.0

Review Questions

1. Explain the concept of supply chain management and its importance in modern business.
2. Discuss the role of eMarketplaces in facilitating efficient supply chain operations.
3. How does omnichannel retailing differ from multichannel retailing? Provide examples.
4. What is Industry 4.0 and how does it impact supply chain management?

Your Advanced Question for Starting Prompt Engineering

- Analyze the role of supply chain visibility and agility in mitigating risks and disruptions. How can organizations build resilient supply chains capable of adapting to unforeseen challenges?
- Examine the impact of emerging technologies such as blockchain, artificial intelligence, and the Internet of Things on supply chain management. How can organizations leverage these technologies to create competitive advantage?
- Discuss the challenges and opportunities for creating sustainable supply chains. How can businesses balance environmental, social, and economic considerations in their supply chain operations?
- Analyze the complexities of managing global supply chains, including factors such as geopolitical risks, trade regulations, and cultural differences. How can organizations effectively navigate these challenges to ensure supply chain continuity?

Business Case

Please read the "B2B Retail Business Case"(No. 8) featuring the companies Shopify, eBay, Salesforce, and SAP and investigate the principles of success in the B2B market.

Further Readings

Jose D. et al (2024) Ai-driven IoT systems for industry 4.0 (Edge Ai in future computing)

Laurent N et al (2022) Digital business models

Walker R (2024) B2B Digital marketing – 3 books in 1: the complete guide to b2b online success through social media, viral, and email marketing

Chapter 10
Digital Business Analysis and Digital Transformation

Abstract

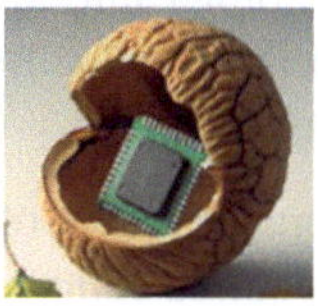

In a nutshell
The chapter outlines the evolution of Digital Business. It covers the transition from analog to digital formats, emphasizing the importance of digital transformation. Key concepts include the creation of new business models, customer interaction, and the role of technology in driving these changes. The text also explores the significance of supply chain management, E-Commerce, and data analytics in the digital landscape. Finally, it highlights the potential of artificial intelligence in revolutionizing business operations.

Keywords Digitalization · Digital transformation · Digital Business · Customer relationship management (CRM) · Business intelligence (BI) · Big data · Artificial intelligence (AI) · Machine learning · Data-driven business

Basic Prompts

- What is the difference between digitization and digital transformation?
- How does a business model change during digital transformation?
- What is the role of technology in Digital Business?
- How can a company improve customer relationships through digitalization?
- What is the importance of data in a Digital Business?

S. Schneider, L. Anderie, *Digital Business Management*,
https://doi.org/10.1007/978-3-031-83177-5_10

10.1 Digitalization and Digital Transformation

Digitalization is the process of converting information from an analog format into a digital format. This involves capturing and encoding data into a series of numbers that can be processed by computers. **Digitization** is about converting data into a digital format.

Digital transformation is the process of changing existing business models and business processes to develop or create new value chains and values for customers. As a result, there are new consumption patterns, socioeconomic structures, legal and policy measures, or cultural/organizational patterns.

Furthermore, it is a process of utilizing digital technologies to fundamentally change or enhance the way businesses operate, deliver value to customers, and interact with their stakeholders. It involves integrating digital technology into all areas of a business, fundamentally changing how it operates and delivers value to customers. Figure 10.1 shows the steps toward a broader digital transformation.

- **Value Creation** or Operating **Model**: Defines the structure and management of E-Business, including organizational hierarchy, workflows, and required competencies as well as business processes. It focuses on how resources are aligned to achieve strategic goals efficiently and effectively.
- **A Value Proposition Model:** Uses the grades of digitalization of products and services. It involves transforming traditional products and services into digital forms. This enhances accessibility, improves customer engagement, allows for innovative features, and creates new revenue channels through digital platforms.
- **Customer Interaction Model**: Tailors how a business engages with its customers through unique value propositions, establishing innovative touchpoints, and enhancing overall customer experience. It's about creating meaningful connections and ensuring satisfaction throughout the customer journey.

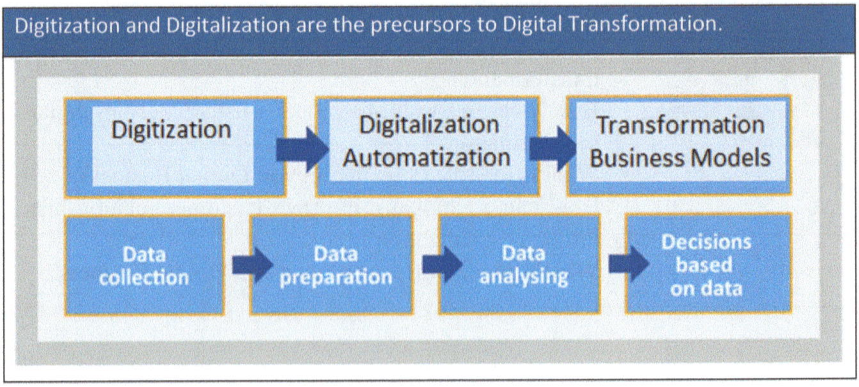

Fig. 10.1 Digitization, digitalization, digital transformation

This leads to a new business model, outlining the rationale for how an organization creates, delivers, and captures value, as articulated in a business model canvas. Figure 10.2 illustrates the process from triggering digital business transformation (e.g., adapting new technologies) until the creation of a new business model.

A Digital Business **framework**, as visualized in Fig. 10.3, can be described as a detailed diagram illustrating the various components and their relationships within the Digital Business environment. Central to the diagram is the concept of Digital Business, which encompasses several interrelated sectors.

On the left side of the diagram, **E-Commerce** is connected to concepts such as eProcurement, eMarketplaces, and a flow toward supplier. This suggests a focus on the commercial transactions that occur electronically on the Internet, especially those involving procurement and marketplaces designed for trading goods and services in the B2B area.

On the right side, **social commerce** seems to imply a form of social commerce that leverages social networks, here depicted as social networks (Web 2.0, blogs, and fake news), indicating the use of modern Internet technologies and platforms, including the consideration of misinformation. This connects to the customer and other people, suggesting the community and social aspect of commerce.

The center of the diagram is labeled **E-Business,** which integrates various subsystems such as **supply chain management (SCM), enterprise resource planning (ERP)**, and **customer relationship management (CRM).** These are foundational components of electronic business that manage company relationships and efficiencies. Underlying the central E-Business section is a layer labeled Extended Digital Business that includes **EAI (Middleware)**—presumably Enterprise Application Integration software that allows for data interchange between different software applications within an enterprise. At the bottom of the diagram, there's a foundation of Big Data **/ BI /** Business Analytics and Wireless/Mobile/Augmented, suggesting the technological base that supports Digital Business with data analysis, mobile connectivity, augmented reality, and artificial intelligence. In today's world, customers and potential customers communicate with each other, known as **social commerce** using social

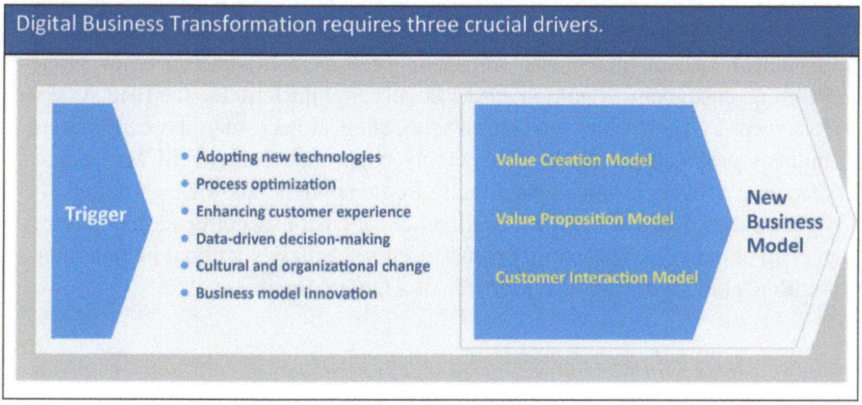

Fig. 10.2 Digital business transformation

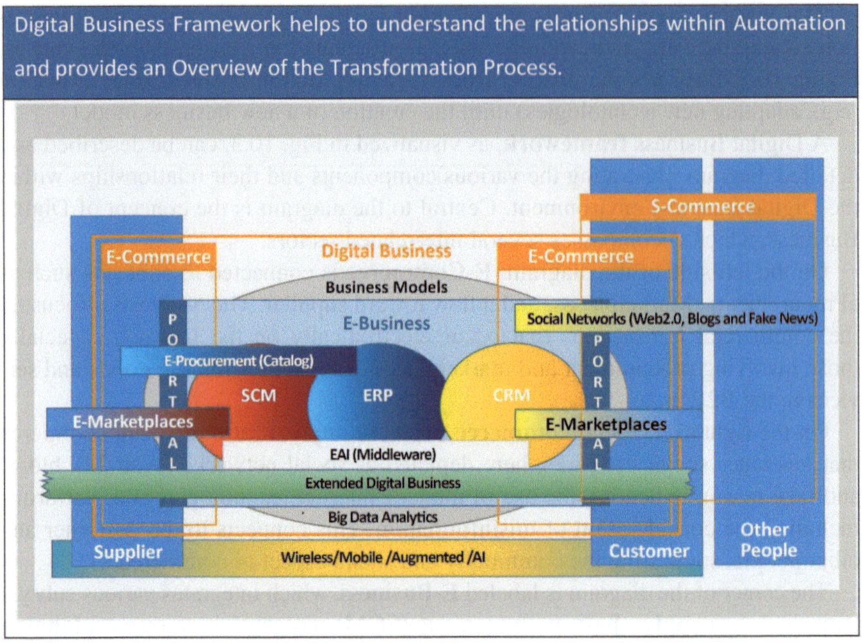

Fig. 10.3 The digital business framework

networks. Digital Businesses seek to leverage the influence of social networks. To support this, they must adopt new business models based on **Big Data analytics** and utilize artificial intelligence (Fig. 10.3 The Digital Business framework).

The diagram outlines a framework of Digital Business, highlighting the interconnected nature of various Online E-Business systems, platforms, and technologies, which collectively support the procurement, sale, and exchange of products and services between suppliers and customers within the **digital economy**.

EXAMPLE Applying the Digital Business Framework: A customer places an online order via a Digital Business 'E-Business portal. The data is captured in the CRM system, potentially triggering personalized suggestions or offers based on customer recognition. Order details are transferred to the ERP system for inventory checks and production scheduling. If necessary, the ERP system initiates procurement through the supply chain management (SCM) system, receiving delivery notifications directly from suppliers. The ERP subsequently updates the CRM with product availability for customer notification regarding pickup or delivery. This entire process occurs seamlessly without human intervention, embodying the core principle of a Digital Business.

10.2 Customer Relationship Management and Business Intelligence

Customer relationship management (CRM) is a comprehensive set of processes and technologies for managing the relationship with potential and current customers and business partners across marketing, sales, and service regardless of the communication channel. CRM can be categorized in three parts: **operational CRM** focuses on automating and improving customer-facing processes like sales, marketing, and service. **Analytical CRM** involves analyzing customer data to gain insights for strategic decision-making. **Collaborative CRM** emphasizes interaction and coordination among various departments to enhance customer relationships, often through shared databases and communication channels. Examples for CRM functionality are performance and profitability analysis involves evaluating business performance and profitability metrics to optimize operations and resource allocation. **One-to-one marketing** and personalization tailors marketing efforts to individual customer preferences and behaviors for enhanced engagement and conversion. **Permission-based marketing** obtains consent from customers before sending marketing communications, fostering trust and compliance. **Viral marketing** utilizes social networks and word-of-mouth to spread marketing messages rapidly among consumers, leveraging their networks for brand promotion. Sales force and marketing automation streamline repetitive tasks, improve efficiency, and enhance communication within sales and marketing teams.

Business intelligence (BI) refers to the technological methods and business practices employed to collect, integrate, analyze, and present business data for decision-making. It transcends mere data storage (as in data warehousing) and focuses on transforming data into actionable insights, unlike the narrower scope of **data mining**.

For BI to be effective, the information must be reliable, timely, pertinent, user-friendly, and contextual. BI tools, like **OLAP analysis** (online analytical processing) and scorecards, provide executives with comparative insights over time to identify trends and inform strategy. Executive dashboards synthesize this information, ensuring it is easily understandable and aids in corporate decision-making. Figure 10.4 illustrates key aspects of Business Intelligence processing.

10.3 Big Data Analytics and Applied Artificial Intelligence

Big Data analytics is the process of examining large volumes of data with the goal of discovering patterns, trends, and other useful information. This data can be structured, unstructured, or a combination of both.

Big Data refers to extremely large datasets that traditional data processing software can't manage efficiently.

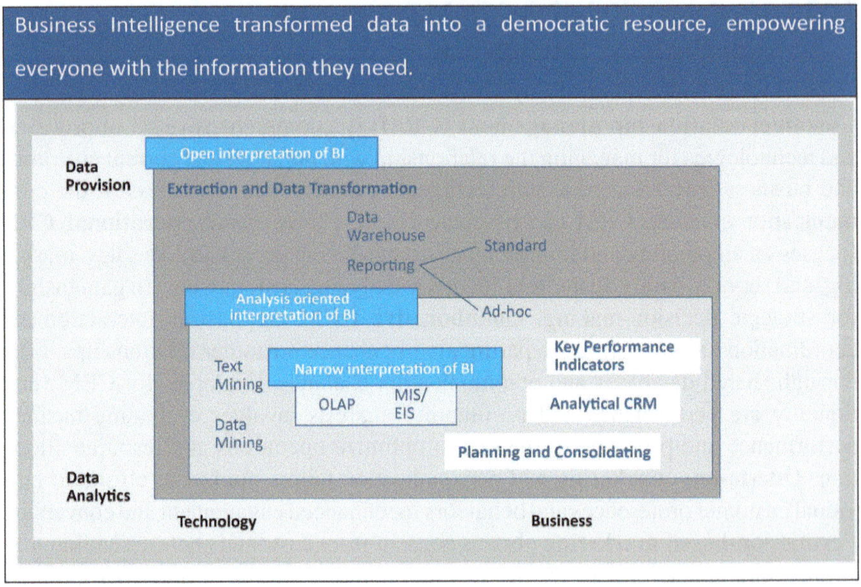

Fig. 10.4 Business intelligence

Big Data is the collection and analysis of large, polystructured data for decision-making using statistical methods and probabilities. These datasets are characterized by their volume, velocity, variety, and complexity. **Big Data analytics** is the process of examining Big Data to uncover hidden patterns, unknown correlations, market trends, customer preferences, and other useful business information. Advanced analytics techniques, including predictive analytics, data mining, and machine learning, are applied to Big Data to help organizations make more informed business decisions, optimize operations, and predict future trends. It is essential for gaining a competitive edge in the data-driven market landscape.

Management information systems (MIS), a blend of business and computer science, have evolved over time, as detailed in Fig. 10.5: the history of management information systems. The requirements have not changed since the 1960s—a decision-maker needs ad hoc information. While such requests took longer in the early days due to mainframes and IT systems with low performance, the introduction of data warehouses with data mining and online analytical processing (OLAP), and subsequently the introduction of Business Intelligence (BI), improved the situation. Better IT performance and more data, as well as advanced Big Data analytics, now make ad hoc data-driven decisions possible. The introduction of self-service BI (SSBI) also accommodates the agile approach.

Figure 10.6 published by Gartner Group outlines the spectrum of **Business Intelligence (BI)** and **Big Data** analytical methods, arranged by increasing complexity and business value. It begins with **reporting** (answering "What happened?"), moves up to **analysis** (understanding "Why it happened?"), then to **monitoring**

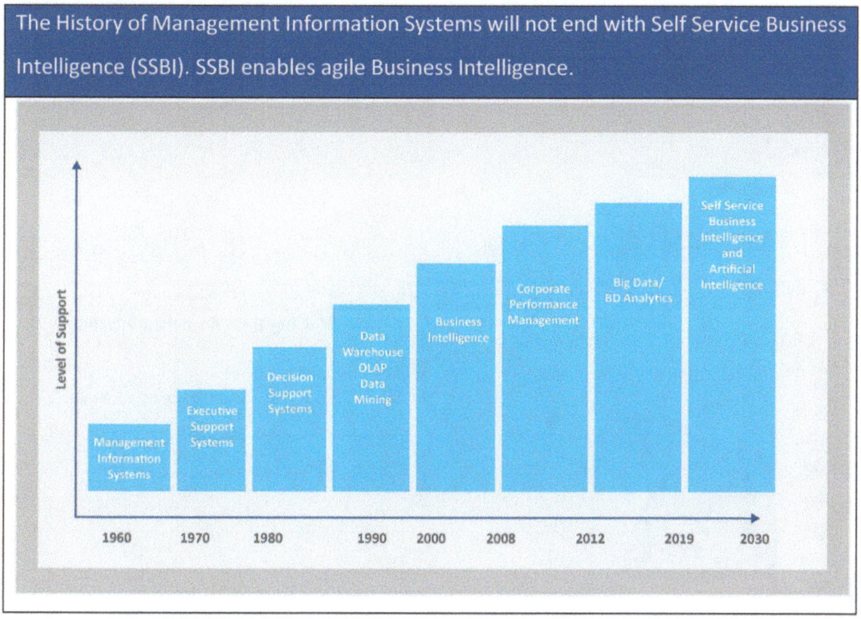

Fig. 10.5 The history of management information systems

(knowing "What's happening now?"), and to **prediction** (forecasting "What might happen?").

The pinnacle is **advice** (deciding "What should be done?"). The x-axis suggests that as the complexity of BI technologies increases, so does the potential business value they offer, spanning from basic query tools to advanced predictive analytics.

AI advice can be risky if it lacks understanding of complex human emotions, ethical nuances, and moral values, potentially leading to decisions that are technically correct but inappropriate or harmful in a broader social and ethical context.

Applied artificial intelligence (AI) is crucial for Digital Business as it empowers organizations to optimize operations, enhance customer experiences, create innovative offerings, and gain a competitive edge. By leveraging technologies like machine learning, natural language processing, computer vision, and robotics, businesses can transform their operations and unlock new growth opportunities.

Artificial intelligence (AI) means a simulation of intelligence. These are systems that mimic human intelligence. A system is considered intelligent if it can solve problems independently and efficiently. Strong AI, or **artificial general intelligence (AGI)**, refers to AI that possesses the ability to understand, learn, and apply knowledge in a way that is indistinguishable from a human. It has a self-aware consciousness and can solve a variety of problems with human-like flexibility. Figure 10.7 indicates the types of AI.

Weak AI, or **narrow AI**, is designed for specific tasks and operates within predefined boundaries. Lacking consciousness and true understanding, it functions

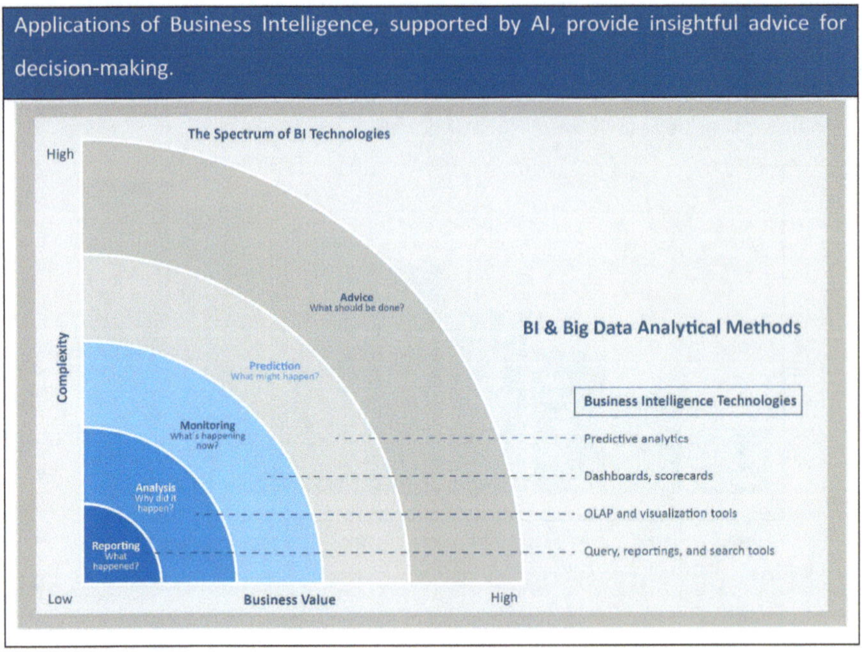

Fig. 10.6 Applications of Business Intelligence. (Adapted from Gartner)

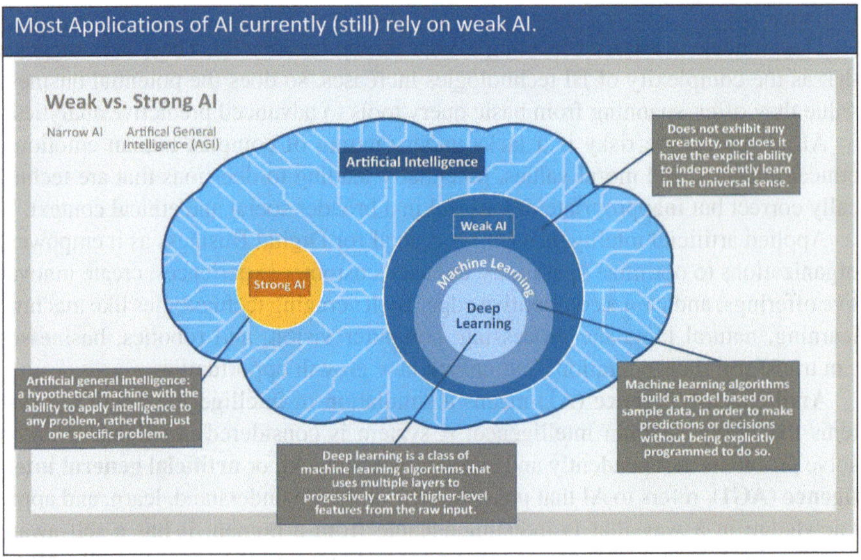

Fig. 10.7 Types of artificial intelligence

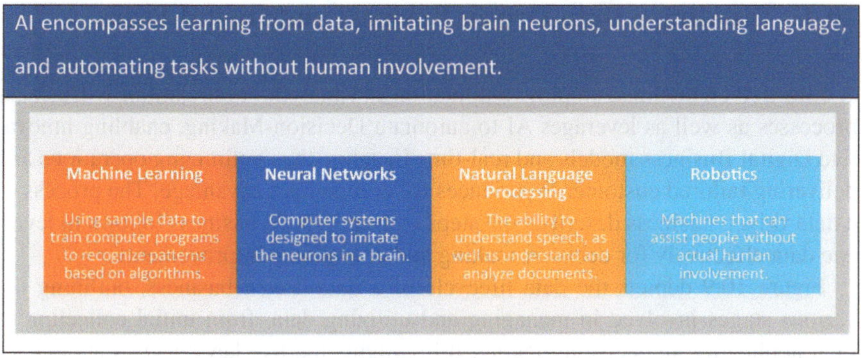

Fig. 10.8 Categorization of artificial intelligence

more like an advanced algorithm. In contrast, **strong AI**, or **artificial general intelligence (AGI)**, aims to replicate human-level intelligence across a wide range of tasks.

Applied artificial intelligence (AI) is crucial for Digital Business as it empowers organizations to optimize operations, enhance customer experiences, create innovative offerings, and gain a competitive edge. By leveraging technologies like machine learning, natural language processing, computer vision, and robotics, businesses can transform their operations and unlock new growth opportunities.

With the launch of **ChatGPT**, a Chat Generative Pre-trained Transformer by **OpenAI** in November 2022, generative AI has seen a renewed focus on **large language models (LLMs)** and image processing, exemplified by tools like DALL-E.

Since the outputs of AI language models are probability-based, they often generate answers that are more or less plausible. Despite continuous improvements through extensive training and vast datasets, hallucinations—instances where the AI fabricates information—can occur. To mitigate this, AI-generated content can be self-verified, and techniques like **retrieval-augmented generation**, which combines information retrieval and text generation, are increasingly employed to bolster accuracy and reliability.

Figure 10.8 provides definitions of four key technologies within the realm of artificial intelligence and robotics. **Machine learning** is described as the use of data to train computers to recognize patterns.

Neural networks are computer systems modeled after the human brain's neurons. **Natural language processing (NLP)** is defined as the capability to comprehend spoken language and analyze text. **Robotics** is referred to as the development of machines that can perform tasks without human intervention. Collectively, these technologies represent the diverse capabilities and applications of AI in mimicking and augmenting human abilities.

10.4 Building a Data-Driven Business and Digital Twins

A **data-driven business** employs automation and analytics to streamline E-Business processes as well as leverages AI to automate Decision-Making, enabling innovative Digital Business models and real-time insights, thus optimizing operations and delivering tailored customer experiences for competitive advantage. The process of a data-driven business describes the steps or stages that a business follows to leverage data effectively for decision-making and operational improvements.

Figure 10.9 depicts the data lifecycle of a data-driven business, outlining the various stages involved in managing and utilizing data, from initial collection to final application in decision-making. It highlights the five key stages (data extraction, data curation, data storage, data analysis, and data usage) and lists key resources, aspects, and activities throughout the process, from extracting data from a database, through evaluation and processing, to automated decision-making.

A **digital twin** is a virtual model designed to accurately reflect a physical object, system, or process. It's used to simulate, analyze, and predict the performance of its real-world counterpart, enabling remote monitoring, proactive maintenance, and in-depth analysis.

Figure 10.10 presents a roadmap for the development of **digital twins**, categorized into four stages: basic, full, enhanced, and next generation from physical and digital perspective. From a physical perspective, the image illustrates the evolution of digital twins, progressing from basic connectivity to advanced capabilities such as additive manufacturing. From a digital perspective, it commences with security considerations and leverages technologies like blockchain and AI.

The benefits of digital twins include enhanced operational efficiency, reduced downtime through predictive maintenance, and improved product development

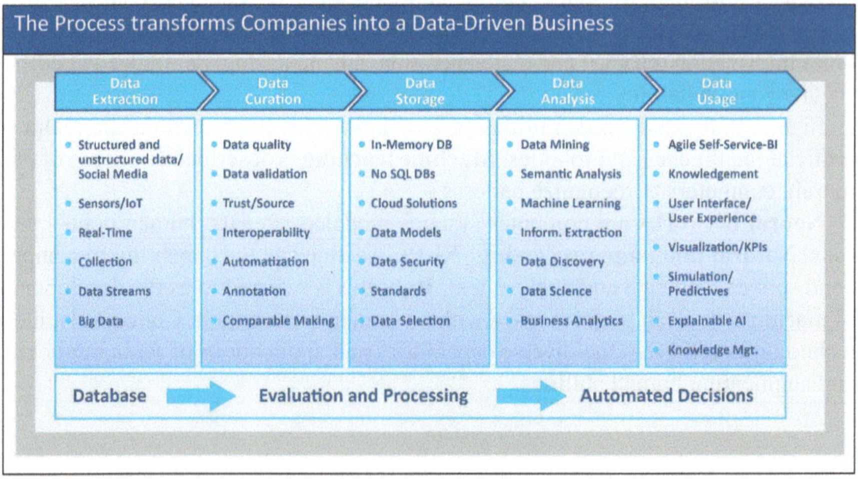

Fig. 10.9 Process of a data-driven business

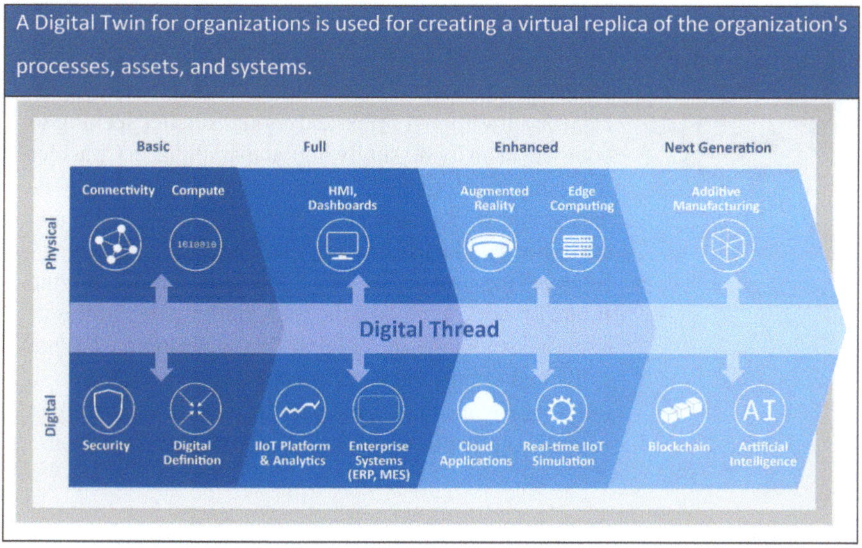

Fig. 10.10 Digital twin

cycles. They allow for safer testing and troubleshooting, provide valuable insights for decision-making, and enable customization in manufacturing. By mirroring the physical world in a digital space, they bridge the gap between physical and digital, facilitating innovation and optimization in various industries.

Review Questions

1. Define digitalization and digital transformation. Explain the key differences between the two concepts and provide examples of each.
2. Discuss the components of a Digital Business framework. How do these components interact to create value for an organization?
3. Explain the role of data analytics and business intelligence in supporting decision-making within a Digital Business.
4. What is the potential impact of artificial intelligence on business models and operations? Discuss the challenges and opportunities associated with AI adoption.

Your Advanced Question for Starting Prompt Engineering

- Develop a comprehensive digital transformation strategy for a traditional brick-and-mortar retailer seeking to compete in an increasingly digital marketplace. Consider the integration of E-Commerce, omnichannel experiences, and data analytics to drive business growth and customer satisfaction.
- Explore the impact of digital transformation on the future of work. How will the roles and responsibilities of employees change in a digital-first environment? What skills and competencies will be essential for success in the future workforce? Analyze the role of supply chain visibility and agility in mitigating risks and disruptions.

Business Case

Please read Business Case No. 9, "Transformations in the Media Industry," featuring Netflix, Disney+, and Amazon Prime Video. How has NETFLIX changed the industry, and will YouTube or social media disrupt it?

Further Readings

Consultoria I (2024) Insights fusion: business intelligence, digital transformation, and AI
Cao J (2024) E-Commerce big data mining and analytics (Advanced studies in E-Commerce)
Grand Bang C (2024) Data-driven decision-making for business

Chapter 11
Digital Business in Digital Worlds

Abstract

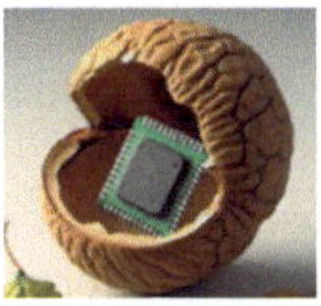

In a nutshell
The digital landscape is rapidly evolving, transitioning from a two-dimensional Internet to an immersive, three-dimensional experience. This chapter delves into the metaverse, a collective virtual space merging the physical and digital realms. We explore key concepts like omniverse, AR, VR, and MR while examining the gaming industry's pivotal role in shaping this future. The chapter concludes with a discussion on the immense potential and challenges of this digital frontier.

Keywords Metaverse · Omniverse · Augmented reality (AR) · Virtual reality (VR) · Mixed reality (MR) · Internet of Things (IoT) · Gamification · Serious games · Spatial computing · Digital Frontrunner (gaming industry)

Basic Prompts

- What is the metaverse and how does it differ from the traditional Internet?
- How does the gaming industry contribute to the development of the metaverse?
- What are the key technologies driving the metaverse and how do they interact?
- What is the omniverse and how does it relate to the metaverse?

S. Schneider, L. Anderie, *Digital Business Management*,
https://doi.org/10.1007/978-3-031-83177-5_11

11.1 Omniverse Versus Metaverse

The Internet, which began utilizing TCP/IP in 1983, is evolving into a three-dimensional Internet, commonly known as the **metaverse.**

Metaverse is often described as a collective virtual shared space, created by the convergence of virtually enhanced physical reality and physically persistent virtual space, including the sum of all virtual worlds, augmented reality, and the Internet. Think of it as a single, interconnected universe where users can interact with each other and digital objects in real time.

Matthew Ball's bestselling business book delineates seven crucial elements for a thriving metaverse.

- **Accessibility:** Ensuring easy access for all users, regardless of device, location, or ability.
- **Persistence:** Maintaining a continuous and consistent existence for the virtual world and its elements.
- **Scalability:** The ability to accommodate growth and increasing user numbers.
- **Interoperability:** Enabling seamless interaction between different platforms and systems.
- **Security:** Protecting users and the metaverse from threats and vulnerabilities.
- **Identity:** Providing a unique and secure identification system for users.
- **Privacy:** Safeguarding user data and protecting personal information.

Omniverse is a broader concept, encompassing multiple metaverses. It's a platform or framework that can simulate and connect different virtual worlds, allowing for interoperability and data sharing between them. In essence, it's a platform for building and operating metaverses.

While **metaverse** and **omniverse** are frequently used interchangeably, Fig. 10.3 clearly differentiates the two by showcasing the distinct advantages of an Omniverse platform in terms of value, time, complexity, and interoperability.

Initially, the Internet served exclusively as a **marketing platform** before high-quality content was generated and **published** (Fig. 11.1). Subsequently, **online transactions** emerged, gradually evolving toward increased **interactivity**. Eventually, all functionalities were adapted for **mobile** devices, creating an ambient augmented mobility environment where smartphones, for instance, offer context-aware assistance to users. This phase marks the advent of the **metaverse**, a realm where individuals can engage with a computer-generated world and interact with other users or their digital representations (avatars).

The **omniverse** serves as a bridge between multiple metaverses and the physical world, facilitated by AR, VR, and complementary technologies like IoT and RFID. The omniverse will emerge from the integration of virtually enhanced physical reality and digital environments. The omniverse is a connection between the Internet and the physical world in the combination of augmented (AR) and virtual reality (VR) technologies, in which people can immerse themselves using avatars and robots in a mixed reality.

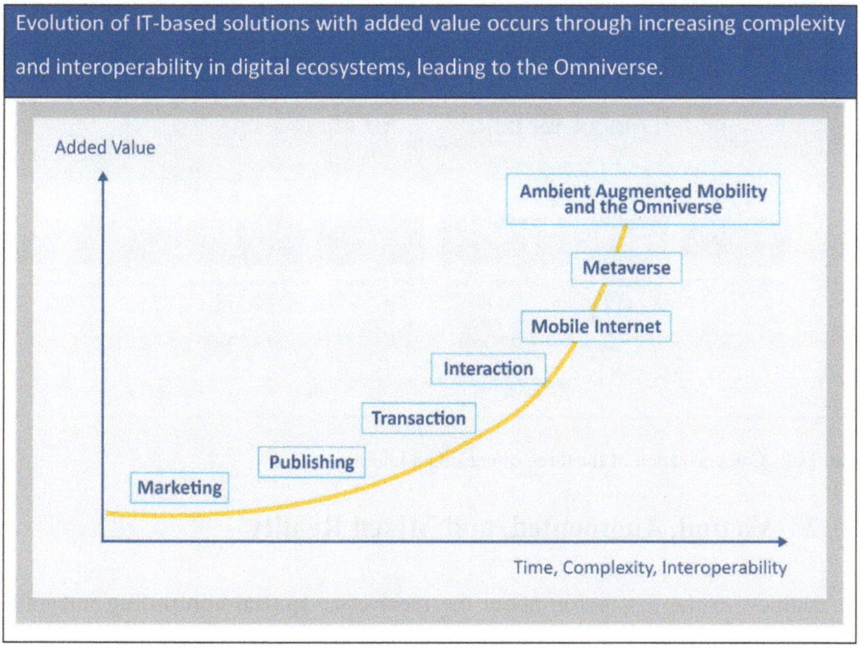

Fig. 11.1 The way to the omniverse

It is likely that there will not be just one metaverse, but many different ones catering to various purposes and originating from diverse manufacturers such as Apple, Google (Alphabet), Microsoft, Meta (formerly Facebook), and companies from the gaming industry. Some will be still mostly virtual, while others already partially connect the physical and virtual worlds, though still very rudimentary. Especially games or social interaction platforms, among other industries, highlight individual experiences and needs (media, tourism, health, etc.). Each operator of such metaverse platforms will try to keep the users as engaged as possible in their environment (**lock-in effect**). However, another development will then require **interoperability**, where values and content or even virtual representations such as avatars can be transferred from one world to another.

Figure 11.2 presents a timeline-like overview of the evolution from early online 3D environments to the anticipated future of the metaverse. It illustrates the progression from early, isolated 3D digital spaces to a more interconnected and immersive metaverse. It highlights the growing interest and involvement of major tech companies in this emerging field. The question marks for Google and Apple suggest uncertainty about their specific roles and the overall competitive landscape in the future metaverse.

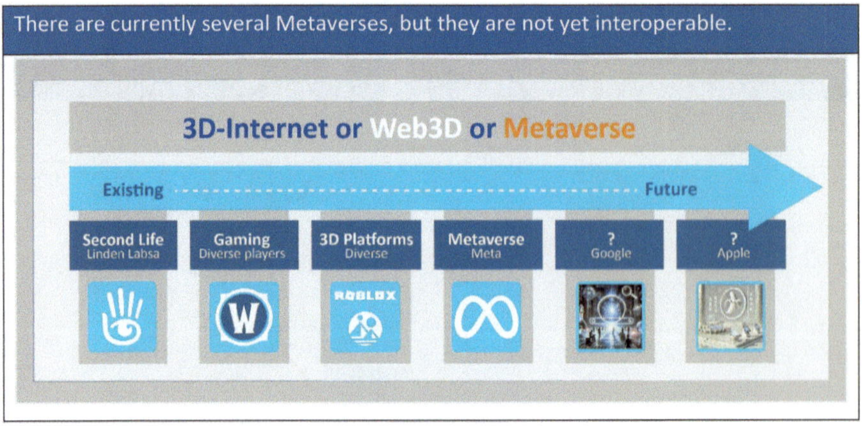

Fig. 11.2 Categorization of the three-dimensional Internet

11.2 Virtual, Augmented, and Mixed Reality

In addition to the discussion about the metaverse, **spatial computing** integrates physical and digital worlds through virtual reality (VR), augmented reality (AR), and artificial intelligence (AI) into one omniverse, enabling interactive, **immersive experiences** with 3D digital content in real environments. Especially augmented reality (AR) and general the human-computer interface are becoming increasingly important.

In this context, distinctions can be made, especially between augmented reality, augmented virtuality, and entirely virtual worlds. **Augmented reality (AR)** overlays digital content onto the real world, enhancing perception and interaction. AR enhances our senses and helps us perceive things faster and more comprehensively than with our natural human senses. It integrates computer-generated information, like images, videos, or 3D models, into the user's environment in real time. AR applications range from gaming and education to navigation and product visualization, offering immersive and interactive experiences. **Augmented virtuality (AV)** blends real-world elements into virtual environments. It enhances virtual experiences by integrating physical objects or environments into computer-generated simulations. AV enables users to interact with both real and virtual elements simultaneously, offering a hybrid reality experience. Paul Milgram proposes an overview in four categories, which he calls **mixed reality**.

Immersive experiences with virtual reality (VR) and augmented reality (AR) create deeply engaging environments. Different virtual worlds and metaverses with interoperability expand the user experience across platforms. Web 3D services, using technologies like WebGL, display 3D graphics directly in Web browsers without extra plugins, making the Web more visually dynamic. Interactivity in 3D environments surpasses traditional Web pages, being responsive to user actions for a more engaging and intuitive experience. Integration with the Internet of Things

(IoT) further enhances connectivity and human-computer interfaces. Additionally, the 3D Internet revolutionizes E-Commerce and marketing, enabling customers to virtually experience products before purchasing.

Figure 11.3 illustrates the spectrum of experiences called mixed reality (MR): combines elements of both real and virtual worlds between the real world and the fully virtual world:

- **Reality:** The physical world as it is.
- **Augmented Reality (AR):** Overlays digital information onto the real world.
- **Augmented Virtuality (AV):** Enhances a virtual environment with real-world elements.
- **Virtual Reality (VR):** A completely immersive digital environment.
- Gaming Industry: The Digital Frontrunner.

The gaming industry serves as a digital trailblazer for Digital Business, driven by several compelling factors:

- Intersection of Technology and Entertainment: At the nexus of cutting-edge technology and the pursuit of entertainment, the gaming industry operates at the forefront of innovation. It demands constant pushing of technological boundaries to deliver immersive and engaging experiences.
- High-Stakes Innovation Environment: The rapidly evolving nature of the gaming market necessitates continuous innovation. With fickle consumer preferences and intense competition, game developers must consistently introduce new features, graphics, and gameplay mechanics to retain player interest. This high-pressure environment drives rapid technological advancement.

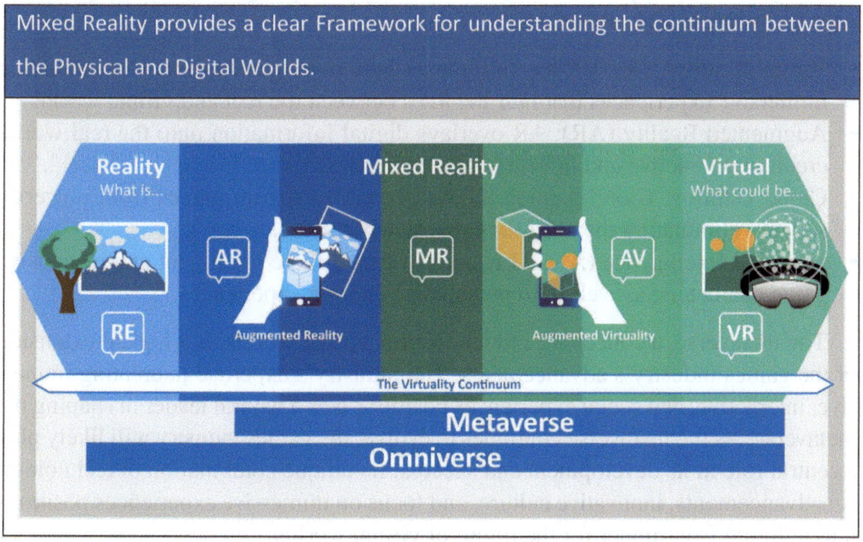

Fig. 11.3 Mixed reality. (Adapted from Milgram)

- Low Brand Loyalty: Unlike traditional industries where brand loyalty is often strong, the gaming industry faces a unique challenge: low player loyalty. Gamers are notoriously fickle, seeking out new experiences and platforms. This forces game developers to be at the cutting edge of technology to attract and retain players.
- Testing Ground for New Technologies: Given the need for constant innovation and the relatively low barriers to entry for new technologies (compared to other industries), the gaming industry becomes an ideal testing ground for emerging technologies. This allows for rapid experimentation and iteration, accelerating the development cycle.
- Talent Pool and Culture: The gaming industry attracts highly skilled and passionate individuals who are comfortable with risk and experimentation. This culture of innovation fosters a fertile ground for technological breakthroughs.

The Games Industry is also a Digital Frontrunner for the metaverse. It has long been a pioneer in digital innovation, consistently pushing the boundaries of technology and user experience. Its unique combination of technological demands, competitive pressures, and a culture of innovation positions it as a leading force in driving advancements that will shape the future of the metaverse.

The industry is known for its relentless pursuit of innovation. Game developers and publishers constantly strive to create immersive, engaging, and visually stunning experiences. This drive has led to significant technological breakthroughs, such as advanced graphics rendering, realistic physics simulations, and sophisticated artificial intelligence. These innovations have not only enhanced gaming experiences but have also found applications in other industries, making the games industry a catalyst for broader technological progress.

The games industry has been at the forefront of adopting and developing cutting-edge technologies. These include:

- Virtual Reality (VR): VR has become a staple in the gaming industry, providing immersive experiences that blur the lines between the real and virtual worlds.
- Augmented Reality (AR): AR overlays digital information onto the real world, creating interactive and informative experiences.
- Cloud Gaming: Cloud gaming allows players to stream games from powerful servers, eliminating the need for expensive hardware.
- Artificial Intelligence (AI): AI is used to create more intelligent and responsive game characters, as well as to personalize gaming experiences.

The metaverse, a concept of interconnected virtual worlds, is a logical extension of the games industry's advancements. The industry's expertise in creating immersive, interactive, and social experiences positions it as a natural leader in shaping the metaverse. As the metaverse continues to evolve, the games industry will likely play a central role in its development and success. Its unique combination of technological advancements, innovative culture, and focus on immersive experiences positions it as a digital frontrunner for the future of virtual worlds.

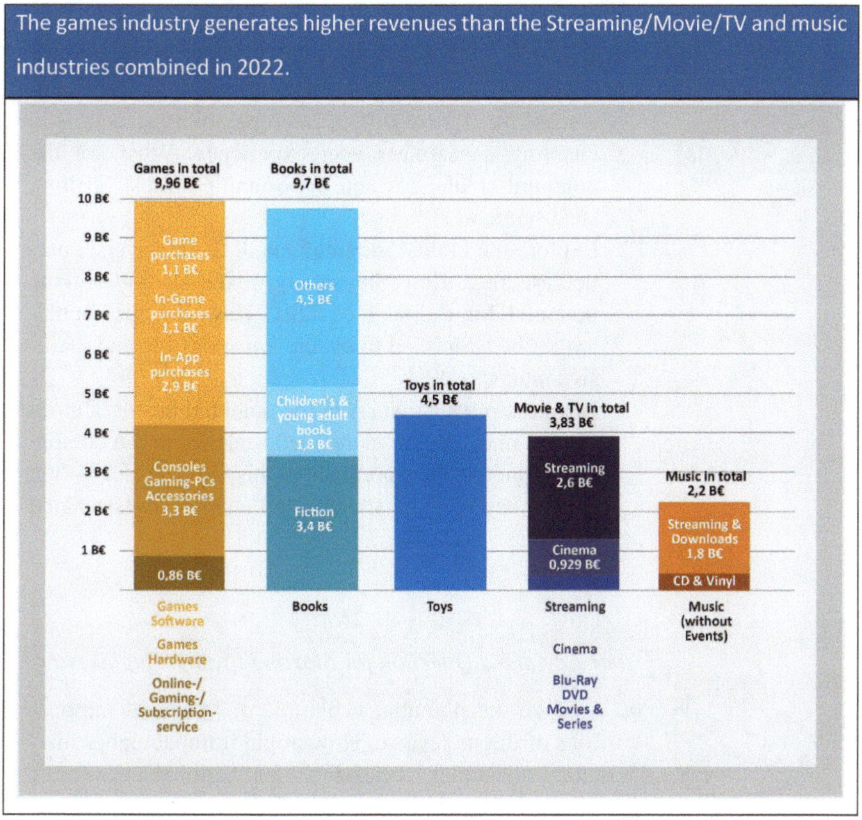

Fig. 11.4 Revenue of the German Gaming Industry according to game and gameswirtschaft.de

It's worth noting that this industry generates more revenue (see Fig. 11.4) than the film and music industries combined. The games industry has evolved from a nascent hobbyist pursuit into a global economic powerhouse. Its trajectory is marked by technological breakthroughs, shifting consumer preferences, and a broadening market scope.

Review Questions

1. Given the potential for multiple, competing metaverses, discuss the critical role of Interoperability standards in enabling a seamless user experience. What are the potential challenges and opportunities in establishing such standards?
2. Explore the ethical implications of the metaverse, particularly regarding data privacy, digital identity, and the potential for digital inequality. How can these challenges be addressed to ensure a responsible and inclusive metaverse?
3. Business models: Analyze the potential business models that may emerge in the metaverse. How can companies monetize their presence in this virtual space? What are the key revenue streams and challenges associated with these models?

Your Advanced Question for Starting Prompt Engineering

- Analyze the potential economic and societal implications of the metaverse. How might it impact labor markets, consumer behavior, and global economic structures? Consider the ethical implications of a virtual economy, including issues of digital ownership, taxation, and inequality.
- Discuss the key technological challenges that must be overcome to fully realize the potential of the metaverse. What are the potential breakthroughs in areas such as artificial intelligence, haptics, and network infrastructure that could accelerate metaverse development? How might these advancements reshape industries and create new business opportunities?

Business Case

Please read Business Case No. 10, "The Potential of Digital Worlds (Metaverse)," featuring Meta (Mmetaverse), Alphabet (Google's metaverse initiative), and Apple (Apple's metaverse initiative). Each has different approaches to designing the metaverse. Please analyze these.

Further Readings

Ball M (2024) The metaverse: building the spatial internet, ISBN-13: 978-1324095286. https://www.matthewball.co/all/themetaverse

Game (2024) https://www.game.de/

Gameswirtschaft (2024) https://www.gameswirtschaft.de/wirtschaft/umsatz-vergleich-games-musik-kino-2023-120724/

Kotler P et al (2023) Marketing 6.0: the future is immersive

Milgram P, Kishino F (2024) A taxonomy of mixed reality visual displays. https://www.linkedin.com/in/paul-milgram-55ba609a/; https://www.cmc.osaka-u.ac.jp/?page_id=213&lang=en

Part III
Industry and Business Cases Prompt Engineering

Chapter 12
Industry and Business Cases

The **following chapters** provide insights into various industries and examines the regularities of change while highlighting the challenges companies face. Most of the **output has been generated** with **large language models (LLMs)** such as ChatGPT and Google's Gemini or others described in the first part of the book.

Use the basic and advanced prompts to **start your own research and discussion** (Prompt Engineering).

Charts and tables illustrating revenue and the number of employees are based on data from the annual reports of the companies, if available.

12.1 Disruption and Self-Driving Cars

Waymo and Tesla

WAYMO

TESLA

Basic Prompt

Describe the self-driving cars industry in 80 words.

S. Schneider, L. Anderie, *Digital Business Management*,
https://doi.org/10.1007/978-3-031-83177-5_12

The **self-driving cars industry** is rapidly evolving, driven by advancements in AI and sensor technology. Key players like Tesla, Waymo, and Uber are pioneering autonomous vehicle development. These vehicles promise to enhance safety, reduce traffic congestion, and provide greater mobility for all. However, challenges such as regulatory hurdles, technological reliability, and public acceptance remain. The self-driving industry, also known as **autonomous driving,** involves the development of vehicles capable of sensing their environment and operating without human intervention. This **industry leverages technologies like AI, machine learning, sensors,** and advanced algorithms to enable vehicles to navigate, recognize obstacles, and make decisions. Key players include tech giants, automotive manufacturers, and startups. The industry aims to enhance safety, reduce traffic congestion, and improve mobility. **Regulatory, ethical, and technical challenges** remain significant hurdles for widespread adoption.

12.1.1 Waymo

Waymo	Waymo is an Alphabet company
Founder(s)	Sebastian Thrun, Stanford Racing Team
Revenue 2023	307 billion USD (Alphabet)
Employees 2023	183k employees (Alphabet)
Year of foundation	2009
Business idea or how the company earn money	Waymo is a pioneer in the development of autonomous driving technologies and operates the Robotaxi service Waymo One in Phoenix. Waymo is the market leader

Figure 12.1 illustrates Waymo's expanding reach, highlighting cities currently served by its Robotaxis. However, in some areas, such as San Francisco and Phoenix, Waymo's initiatives have encountered challenges, including regulatory hurdles and technical issues.

About Waymo

Basic Prompt

Describe the history, products, and business model of Waymo in 200 words.

Fig. 12.1 Places where Waymo's Robotaxis are already operating

Waymo, originating as **Google's self-driving car project in 2009,** transitioned to a stand-alone subsidiary of Alphabet Inc. in 2016. Initially part of Google X, the project aimed to **develop safe, autonomous driving technology.** Renamed Waymo, short for "a new way forward in mobility," it quickly became an industry leader, conducting extensive testing to refine its systems.

Waymo's primary products are its autonomous driving systems, integrated into vehicles like the Chrysler Pacifica minivans and Jaguar I-PACE electric SUVs. **The technology combines sensors, including LiDAR, radar, and cameras, with advanced machine learning algorithms.** Each vehicle is equipped with over 29 cameras, 6 radars, 5 LiDAR sensors, and microphones that collect millions of data points every second. This makes the vehicles comparable to a highly sophisticated supercomputer. The Waymo Driver, a versatile autonomous driving system, is adaptable to various vehicle types, including trucks and passenger cars.

Waymo's **business model revolves around autonomous mobility services and technology licensing.** Its flagship service, Waymo One, is a commercial Robotaxi service in Phoenix, Arizona, and San Francisco offering autonomous rides via a mobile app. This service represents a significant step toward commercializing autonomous driving technology.

Context

Your Advanced Question for Starting Prompt Engineering

Describe the industry environment, including major players, company culture, and historical context. Consider how suppliers and customers perceive the industry?

The electric vehicle industry, closely linked to the self-driving car sector, is highly competitive. Major players include Tesla, General Motors, and Ford, alongside emerging companies like Rivian and Lucid Motors. The industry emphasizes innovation, sustainability, and rapid technological advancement. Historically, the shift from internal combustion engines to electric powertrains marks a significant transition. Suppliers focus on advanced batteries and efficient powertrains, while customers prioritize sustainability, performance, and cost-effectiveness. Governments worldwide incentivize electric vehicles adoption through subsidies and regulations, further driving market growth. The industry is characterized by dynamic changes, increased consumer acceptance, and significant investments shaping its future.

Challenges and Opportunities

Basic Prompt

How did Waymo change or disrupt the industry? How does competitors or the government or customers react? Limit your response to 100 words.

Waymo revolutionized the industry by **achieving significant milestones in autonomous driving technology, including the launch of the first commercial Robotaxi service.** Competitors like Tesla and Uber accelerated their own autonomous efforts in response. Governments are actively developing regulations to ensure safety and integration of autonomous vehicles, often looking to Waymo's advancements as benchmarks. Customers, intrigued by the promise of safer, more efficient transport, show growing interest and acceptance, though some remain cautious. Waymo's success has set high standards, pushing the entire industry toward faster innovation and broader adoption of autonomous driving technologies. **Waymo is also working on a driverless delivery service and package delivery.**

Discussion and Lessons Learned

Your Advanced Question for Starting Prompt Engineering

Explain the actions taken to address the challenge or capitalize on the opportunity. This could involve strategies implemented, decisions made, or interventions undertaken. What happened recently? Limit your response to 100 words.

To address challenges and capitalize on opportunities, Waymo **expanded its Waymo One Robotaxi service to more cities**, enhancing market presence and customer access. They partnered with automakers like Volvo and Stellantis to integrate their autonomous technology into new vehicle models. **Waymo also launched a dedicated trucking unit,** Waymo Via, to tap into the logistics sector. Recently, they secured significant investments to fuel further development and deployment. Additionally, Waymo intensified safety measures and regulatory collaboration to build trust and comply with evolving laws. These strategic actions aim to strengthen Waymo's market leadership and accelerate autonomous technology adoption.

12.1.2 Tesla

Tesla	
Founder(s)	Martin Eberhard and Marc Tarpenning, acquired by Elon Musk (2024)
Revenue 2023	96 billion USD
Employees 2023	127k employees
Year of foundation	2003
Business idea or how the company earn money	Tesla, a **manufacturer of electric vehicles**, is renowned for its autopilot system, which offers advanced driver assistance features. The company is actively working on **developing fully autonomous vehicles**, particularly in collaboration with Chinese partners

Figure 12.2 highlights Tesla's position as the leading company in the electric car industry and includes a SWOT analysis to provide a comprehensive overview of its strengths, weaknesses, opportunities, and threats.

Fig. 12.2 Tesla is the leader in electric cars, while Waymo excels in self-driving technology

About Tesla

Basic Prompt

Describe the history, products, and business model of Tesla in 200 words.

Tesla, Inc., founded in 2003 by Martin Eberhard and Marc Tarpenning, gained prominence under the leadership of Elon Musk, who joined shortly after and significantly shaped the company's vision. Tesla's mission is to accelerate the world's **transition to sustainable energy.** The company started with the Tesla Roadster in 2008, the first fully electric sports car, demonstrating the viability of electric vehicles.

Tesla's product lineup includes the Model S sedan, Model X SUV, Model 3 sedan, and Model Y compact SUV, all of which are fully electric. Additionally, TESLA offers the Cybertruck, an electric pickup truck, and the Tesla Semi, an electric truck for commercial use. The company also produces energy products such as the Powerwall, Powerpack, and Solar Roof, integrating renewable energy solutions for homes and businesses. **Tesla's autopilot and full self-driving (FSD)** technologies are key features, aiming to bring autonomous driving to the mass market.

Tesla's **business model focuses on direct sales** through its online platform and a network of company-owned showrooms, bypassing traditional dealerships. This approach allows for greater control over customer experience and pricing. Tesla also **invests heavily in its Supercharger network,** providing fast-charging solutions for its vehicles. Revenue streams include vehicle sales, energy products, software upgrades (like FSD), and regulatory credits. By vertically integrating its supply chain, Tesla ensures control over production and innovation, driving down costs and improving margins. This comprehensive approach has positioned Tesla as a leader in the EV and renewable energy sectors.

Context

Your Advanced Question for Starting Prompt Engineering

Describe Tesla's situation and the industry environment. This should include major industry players, company culture, and historical context. Additionally, consider how suppliers and customers perceive Tesla and the industry? Limit your response to 100 words.

Tesla operates in the highly competitive electric vehicle and self-driving car industry, alongside key players such as Volkswagen, General Motors, and BYD. Known for its innovative autopilot system, Tesla fosters a culture of innovation and rapid development. **Historically, Tesla has been a market disruptor, pushing advancements in battery technology and autonomous driving**. Suppliers view Tesla as demanding but prestigious, while customers appreciate its cutting-edge technology and brand prestige. Challenges include supply chain constraints and regulatory hurdles, especially as it collaborates with Chinese partners to expand its autonomous vehicle capabilities.

Challenges and Opportunities

Basic Prompt

How did Tesla change or disrupt the industry? How do competitors, the government, or customers react?

Tesla revolutionized the automotive industry by **proving the viability of high-performance electric vehicles and pioneering innovations like long-range batteries** and autonomous driving technologies. Competitors accelerated their electric vehicle initiatives, with automakers like GM and Ford investing heavily in electric and autonomous vehicles. Governments globally implemented stricter environmental regulations and offered incentives for electric vehicles adoption, spurred by Tesla's success. Customers embraced Tesla for its innovation, performance, and sustainability, driving broader market acceptance and demand for electric vehicles. Tesla's influence significantly accelerated the global shift toward sustainable transportation and set new standards for the industry.

Discussion and Lessons Learned

Your Advanced Question for Starting Prompt Engineering

Explain the actions taken to address the challenge or capitalize on the opportunity. This could involve strategies implemented, decisions made, or interventions undertaken. What happened recently? Limit your response to 100 words.

Tesla revolutionized the automotive industry by proving the viability of high-performance electric vehicles and pioneering innovations like long-range batteries and autonomous driving technologies. **Competitors responded by accelerating their own electric vehicles programs,** with major automakers like GM, Ford, and Volkswagen investing heavily in electric and autonomous vehicle development. **Governments worldwide implemented more aggressive environmental regulations and offered incentives for electric vehicles adoption**, spurred by Tesla's success. Customers embraced Tesla's products for their performance, cutting-edge technology, and environmental benefits, driving broader market acceptance and demand for electric vehicles. Tesla's influence has significantly accelerated the global transition to sustainable transportation. Tesla takes a different approach than WAYMO. Tesla tries to equip its cars with fewer and more standard sensors, while WAYMO uses more and more specialized sensors, which, however, significantly increases production costs.

12.1.3 Review: Problems and Challenges of Disruptions

Basic Prompt

What are the problems and challenges in the self-driving cars and electrical vehicle industry?

The self-driving car and electric vehicle industries face several significant challenges. Ensuring technological reliability is crucial, as autonomous vehicles must operate safely in all conditions, including extreme weather and complex urban environments. Regulatory hurdles add complexity, with the need to develop and harmonize standards across different regions to ensure safety without stifling innovation. Public acceptance is another major concern, as skepticism about safety, privacy, and job losses in driving professions remains high.

High costs are a barrier, as developing, testing, and deploying autonomous and electric vehicle technology requires substantial financial investment. Cybersecurity is critical, with the need to protect vehicles from hacking and ensure data privacy. Ethical dilemmas also arise, particularly in decision-making during unavoidable accident scenarios. Infrastructure requirements are significant, as many autonomous vehicle systems rely on high-definition maps and consistent road infrastructure, necessitating upgrades and maintenance.

Interoperability is essential, ensuring that autonomous vehicles from different manufacturers can communicate and operate seamlessly with each other and traditional vehicles. Despite these challenges, the industry continues to push forward, driven by the promise of enhanced safety, reduced traffic congestion, and greater mobility. Key players like Tesla, Waymo, and Uber are at the forefront, investing heavily in research and development to overcome these obstacles and pave the way for future in transportation a transformative.

Side Bar: Other players in the autonomous vehicles industry are:

General Motors **(Cruise):** GM is heavily investing in self-driving technologies through its subsidiary Cruise and plans to introduce autonomous vehicles without steering wheels or other manual controls. Stops the rollout of Robotaxis has shifted the initiative back into a project status.

Ford: In collaboration with Argo AI, Ford is testing autonomous vehicles in several US cities and plans to launch its first commercial autonomous vehicle fleet soon—but no date has been announced yet.

Baidu: The Chinese technology company operates one of the most advanced Robotaxi services with its Apollo platform and has extensive partnerships to promote its autonomous technologies. Operates only in China.

Further Readings

Alphabet (2024) https://abc.xyz/investor/
Tesla (2024) https://ir.tesla.com/
Waymo (2024) https://waymo.com/about/

Questions

1. Create an OpenAI/ChatGPT prompt to discuss the key challenges of autonomous driving.
2. Discuss the most important problems related to autonomous driving. Consider factors such as technological limitations, safety concerns, regulatory hurdles, ethical dilemmas, public acceptance, and infrastructure requirements.
3. How do these challenges impact the development and deployment of autonomous vehicles, and what potential solutions exist to address them?

12.2 Shared Economy and On-Demand Service Companies

Airbnb and Uber

Basic Prompt

Describe on-demand service companies in 80 words.

On-demand service companies are technology-driven and operate platforms that connect consumers with immediate access to goods and services in real time or on a short-term basis. These companies leverage technology, typically through mobile apps or websites, to offer a wide range of services that customers can request with just a few clicks. The services are **flexible** (offer services that are adaptable to customer schedules and preferences) and **scalable** (capable of adjusting service availability based on demand). Customer-centric and convenience are the basis of on-demand services.

12.2.1 Airbnb

Airbnb	
Founder(s)	Brian Chesky, Nathan Blecharczyk and Joe Gebbia
Revenue 2023	10 billion USD
Employees	7k employees
Year of foundation	2007
Business idea or how the company earn money	Airbnb makes money by charging both hosts and guests (two-sided market) a commission fee for each booking made on their platform

Figure 12.3 illustrates how Airbnb facilitates the interaction between hosts and guests. Hosts provide access to their rooms via Airbnb's platform, paying a 3% service fee, while guests can search for and book rooms, paying a 5–12% service fee. Both hosts and guests can leave reviews after transactions, ensuring transparency and trust within the marketplace.

About Airbnb

Basic Prompt

Describe the history, products, and business model of Airbnb in 200 words.

Airbnb began in 2007 when two roommates struggled to pay rent and inflated an air mattress to accommodate guests for a conference. From there, **it grew into a massive online for unique stays around the world establishing a platform** business in the shared economy. **Airbnb doesn't own any physical products;** it's about intangible products—bringing customer and home owner together by information sharing. Their platform acts as a two-sided marketplace connecting travelers (guests)

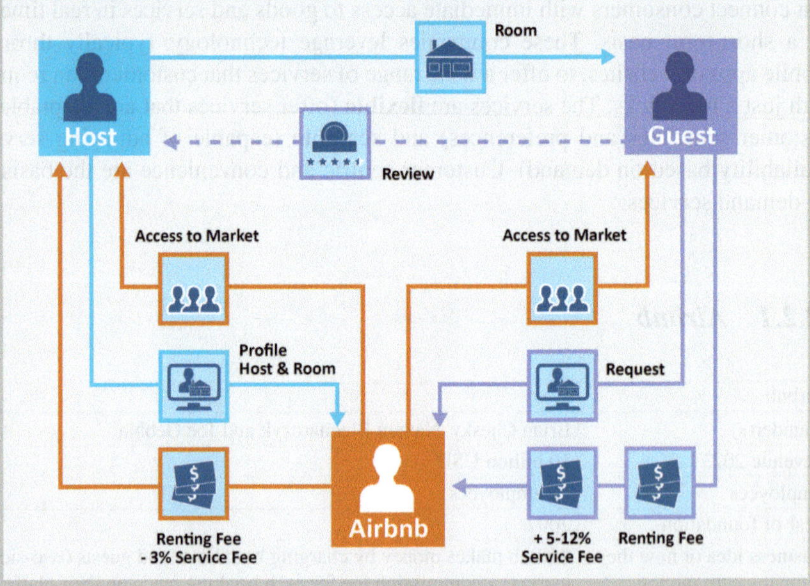

Fig. 12.3 The two-sided market business of Airbnb

with property owners (hosts). They offer a variety of unique accommodations, from apartments to castles.

Airbnb's key to **making money is its commission fees** (transaction fee-based revenue model). They take a cut, typically 3–5% from hosts and 0–20% from guests, for each booking completed through their platform. This two-sided model with commission fees on transactions is what fuels their business.

This novel approach offered a convenient alternative to traditional hotels or apartments, prioritizing efficiency and clear dynamic pricing. Airbnb revenue model included earning commissions per stay.

Context

Your Advanced Question for Starting Prompt Engineering

Describe the industry environment, including major players, company culture, and historical context. Consider how suppliers and customers perceive the industry? Limit your response to 100 words.

Airbnb faces a dynamic industry. Sharing economy rivals like VRBO and Booking.com offer similar rentals. Hotels remain competitors, and some regions have regulations aiming to restrict short-term rentals like the city of Frankfurt. Amidst regulatory challenges and changing consumer demands, the industry emphasizes safety, authenticity, and convenience. Expanding into new markets and diversifying offerings remain crucial strategies for Airbnb's growth, as it navigates a dynamic environment shaped by evolving consumer behaviors and emerging technologies.

Challenges and Opportunities

Basic Prompt

How did Airbnb change or disrupt the industry? How do competitors, the government, or customers react? Limit your response to 100 words.

Airbnb **disrupted the hospitality industry by introducing a peer-to-peer model,** allowing individuals to rent out their homes to travelers. This created a vast network of unique accommodations and experiences, challenging traditional hotels. Competitors initially reacted with skepticism but soon adapted, with companies like Vrbo and Booking.com expanding their offerings to include vacation rentals. Governments responded with regulations aimed at addressing **concerns about safety, zoning, and taxation.** Customers embraced Airbnb's flexibility, affordability, and personalized experiences, driving its rapid growth. However, concerns over regulatory compliance, safety standards, and impact on local housing markets remain ongoing challenges for the company.

Discussion and Lessons Learned

Your Advanced Question for Starting Prompt Engineering

Explain the actions taken to address the challenge or capitalize on the opportunity. This could involve strategies implemented, decisions made, or interventions undertaken. What happened recently? Limit your response to 100 words

To address regulatory challenges, Airbnb **collaborates with governments** on taxation and safety regulations. Enhanced safety measures include stricter verification and 24/7 support. They highlight positive economic impact and community support. Recent scrutiny over housing affordability prompts renewed collaboration and advocacy. They also introduced a **rating system for renters and apartment owners** to prevent damage and make more realistic description of the offered apartments.

12.2.2 *Uber*

Uber	
Founder(s)	Travis Kalanick, Garrett Camp
Revenue 2023	37 billion USD
Employees 2023	30k employees
Year of foundation	2009
Business idea or how the company earn money	Uber connects riders with drivers through a smartphone app. You hail a ride electronically, track its arrival on a map, and pay cashless after the trip. It disrupts traditional taxis by offering transparency, convenience, and potentially lower fares

Figure 12.4 illustrates the business model and the two-sided market business model of Uber. The chart explains Uber's two-sided marketplace model, where clients place orders and vendors (or drivers) receive them. Uber connects clients and drivers, facilitating transportation and handling payments between both sides. The flow highlights how Uber profits by charging fees to both the client and the driver while ensuring that the transportation is completed efficiently.

About Uber

Basic Prompt

Describe the history, products, and business model of Uber in 200 words.

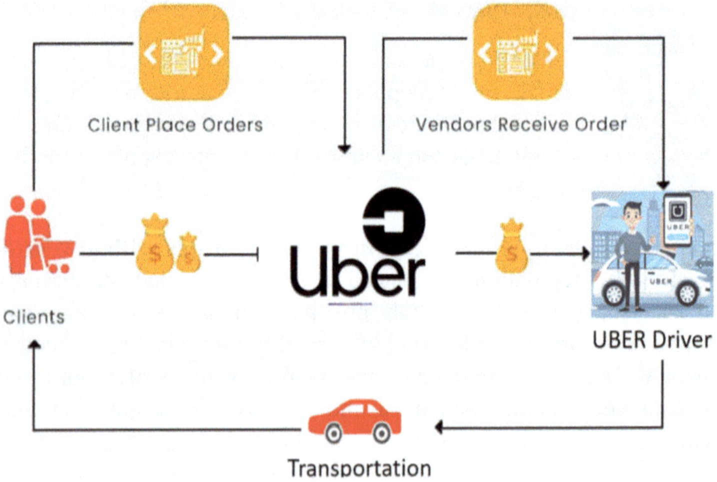

Fig. 12.4 The two-sided market business model of Uber

Founded in 2009, UBER **revolutionized urban transportation with its app-based ride-hailing service** (on-demand transportation service via mobile apps **connecting passengers with drivers** for convenient, flexible travel arrangements in real time). Initially, it connected **riders with independent drivers offering a cheaper and more convenient alternative to taxis.**

Uber's core product remains ride-hailing, but it has **expanded into food delivery** (Uber Eats) and other delivery services. Its business model thrives on being a multi-sided platform. It takes a commission on each transaction **(transaction-based revenue model),** connecting riders willing to pay for a service with drivers seeking income. This light-asset model bypasses owning vehicles or employing drivers directly, allowing for rapid global expansion. Despite early controversies, Uber's innovative approach has transformed how people get around and what they get delivered.

Context

Your Advanced Question for Starting Prompt Engineering

Describe the situation of Uber and the environment surrounding the industry. This might include other major industry players, company culture, or historical context, depending on the subject. How do suppliers or customers perceive this? Limit your response to 100 words.

Uber operates in the **highly competitive ride-sharing industry, facing rivals like Lyft, Didi Chuxing,** and traditional taxi services. Uber's company culture emphasizes innovation and rapid scalability. **Historically, Uber has disrupted transportation by leveraging technology to connect drivers with passengers efficiently.** Suppliers (drivers) appreciate the flexible work opportunities, while customers enjoy the convenience and affordability. The company's continuous efforts in autonomous vehicle development and **expansion into food delivery with Uber Eats** show its adaptability and forward-thinking approach.

Challenges and Opportunities

Basic Prompt

How did the Uber change or disrupt the industry? How do competitors, the government, or customers react? Limit your response to 200 words.

On-demand transportation service via mobile apps **connecting passengers with drivers** for convenient, flexible travel arrangements in real-time. This novel approach offered a convenient **alternative to traditional transportation, prioritizing efficiency and clear dynamic pricing.** Uber's revenue model included earning commissions per trip. Yet, challenges arose concerning labor rights and industry competition amid rapid evolution in on-demand services. **Uber disrupted the transportation industry** by introducing an **innovative model of on-demand ride-hailing,** challenging traditional taxi services. Its use of technology for seamless booking and payment transformed urban mobility. Competitors responded with similar platforms, fostering healthy competition. **Governments reacted with regulatory scrutiny, addressing concerns about safety, labor rights, and market fairness.** Customers embraced the convenience and affordability, contributing to Uber's rapid growth despite occasional controversies. Uber has introduced a **rating system for drivers and customers to increase trustworthiness and safety.**

Discussion and Lessons Learned

Your Advanced Question for Starting Prompt Engineering

Explain the actions taken to address the challenge or capitalize on the opportunity. This could involve strategies implemented, decisions made, or interventions undertaken. What happened recently? Limit your response to 100 words.

To address regulatory challenges and **improve its public image,** Uber has implemented various strategies. This includes enhancing safety measures for both riders and drivers, such as background checks and in-app emergency features. Additionally, Uber has engaged in **dialogue with governments** to establish clearer regulations and partnerships, promoting a more cooperative relationship. Recently, Uber has expanded its services beyond ride-hailing, such as investing in food delivery with Uber Eats. This **diversification mitigates risks** and capitalizes on emerging market trends, strengthening Uber's position in the industry.

12.2.3 Review: Problems and Challenges of On-Demand Services

One major problem is **regulatory compliance** (local rules). These firms often operate in heavily **regulated industries** like transportation and hospitality, requiring compliance with local, regional, and national regulations. Navigating this complex regulatory landscape can be time-consuming and costly. There are a lot of **driver treatment and employment issues**/labor issues or owners of neighboring apartments complain about the constant "visitor turnover." The classification of workers as independent contractors rather than employees has sparked debates over labor rights, wages, and benefits. This classification can lead to legal battles and disputes over worker classification and protections. Concerns arise over the **classification of drivers as independent**. There are still trust and safety concerns. Ensuring the safety and security of both users and providers is paramount. Incidents such as accidents, theft, or fraudulent activities can erode trust and damage the company's reputation.

On-demand service markets are often **saturated with competitors** vying for market share. Rivalry from established players and new entrants can intensify pricing pressure and reduce profit margins. Contractors face challenges, leading to debates about fair compensation, benefits, and working conditions. Additionally, acquiring and retaining customers in a competitive market can be challenging. Providing high-quality service, maintaining competitive pricing, and offering incentives are essential to attract and retain users and need to collect and analyze a lot of customer data.

Managing **operations efficiently,** especially during peak demand periods, can be difficult. Balancing supply and demand, optimizing routes, and ensuring timely service delivery are critical for customer satisfaction. Risk primarily revolves around operational scalability, regulatory compliance, and dependency on gig workers and apartment owners. Guarantees are crucial for building trust; therefore, businesses often offer satisfaction guarantees and responsive customer support to mitigate risk and enhance reliability by having rating systems.

On-demand service companies must collaborate with regulators to develop regulatory frameworks that balance innovation with consumer protection. Improving labor relations by offering fair wages, benefits, and opportunities for advancement can enhance worker satisfaction and reduce turnover. Investing in safety measures, such as background checks and training programs, can help mitigate risks and build trust among users.

Further Readings

Airbnb (2024) https://investors.airbnb.com/home/default.aspx
Uber (2024) https://investor.uber.com/home/default.aspx

Questions

1. Conduct an OpenAI/ChatGPT search to examine whether Uber drivers are genuinely independent contractors. Discuss the findings on the autonomy and employment status of Uber drivers.
2. How have traditional competitors responded to Airbnb?

12.3 Scaling Effects of Cloud Service Business

Amazon Web Services (AWS) and Microsoft Azure

Basic Prompt

Describe Cloud Service Provider in 80 words.

AWS and Microsoft Azure offer **on-demand services for cloud computing**, enabling users to **scale resources** as needed. With AWS, users pay for compute power, storage, and other services without upfront costs (IaaS, PaaS, SaaS), allowing flexibility and cost-efficiency. Azure's on-demand model similarly provides a wide array of services like virtual machines and databases, all billed based on usage. These platforms empower businesses to swiftly deploy, manage, and scale applications, **ensuring optimal performance and cost-effectiveness** in a rapidly changing digital landscape. Hyperscalers are large-scale data centers that provide extensive computing resources through elastic cloud platforms, supporting applications requiring significant computational power and storage. Key players in this space include Amazon Web Services (AWS), Microsoft Azure, Google Cloud Platform (GCP), IBM Cloud, and Alibaba Cloud.

12.3.1 Amazon Web Services (AWS)

AWS	
Founder(s)	Jeff Bezos
Revenue 2023	575 billion USD
Employees (2023)	1.6 K employees
Year of foundation	1994 (AWS services since 2006)
Business idea or how the company earn money	AWS earns money through a **pay-as-you-go model,** charging for cloud computing services based on usage. Businesses and individuals pay for resources like storage, compute power, and databases, without upfront costs. This allows **clients to scale resources as needed, offering flexibility and cost-efficiency** in deploying and managing applications in the cloud

Figure 12.5 shows that nearly three-quarters of Amazon's revenue is generated by its cloud business. The chart shows Amazon's revenue growing steadily, reaching $470 billion by 2021. Additionally, it highlights that 74% of its $25 billion operating profit comes from one major segment, likely AWS.

About Amazon Web Services (AWS)

Basic Prompt

Describe the history, products, and business model of AWS in 200 words.

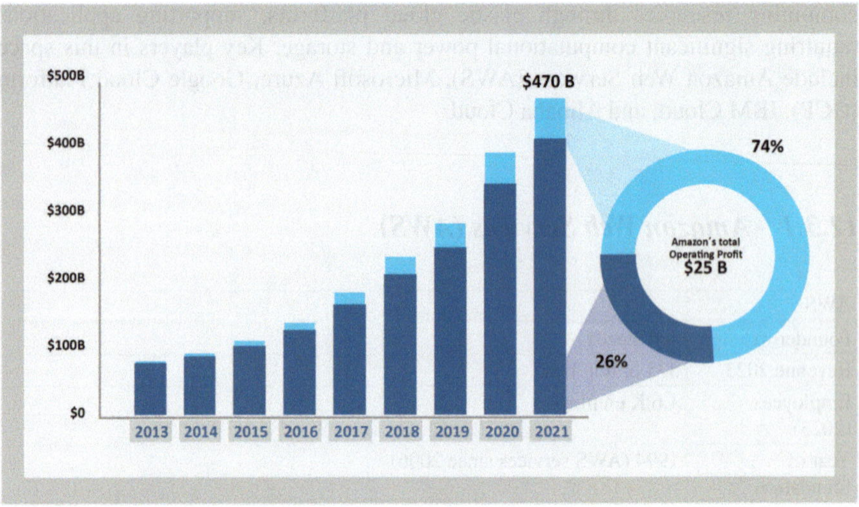

Fig. 12.5 Almost 3/4 of Amazon's profit results out of the cloud business

History: In 2006, Amazon.com unveiled Amazon Web Services (AWS), **initially developed as an internal project and invented cloud computing** to fortify their E-Commerce infrastructure. Recognizing its potential beyond Amazon's walls, AWS officially launched, heralding a new era in cloud computing. Its mission: democratize access to scalable, reliable computing power.

AWS boasts a comprehensive portfolio of cloud services, including Amazon Elastic Compute Cloud (EC2) for scalable virtual servers, Amazon Simple Storage Service (S3) for robust object storage, and Amazon Relational Database Service (RDS) for managing databases. Its suite extends to Amazon Aurora for high-performance relational databases, AWS Lambda for serverless computing, and Amazon SageMaker for machine learning. AWS business model is more and more subscription based. At the core of AWS's success lies its **innovative pay-as-you-go model**. Businesses pay only for the computing resources they use, without upfront costs or long-term contracts. This utility-based pricing model revolutionized the industry, enabling scalability, flexibility, and cost-efficiency. AWS aims to **expand its cloud computing services globally, innovate with new technologies like AI,** and maintain market leadership through customer-centric strategies.

Context

Your Advanced Question for Starting Prompt Engineering

What is the current landscape of the industry? Include key players, company culture, and relevant historical context. Additionally, discuss the perspectives of suppliers and customers within this environment. Limit your response to 100 words.

Industry Landscape: AWS operates in a fiercely competitive **growing cloud computing market,** with major players like Microsoft Azure and Google Cloud Platform vying for dominance. This environment fuels innovation and drives companies to offer cutting-edge solutions by achieving very good profit margins. AWS Culture is known for its **customer-centric** approach and culture of innovation. AWS fosters a dynamic and collaborative work environment. It prioritizes customer feedback, agility, and a "builder" mentality among its employees.

Challenges and Opportunities

Basic Prompt

How did the company change or disrupt the industry? How does competitors or the government or customers react? Limit your response to 100 words.

AWS disrupted the industry by democratizing access to computing power with its pay-as-you-go model. This shifted the paradigm, allowing businesses to scale without hefty upfront costs.

Competitor Response: Competitors like Microsoft Azure and Google Cloud intensified innovation, benefiting customers with advanced technologies and cost-effective solutions. **Governments monitor AWS and cloud giants** for data privacy and antitrust concerns. AWS's compliance and dialogue with regulators maintain.

Discussion and Lessons Learned

Your Advanced Question for Starting Prompt Engineering

Explain the actions taken to address the challenge or capitalize on the opportunity. This could involve strategies implemented, decisions made, or interventions undertaken. What happened recently? Limit your response to 100 words.

AWS continually innovates to address challenges and capitalize on opportunities. Recent initiatives include:

- Expansion of Services: Introducing new services like Amazon Aurora Serverless and AWS Outposts for on-premises computing.
- Partnerships: Collaborations with industry leaders to enhance offerings, such as the AWS IoT Greengrass with Intel.
- Hybrid Cloud Solutions: Enhancing hybrid cloud capabilities with solutions like AWS Hybrid Cloud.

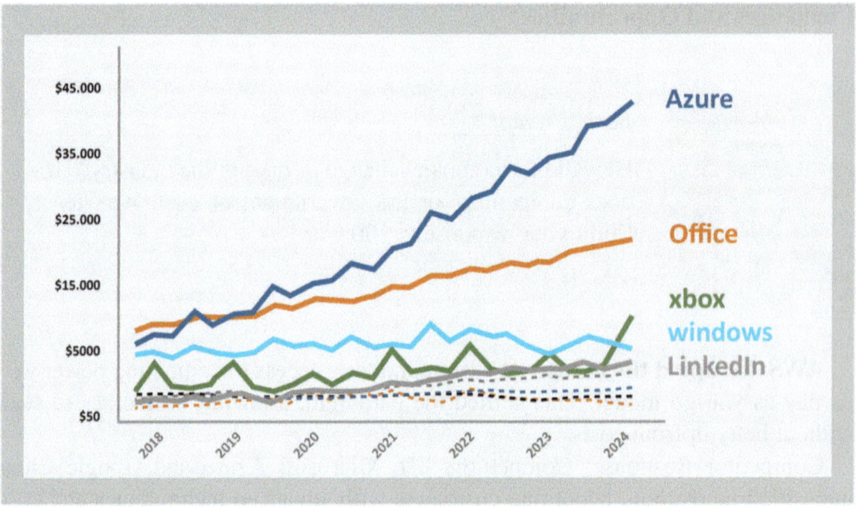

Fig. 12.6 Contribution of cloud business to Microsoft's overall success

12.3.2 Microsoft Azure

Microsoft Azure	
Founder(s)	Bill Gates and Paul Allen
Revenue 2022	245 billion USD (Microsoft)
Employees (2022)	221k employees (Microsoft)
Year of foundation	1975 (Azure 2010)
Business Idea or how the company earn money	Microsoft Azure **provides cloud computing services**, earning revenue through a **pay-as-you-go model** Businesses pay for services such as virtual machines, storage, and databases based on usage, enabling **scalability and cost-efficiency** in deploying and managing applications in the cloud.

Figure 12.6 illustrates how Microsoft's cloud business significantly contributes to the company's overall success.

About Microsoft Azure

Basic Prompt

Describe the history, products, and business model of Microsoft Azure in 200 words.

Microsoft Azure, launched in 2010, is Microsoft's cloud computing platform, marking a pivotal moment in the company's evolution. It began as an effort to bolster Microsoft's services and products, expanding into a comprehensive **cloud offering for businesses worldwide.** Microsoft's product is called **Azure, which offers a diverse range of cloud services, catering to computing, analytics, storage, networking, machine learning**, and more. Core products include Azure Virtual Machines for scalable computing power, Azure Blob Storage for object storage, Azure SQL Database for managed databases, and Azure AI for machine learning capabilities. Microsoft offers also hybrid solutions. Azure Hybrid Solutions enable seamless integration between on-premises and cloud environments, allowing businesses to leverage existing infrastructure while benefiting from cloud scalability and innovation.

Microsoft business model operates on a **pay-as-you-go model, similar to its competitor** AWS, where customers pay for the computing resources, storage, and services they use. This flexible pricing model enables businesses to scale resources based on demand, promoting cost-efficiency and agility.

Enterprise Focus: Azure's business model caters to enterprises of all sizes, offering solutions tailored to diverse industries such as healthcare, finance, government, and education. Azure Government, for instance, provides cloud services specifically for U.S. federal, state, local, and tribal governments. Microsoft Azure **has forged strategic partnerships with industry leaders,** integrating services such as SAP HANA, Oracle Cloud, and Adobe Experience Cloud. These collaborations enhance Azure's capabilities, providing customers with a broader range of solutions. Azure's **global presence** spans over 60 regions worldwide, ensuring low-latency access to services. This expansive network of data centers adheres to strict security and compliance standards, earning the trust of customers across industries.

Context

Your Advanced Question for Starting Prompt Engineering

What is the current landscape of the industry, including major players, company culture, and relevant historical context? Additionally, outline how suppliers and customers perceive this environment. Limit your response to 100 words.

Microsoft Azure operates in a competitive landscape alongside major players like AWS and Google Cloud Platform. Supplier and Customer Perspectives: **suppliers appreciate Azure's reliability and global reach**, often partnering for integrated solutions. Customers value Azure's robust security, scalability, and industry-specific offerings, trusting the platform for critical workloads and digital transformation initiatives.

Challenges and Opportunities

Basic Prompt

How did MS Azure change or disrupt the industry? How do competitors or the government or customers react? Limit your response to 100 words.

Azure revolutionized cloud computing, **democratizing access to powerful tools** for businesses worldwide. Its diverse services and hybrid solutions changed the landscape, enabling digital transformation at scale. **Governments closely monitor**

Azure for compliance with data privacy and antitrust regulations, acknowledging its impact and market influence.

Customers embraced Azure for its versatility and reliability, integrating it into their operations for seamless scalability and digital innovation. This widespread adoption solidified Azure as a leader in the cloud computing industry.

Discussion and Lessons Learned

Your Advanced Question for Starting Prompt Engineering

Explain the actions taken to address the challenge or capitalize on the opportunity. This could involve strategies implemented, decisions made, or interventions undertaken. What happened recently? Limit your response to 100 words.

Azure has responded to industry challenges by developing **industry-specific solutions** like Azure Healthcare APIs for the healthcare sector. **Azure Arc addresses the need for seamless hybrid cloud management across environments.** Significant advancements in AI and machine learning, exemplified by Azure Machine Learning, cater to evolving customer needs. Moreover, Azure's commitment to sustainability is evident through initiatives such as the Azure Sustainability Calculator, demonstrating a holistic approach to innovation and addressing customer requirements. These actions reflect Azure's ongoing efforts to stay at the forefront of cloud computing, providing tailored solutions and fostering sustainable practices.

12.3.3 Review: Problems and Challenges of Cloud Service Provider

The **scaling effects of cloud service businesses primarily involve cost efficiency, flexibility**, and market responsiveness. All cloud providers typically operate under a similar business model, which is often based on a pay-as-you-go structure. For customers to **avoid vendor lock**-in, many of them implement a **multi-cloud management strategy**, which involves using services from multiple cloud providers.

Figure 12.7 illustrates the distribution of market share among leading companies in the cloud computing industry.

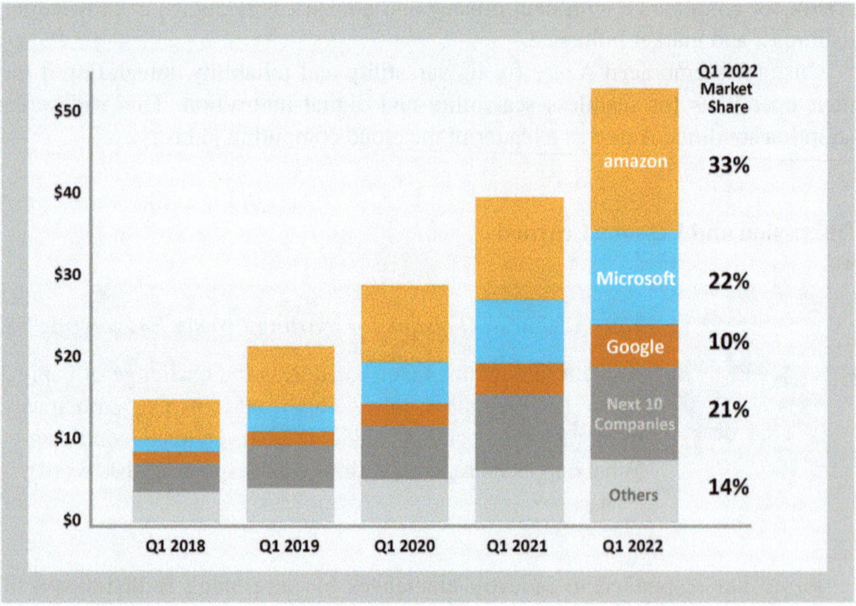

Fig. 12.7 Market shares in cloud computing (in billions)

This approach offers several benefits: so, they can **mitigate risk by diversifying their cloud service providers.** They are more flexible and allow organizations to choose the best services from different providers. This also can **leverage price competition** among cloud providers, choosing more cost-effective solutions for different tasks. By using multiple clouds, companies can more easily comply with data residency laws and reduce latency by locating services closer to users.

The primary objective of cloud computing is to transform fixed costs into variable costs. In an IT context, fixed costs represent consistent expenses like salaries for permanent staff or leasing office space. Variable costs fluctuate based on usage, such as software licenses or data storage fees, which increase with greater usage. But many customers still have security concerns. Both Microsoft Azure and AWS face challenges in ensuring data security and compliance with regulations. The vast amounts of sensitive data stored in the cloud necessitate robust security measures to prevent breaches and maintain customer trust. Privacy regulations such as GDPR and CCPA pose challenges for both Azure and AWS. Ensuring **compliance** with these regulations while offering global services requires intricate data management and privacy protection mechanisms. Customers often struggle with managing costs effectively in the cloud. The **pay-as-you-go model**, while offering flexibility, can lead to unexpected expenses if not monitored closely. Azure and AWS offer cost management tools, but optimizing usage remains a challenge. The offering is getting more and more complex. The extensive range of services and features offered by Azure and AWS can be overwhelming for customers. Navigating through various options, selecting the right services, and integrating them into existing systems can be complex and time-consuming. Important is the **reliability and downtime.** Both Azure and AWS strive for high availability, but downtime can still occur. Outages can disrupt business operations, leading to loss of productivity and revenue for customers. Companies try to avoid **vendor lock-in.** Customers may fear becoming too reliant on a single cloud provider. Azure and AWS work to provide interoperability and open-source solutions, but avoiding vendor lock-in entirely remains a challenge. While Azure and AWS **offer scalability,** customers must design their applications to take full advantage of these capabilities. Ensuring optimal performance as workloads fluctuate requires careful planning and monitoring. Because of the skill shortage, cloud business will increase. Managing cloud services effectively requires specialized skills. Organizations often face challenges in finding and retaining skilled personnel proficient in Azure and AWS technologies. Avoid losing the IT competence inside the company.

Addressing these challenges requires continuous innovation, transparent communication, and a strong commitment to customer satisfaction from both Microsoft Azure and AWS. Both companies strive to provide tools, services, and support to help customers navigate these complexities and maximize the benefits of cloud computing.

Further Readings

Amazon (2024) https://ir.aboutamazon.com/overview/default.aspx
Microsoft (2024) https://www.microsoft.com/en-us/investor/default

Questions

1. What are the benefits of transforming into cloud computing?
2. Use OpenAI/ChatGPT to discuss the benefits of edge computing and cloud computing.
3. Explore the impact of cloud computing on modern businesses. Discuss how cloud services have transformed traditional IT infrastructure, focusing on scalability, cost management, and innovation. Consider both the benefits and challenges, such as security, compliance, and vendor lock-in. Use OpenAI/ChatGPT to dive into the Industry.

12.4 B2C E-Commerce Online Shops

Temu, Shein, Amazon, Alibaba, and Otto

Basic Prompt

Describe the competitive landscape of the B2C e-commerce online shops industry in 80 words.

B2C E-commerce online shops face intense competition. Giants like Amazon and Alibaba dominate the market, leveraging their vast customer bases, efficient logistics, and diverse product offerings. Smaller players compete by specializing in niche markets, offering unique customer experiences, or focusing on specific regions. The industry is characterized by rapid technological advancements, changing consumer preferences, and global economic fluctuations, making it a dynamic and challenging environment for businesses. New entrants like Temu and Shein have disrupted the market with their aggressive pricing strategies, fast fashion models, and targeted marketing campaigns. These companies have gained significant market share, particularly among younger consumers, posing a serious challenge to established players.

12.4.1 Temu

Temu	Temu is part of the PPD Holding
Founder(s)	PDD Holdings (formerly known as Pinduoduo)
Revenue 2023	35 billion USD
Employees 2022	17k employees
Year of foundation	2010
Business idea or how the company earn money	Temu Company **connects global craftsman and traders** with consumers through its E-Commerce platform. It earns **revenue via commission fees on sales facilitated through its platform**. Additionally, Temu offers **premium subscription** services to artisans, providing them with enhanced visibility and marketing tools to reach a wider audience and increase sales

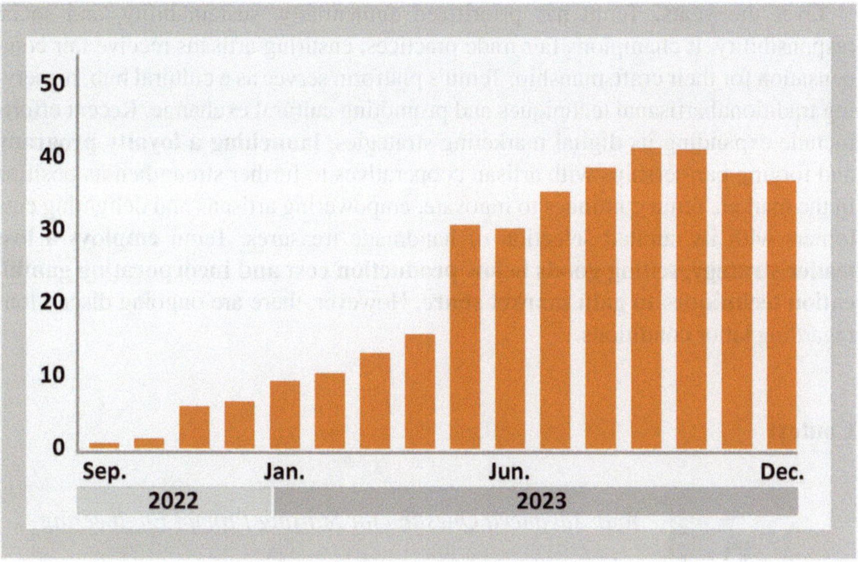

Fig. 12.8 Temu revenues (in billion dollar)

Figure 12.8 indicates the revenue development of Temu, consumer benefits and the "look and feel" of the App.

About Temu

Basic Prompt

Describe the history, products, and business model of the company in 300 words.

Temu is an E-Commerce platform that connects consumers with a wide range of products from various manufacturers and brands. Initially a small marketplace, it evolved into a premier destination for artisanal goods like Etsy. Temu offers a diverse range of products, including handmade jewelry, textiles, ceramics, and home decor, sourced directly from artisans worldwide. The company's **business model revolves around a commission-based system, earning revenue by facilitating sales on its platform.** Additionally, Temu provides premium subscription services to artisans for enhanced visibility and marketing support.

Over the years, Temu has prioritized authenticity, sustainability, and social responsibility. It champions fair trade practices, ensuring artisans receive fair compensation for their craftsmanship. Temu's platform serves as a cultural hub, preserving traditional artisanal techniques and promoting cultural exchange. Recent efforts include expanding its digital marketing strategies, **launching a loyalty program,** and forging partnerships with artisan cooperatives to further strengthen its position in the market. Temu continues to innovate, empowering artisans and delighting customers with its curated selection of handmade treasures. Temu **employs a loss leader strategy, selling goods below production cost and incorporating gamification techniques to gain market share.** However, there are ongoing discussions regarding labor conditions.

Context

Your Advanced Question for Starting Prompt Engineering

What is the industry landscape, including major players, company culture, and historical context? Additionally, consider how suppliers and customers perceive the industry. Limit your response to 200 words.

Temu operates in the highly competitive B2C e-commerce industry, which includes major players like Amazon, Alibaba, and eBay. These giants dominate the market with their extensive logistics networks, advanced technology, and strong brand recognition. Company culture in this industry often emphasizes innovation, customer satisfaction, and efficiency. E-Commerce companies typically foster a fast-paced, dynamic work environment to keep up with rapidly changing market demands. Historically, the industry has evolved significantly with the rise of the Internet and mobile technology, shifting from traditional brick-and-mortar stores to online platforms. This transformation has been driven by technological advancements, changes in consumer behavior, and the increasing importance of data analytics.

From Temu's perspective, the platform differentiates itself by offering competitive prices and a wide range of products. Suppliers might appreciate Temu's ability to reach a broad audience and its focus on affordability, which can drive higher sales volumes. Customers, on the other hand, may value the platform for its cost-effective options and diverse product selection, though they might also be cautious about product quality and delivery times.

Challenges and Opportunities

Basic Prompt

How did the company change or disrupt the industry? How do competitors or the government or react? Limit your response to 100 words.

Temu Company **revolutionized the artisanal goods industry by establishing a direct-to-consumer model**, enabling artisans to reach a global audience through its E-Commerce platform. By **bypassing traditional intermediaries**, Temu empowers artisans to earn higher profits while offering customers authentic, handcrafted products. Its emphasis on cultural preservation distinguishes it from mass-market retailers, garnering positive reactions from customers who value authenticity and ethical sourcing. Competitors may adjust strategies to compete, while **government entities may consider regulatory implications**. Overall, Temu's disruptive innovation reshapes the industry landscape, empowering artisans, delighting customers, and fostering a more equitable and sustainable marketplace for handmade goods. Temu ships a large number of packages that fall below the German customs threshold.

Discussion and Lessons Learned

Your Advanced Question for Starting Prompt Engineering

Explain the actions taken to address the challenge or capitalize on the opportunity. This could involve strategies implemented, decisions made, or interventions undertaken. What happened recently? Limit your response to 100 words.

To address the challenge of increasing competition in the artisanal goods market, Temu Company recently implemented several strategic initiatives. This includes enhancing its **digital marketing efforts to reach a wider audience, expanding its product offerings to cater to diverse consumer preferences,** and forging partnerships with artisan cooperatives to source unique products. Additionally, Temu **launched a loyalty program** to reward repeat customers and improve customer retention. These actions have helped Temu capitalize on the opportunity to further establish itself as a leading destination for authentic, ethically sourced artisanal goods while staying ahead of competitors in the rapidly evolving E-Commerce landscape.

Now Temu is **offering a wide range of heavily discounted products by directly sourcing from manufacturers, reducing intermediary costs.** It utilizes aggressive marketing strategies, including social media and high-profile ads, to attract customers.

12.4.2 Amazon

Amazon	
Founder(s)	Jeff Bezos
Revenue 2023	575 billion USD
Employees	1.6 M employees
Year of foundation	1994
Business idea or how the company earn money	Amazon operates as an **E-Commerce giant,** earning money through a variety of channels. Its **primary revenue streams include retail sales of a vast range of products, subscription services such as Amazon Prime, advertising services, cloud computing (most profits)** through Amazon Web Services (AWS), and third-party seller fees on its platform (most revenue)

Figure 12.9 indicates some of the businesses Amazon is involved with. The chart displays Amazon‘s vast ownership network, showcasing its subsidiaries, including Whole Foods, Audible, Twitch, IMDb, and Zappos. This highlights Amazon‘s diverse portfolio, spanning various industries such as e-commerce, streaming, groceries, and entertainment.

About Amazon

Basic Prompt

Describe the history, products, and business model of the company in 100 words.

Amazon, founded by Jeff Bezos in 1994, **started as an online bookstore** before expanding into a global E-Commerce powerhouse. Its product range now spans virtually every category, including electronics, apparel, groceries, and digital content. **Amazon's business model centers on convenience, offering customers a seamless shopping** experience, fast delivery through **Prime membership**, and competitive pricing.

Throughout its history, Amazon has prioritized customer satisfaction and innovation, constantly evolving to meet changing market demands. Its commitment to efficiency and investment in technology, **logistics**, and infrastructure have cemented

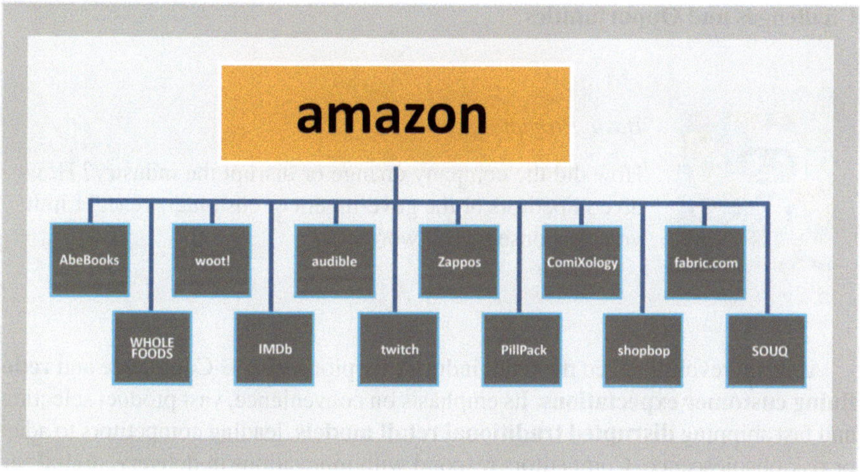

Fig. 12.9 Amazon´s Business Cosmos

its position as one of the world's most valuable companies, driving continued growth and dominance in the E-Commerce and tech industries.

Context

Your Advanced Question for Starting Prompt Engineering

Describe the situation or environment surrounding the industry. This might include major industry players, company culture, or historical context, depending on the subject. How do suppliers or customers perceive this? Limit your response to 100 words.

In the E-Commerce industry, Amazon operates with high **competition from both traditional retailers and online marketplaces.** Major players like Walmart, Alibaba, and eBay vie for market share, each offering unique advantages and services. Amazon's company culture emphasizes innovation, customer obsession, and operational excellence, resonating with both suppliers and customers. Suppliers value Amazon's vast reach and **efficient logistics network**, while customers appreciate its wide product selection, competitive pricing, and fast delivery (same-day delivery) through Prime membership. However, concerns about labor practices, antitrust issues, and environmental impact have sparked debates about Amazon's influence and responsibilities in shaping the industry's future.

Challenges and Opportunities

Basic Prompt

How did the company change or disrupt the industry? How do competitors or the government or customers react? Limit your response to 100 words.

Amazon revolutionized the retail industry by pioneering E-Commerce and **redefining customer expectations.** Its emphasis on convenience, vast product selection, and fast shipping **disrupted traditional retail models**, leading competitors to adapt or risk obsolescence. Competitors respond with innovations in delivery, digital services, and pricing strategies to stay competitive. **Governments scrutinize Amazon's market dominance, leading to antitrust investigations** and regulatory scrutiny. Customers embrace Amazon's convenience and value proposition but express concerns about worker conditions, data privacy, and environmental impact, fueling calls for accountability and ethical business practices.

Discussion and Lessons Learned

Your Advanced Question for Starting Prompt Engineering

Explain the actions taken to address the challenge or capitalize on the opportunity. This could involve strategies implemented, decisions made, or interventions undertaken. What happened recently? Limit your response to 100 words.

To address challenges and capitalize on opportunities, Amazon has **invested heavily in technology, expanding its product offerings, and enhancing its logistics network**. Recent actions include expanding its grocery delivery services, investing in renewable energy projects to mitigate environmental impact, and launching initiatives to improve worker conditions and diversity. Additionally, Amazon continues to innovate with new **products like Amazon Pharmacy and Amazon Fresh stores.** These strategies aim to maintain Amazon's competitive edge, satisfy customer demands, and navigate regulatory challenges while further solidifying its position as a leader in E-Commerce, technology, and logistics. Amazon **expand the business to Amazon store (local automated and autonomous supermarkets**) and Amazon fresh (delivery services).

12.4.3 Shein

Shein	
Founder(s)	Chris Xu
Revenue 2023	33 billion USD
Employees	10k employees
Year of foundation	2008
Business idea or how the company earn money	Shein generates revenue as an **online fashion retailer by selling clothes at low prices and high volume**. Their business model is summarized as follows: sourcing **trendy and affordable fashion** items, leveraging economies of scale for cost efficiency, utilizing targeted online marketing to reach a wide audience, and maintaining a **fast supply chain to quickly respond to market** trends

Shein was founded in China and relocated to Singapore in 2020. The graphic illustrates typical working and manufacturing processes in Asia, as indicated as an example in Fig. 12.10.

About Shein

Basic Prompt

Describe the history, products, and business model of Shein in 300 words.

Shein's journey **began in 2008 as a wedding dress website**. Than transformed into a fast-fashion giant by 2012, offering trendy clothing at incredibly low prices. Initially, they sourced their products from wholesale markets, but later built a **strong network of suppliers in China**. This shift allowed for more control and flexibility in their offerings.

Shein's success can be attributed to three key factors. First, they **utilize a fast-fashion** model. This means producing trendy styles in small batches. This minimizes waste and allows them to quickly adapt to current trends, ensuring their clothing reflects what's hot right now. Second, **Shein is data-driven.** They analyze data to predict what styles will be popular, allowing them to produce what customers want and keep prices low. This approach minimizes the risk of manufacturing clothes that won't sell.

Finally, **Shein is social media savvy and doing gamification.** They target young shoppers through influencer marketing and strategic social media advertising. **Partnering with influencers** allows them to tap into a vast audience who trusts the recommendations of these online personalities. Strategic social media advertising

Fig. 12.10 Example of working and manufacturing in Asia

further expands their reach, ensuring they stay at the forefront of young consumers' minds. By combining trendy styles, data-driven production, and social media expertise, Shein has transformed from a wedding dress website to a global online fashion leader. Shein implemented a good test and replenish system with low charges and just in **time production.**

Context

Your Advanced Question for Starting Prompt Engineering

Describe the situation or environment surrounding the industry. This might include other (big) industry players, company culture, or historical context depending on the subject. How do competitors, the government, or customers react? Limit your response to 100 words.

Shein thrives in the fast-fashion industry, a cutthroat world of **constant trend cycles, high volume, and slim profits**. Competitors like H&M and Zara share the space, but Shein carves a niche with its rock-bOTTOm prices and lightning-fast trend adaptation. **Suppliers in China welcome Shein's bulk orders, but labor**

practices and environmental impact raise concerns. Customers love the affordability and trendy styles, yet ethical considerations and inconsistent quality remain topics of debate.

Challenges and Opportunities

Basic Prompt

How did the company change or disrupt the industry? How do competitors or the government or customers react? Limit your response to 100 words.

Shein shook up fast fashion with **"ultra-fast fashion,"** producing trendy clothes in tiny batches at breakneck speed. Data predicts what sells, minimizing waste and keeping **prices ultra-low**. They mastered social media, reaching young trendsetters. Competitors scramble to keep up, while governments raise an eyebrow at labor practices in China. Customers enjoy the affordability but wrestle with **ethical dilemmas and inconsistent quality.**

Discussion and Lessons Learned

Your Advanced Question for Starting Prompt Engineering

Explain the actions taken to address the challenge or capitalize on the opportunity. This could involve strategies implemented, decisions made, or interventions undertaken. What happened recently? Limit your response to 100 words.

Shein battles criticism over **labor practices and inconsistent quality.** They're fighting back with pledges for supply chain transparency, launching eco-friendly lines, and likely upping quality control. The jury's still out on how well it works. Meanwhile, Shein keeps **growing globally and might be using AI to personalize your shopping experience.** They're addressing challenges while capitalizing on their strengths to stay ahead.

12.4.4 Otto

Otto	
Founder(s)	Werner OTTO
Revenue 2023	16 billion USD
Employees	41k employees
Founded year	1949
Business idea or how the company earn money	Otto, a major German online retailer, makes money in two ways: **commissions like Amazon.** They take a cut from sales made by other retailers on their platform**. Direct sales:** They also sell their own inventory, profiting from the difference between buying and selling prices. They **focus on quality by having high standards** for marketplace sellers and offering their own curated selection

Otto has an extensive logistics network of its own, similar to Amazon, which is depicted in the Fig. 12.11. This network supports Otto's operations with its own logistics infrastructure (Fig. 12.11).

About Otto

Basic Prompt

Describe the history, products, and business model of the company in 200 words.

Otto's story began in 1949 as a **mail-order company in Hamburg, Germany.** It quickly rose to prominence, offering a vast selection of products through **catalogs delivered to homes across the country.** By the 1990s, Otto embraced the digital revolution, launching its **online store in 1995.** This move cemented their position as a retail leader, adapting to the changing consumer landscape.

Today, Otto **offers a diverse range of products,** acting as both a marketplace and a traditional retailer. Their marketplace allows established brands to sell their wares on the Otto.de platform, reaching a wide audience of German online shoppers. This approach expands their product selection significantly without needing to manage a massive in-house inventory. By combining these strategies, Otto has become a dominant force in German online retail. **Their focus on quality extends to both aspects of their business model**. They have **strict criteria for**

Fig. 12.11 Logistics network at Otto

marketplace sellers, ensuring a positive customer experience. Additionally, their curated selection allows them to maintain **high-quality standards for the products they directly sell.** This combination of a vast product selection, a commitment to quality, and a two-pronged revenue stream has solidified Otto's position as a leader in the German online retail market.

Context

Your Advanced Question for Starting Prompt Engineering

Describe the industry landscape, including major players, company culture, and historical context. Additionally, consider how suppliers and customers perceive the industry? Limit your response to 100 words.

Otto thrives in Germany's booming E-Commerce market, facing competition from Amazon and local players. Their focus on quality curation sets them apart. **Customers value their diverse offerings and emphasis on a positive shopping experience.** Suppliers appreciate Otto's large platform reach and strict selection process, ensuring a reliable sales channel.

Challenges and Opportunities

Basic Prompt

How did the company change or disrupt the industry? How does competitors or the government or customers react? Limit your response to 100 words.

Otto didn't disrupt the industry, but rather adapted. They **transitioned from mail-order leader to a successful online retailer** in the 1990s, paving the way for others. Competitors scramble to keep pace with their vast product range and quality focus. The government likely views them positively for their contribution to E-Commerce growth. Customers appreciate their smooth online shopping experience. Otto **is developing an AI tool to predict customer product returns.** Additionally, the company is advancing its internationalization efforts and partner programs, focusing on sustainability initiatives.

Discussion and Lessons Learned

Your Advanced Question for Starting Prompt Engineering

Explain the actions taken to address the challenge or capitalize on the opportunity. This could involve strategies implemented, decisions made, or interventions undertaken. What happened recently? Limit your response to 100 words.

Otto constantly refines its strategy to stay ahead. They **meticulously curate their marketplace sellers, ensuring a high-quality experience** for customers. Additionally, they invest in platform improvements, potentially focusing on areas like **personalization** or **faster delivery**, to stay competitive. Recent developments might be less about major announcements and more about ongoing efforts to adapt and enhance the customer journey.

12.4.5 Alibaba

Alibaba	
Founder(s)	Jack Ma
Revenue 2023	130 billion USD
Employees	205k employees
Year of foundation	1999
Business idea or how the company earn money	E-Commerce giant, B2B, B2C, C2C marketplaces (Alibaba.com, Taobao, Tmall), cloud computing (Alibaba Cloud), digital payments (Alipay), logistics (Cainiao), entertainment (Youku), Big Data. **Revenue: commissions, advertising, subscription fees, transaction fees, cloud services, and logistics services**

Alibaba's Financial Performance: revenue, sales and marketing, and gross margin are shown in Fig. 12.12.

About Alibaba

Basic Prompt

Describe the history, products, and business model of the company in 300 words.

Alibaba, founded by Jack Ma in 1999 in Hangzhou, China, **started as a business-to-business (B2B) marketplace aimed at connecting Chinese manufacturers with overseas buyers.** Initially, the platform provided a space for small and medium-sized enterprises (SMEs) to expand their market reach.

Over the years, Alibaba expanded its services to include **business-to-consumer (B2C)** and **consumer-to-consumer (C2C)** marketplaces. **Taobao (first** Alibaba **platform),** launched in 2003, is a C2C platform similar to eBay, where individuals can sell products directly to consumers. Tmall, introduced in 2008, serves as a B2C marketplace for established brands, offering a more premium shopping experience.

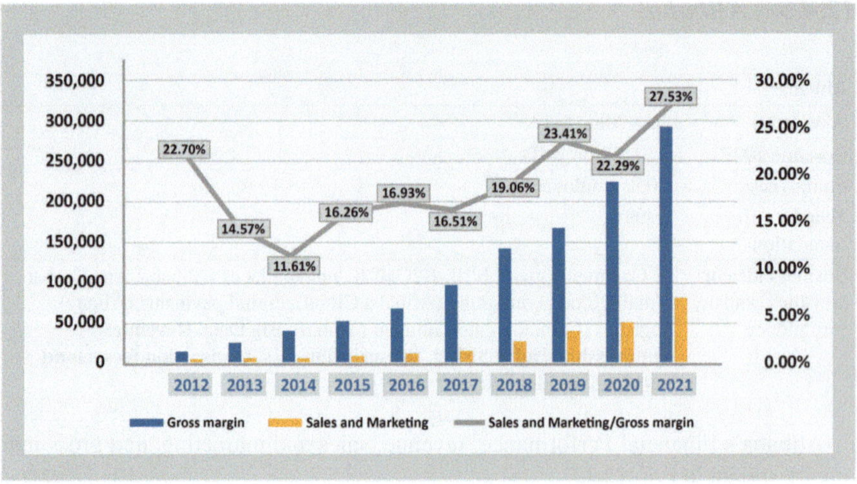

Fig. 12.12 Revenue, sales and marketing, and gross margin development of Alibaba (in billion dollars)

Alibaba's ecosystem encompasses a variety of services beyond E-Commerce. The company also **operates Alipay, a digital payment platform** that has grown to become one of the largest mobile payment services globally. **Cainiao,** Alibaba**'s logistics arm,** ensures efficient delivery and supply chain management, enhancing the overall user experience.

In the **entertainment sector,** Alibaba **owns Youku**, a video streaming platform akin to YouTube, and has invested in various media and film ventures. The company also delves into Big Data and artificial intelligence through its Alibaba DAMO Academy, driving innovation and technological advancement.

Alibaba's **business model is diversified.** It earns revenue through various channels: commissions on transactions from its marketplaces, advertising fees from merchants wanting to **promote their products, subscription fees for premium services, and transaction fees from Alipay.** Alibaba **Cloud** contributes significantly with its pay-as-you-go model for cloud services. Additionally, logistics and delivery services generate income through Cainiao. Overall, Alibaba has evolved from a simple online marketplace to a multifaceted conglomerate, driving E-Commerce, technology, and financial innovation globally.

Context

Your Advanced Question for Starting Prompt Engineering

Describe the situation or environment surrounding the industry. This might include other (big) industry players, company culture, or historical context depending on the subject. How does competitors or the government or customers react? Limit your response to 100 words.

The E-Commerce industry, where Alibaba operates, is highly competitive and rapidly evolving. Major **players include Amazon, JD.com, and** eBay**, all vying for market share** through innovation and extensive logistics networks.

Suppliers value Alibaba for its vast reach and data insights, which help optimize sales strategies. Customers appreciate the diverse product range, competitive prices, and seamless shopping experience. Alibaba's company culture emphasizes innovation, **customer-centricity, and resilience, driving continuous growth and adaptation** in a dynamic market landscape. Historical context shows Alibaba as a pioneer in transforming China's digital economy.

Challenges and Opportunities

Basic Prompt

How did the company change or disrupt the industry? How do competitors or the government or customers react? Limit your response to 100 words.

Alibaba revolutionized the E-Commerce industry by **creating a comprehensive digital ecosystem that seamlessly integrates online marketplaces, cloud computing, digital payments, and logistics.** This holistic approach disrupted traditional retail, forcing competitors like Amazon and JD.com to enhance their service offerings and innovate constantly. The Chinese government supports Alibaba's growth, seeing it as a driver of economic development, though it imposes regulations to ensure fair competition and data security. Customers benefit from Alibaba's diverse product selection, competitive pricing, and efficient delivery, which have set new standards for convenience and accessibility in online shopping. Competitors strive to match Alibaba's extensive infrastructure and technological advancements.

Discussion and Lessons Learned

Your Advanced Question for Starting Prompt Engineering

Explain the actions taken to address the challenge or capitalize on the opportunity. This could involve strategies implemented, decisions made, or interventions undertaken. What happened recently? Limit your response to 100 words.

To address challenges and capitalize on opportunities, Alibaba has implemented several strategic actions. It **expanded its cloud computing** services through Alibaba Cloud, enhancing technological capabilities and tapping into the growing demand for digital transformation. The company also **invested heavily in artificial intelligence and Big Data** through the DAMO Academy, driving innovation and operational efficiency.

Recently, Alibaba **restructured into six distinct business groups to increase agility** and foster growth, each focusing on different sectors like E-Commerce, cloud, and **logistics**. This move aims to enhance responsiveness to market changes and regulatory pressures, positioning Alibaba to better compete and innovate in a dynamic industry landscape.

12.4.6 Review: Problems and Challenges of E-Commerce

Basic Prompt

Describe the challenges that affect the industry. What are the common findings?

The industry with E-Commerce faces several challenges and problems, including:

- **Competition:** The on-demand E-Commerce market is highly competitive, with numerous players vying for market share. Competing with established giants like Amazon, Alibaba, and eBay requires innovative strategies and significant investments in technology and marketing.

- **Customer Acquisition and Retention:** Acquiring and retaining customers in a crowded marketplace can be challenging. Companies must differentiate themselves through unique offerings, personalized experiences, and exceptional customer service to attract and retain loyal customers.
- **Logistics and Fulfillment:** Efficient logistics and fulfillment are critical for on-demand E-Commerce companies. Meeting customer expectations for fast and reliable delivery while minimizing costs and reducing environmental impact requires sophisticated logistics infrastructure and optimization algorithms.
- **Supply Chain Disruptions:** On-demand E-Commerce companies are vulnerable to supply chain disruptions, such as global shipping delays, inventory shortages, or supplier issues. Proactively managing supply chain risks and diversifying suppliers can help mitigate these challenges.
- **Fraud and Security Concerns:** On-demand E-Commerce platforms are susceptible to fraud, cybersecurity threats, and data breaches. Implementing robust security measures, fraud detection systems, and encryption protocols is essential to protect customer data and maintain trust.
- **Regulatory Compliance:** On-demand E-Commerce companies must comply with a myriad of regulations, including consumer protection laws, privacy regulations, and tax laws. Staying abreast of regulatory changes and ensuring compliance across multiple jurisdictions can be complex and time-consuming.
- **Customer Experience:** Delivering a seamless and personalized customer experience across multiple touchpoints is a significant challenge. Companies must invest in user-friendly interfaces, responsive customer support, and data-driven personalization to meet evolving customer expectations.
- **Sustainability:** Increasing consumer awareness and concern about environmental sustainability pose a challenge for on-demand E-Commerce companies. Adopting eco-friendly practices, such as sustainable packaging, carbon-neutral shipping options, and responsible sourcing, is becoming increasingly important to attract environmentally conscious consumers.

Further Readings

Alibaba (2024) https://www.alibabagroup.com/en-US/investor-relations
Amazon (2024) https://ir.aboutamazon.com/overview/default.aspx
Otto (2024) https://investor.pddholdings.com/
PDD Holding (2024) https://investor.pddholdings.com/
SHEIN Group (2024) https://www.sheingroup.com/

Questions

1. Explore the impact of cloud computing on modern businesses. Discuss how cloud services have transformed traditional IT infrastructure, focusing on scalability, cost management, and innovation. Consider both the benefits and challenges, such as security, compliance, and vendor lock-in.
2. Use OpenAI/ChatGPT to dive into the E-Commerce industry by developing a prompt which leads you to future developments of this companies.

12.5 Search Engine Market

Alphabet/Google, MetaGer, and Microsoft /Bing

Alphabet Google metaGer Microsoft Bing

Basic Prompt

Describe the search engine market in 80 words.

The search engine market is competitive and **dominated by a few major players** such as Google, Bing, and Yahoo. These search engines index vast amounts of web content and use complex algorithms to **deliver relevant search results to users. Google, with its dominant market share, sets the standard for search technology and advertising.** Competition exists in areas like specialized search engines, vertical search, and emerging technologies such as voice search and AI-driven search assistants, shaping the landscape of digital information retrieval.

12.5.1 *Google/Alphabet*

Google/Alphabet	
Founder(s)	Larry Page & Sergey Brin
Revenue 2023	307 billion USD (Alphabet)
Employees	183k employees (Alphabet)
Year of foundation	1998
Business Idea or how the company earn money	Google **earns money primarily through advertising,** particularly through its **AdWords** program, where businesses pay to have their ads displayed in Google search results and on other websites within the Google Display Network. Additionally, Google offers **premium services such as Google Workspace and cloud storage through Google Cloud,** generating further revenue

Figure 12.13 shows the market share of Google. The chart illustrates the market share of search engines, with Google dominating at 92.3%. Bing follows with a 3% share, while other search engines collectively account for 4.7%, indicating Google's overwhelming control of the search engine market.

About Google

Basic Prompt

Describe the history, products, and business model of the company in 200 words.

Google, founded in 1998 by Larry Page and Sergey Brin while they were Ph.D. students at Stanford University, has become one of the **most influential and ubiquitous technology companies globally.** Initially, Google started as a research project to develop a **more efficient search engine.** Their **breakthrough algorithm, PageRank** (explanation see below), revolutionized Web search by ranking pages based on their relevance and authority, rather than just keyword density. This innovation propelled Google to dominance in the search engine market.

Over the years, Google **expanded its product portfolio** beyond search. In 2004, it launched **Gmail**, a free email service that offered large storage capacity and powerful search capabilities. Google **Maps**, introduced in 2005, provided users with detailed maps, satellite imagery, and route planning. In 2006, Google **acquired**

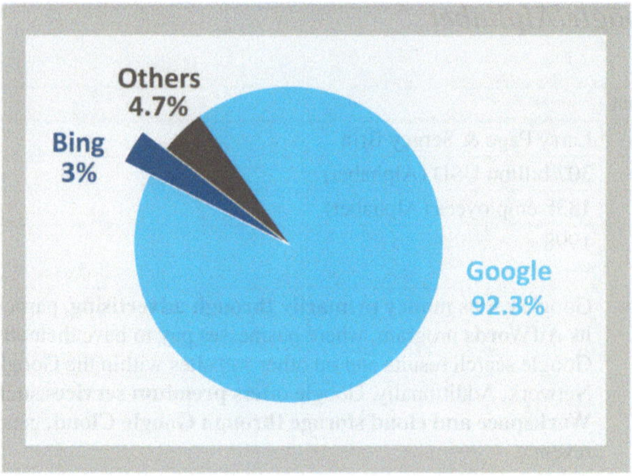

Fig. 12.13 Global search engine market share (2023 without China)

YouTube, the world's largest video-sharing platform, further diversifying its offerings. Other notable products include Google **Drive**, Google **Photos**, and Google **Chrome**.

Google's **business model primarily revolves around advertising**. Its search engine, Gmail, YouTube, and other services are offered to users for free, with revenue generated through targeted advertising. Google**'s sophisticated algorithms analyze user data to deliver personalized ads, making its advertising platform highly effective and lucrative.**

In addition to advertising, Google has ventured into hardware with products like Pixel smartphones, Chromecast, and Nest smart home devices. It also offers enterprise solutions through Google Cloud Platform, **providing cloud computing services,** infrastructure, and productivity tools to businesses. Google's success is attributed to its relentless focus on innovation, user-centric approach, and ability to leverage data effectively. Its mission to organize the world's information and make it universally accessible and useful has guided its product development and expansion strategies.

Context

Your Advanced Question for Starting Prompt Engineering

Describe the situation or environment surrounding the industry. This might include other (big) industry players, company culture, or historical context depending on the subject. How do suppliers or customers react? Limit your response to 100 words.

In the tech industry, Google faces competition from major players like Amazon, Apple, and Microsoft, particularly in areas such as cloud computing, hardware, and artificial intelligence. Its company culture emphasizes innovation, collaboration, and a focus on user experience. Despite criticism over data privacy and antitrust concerns, many **suppliers and customers view Google as an essential partner** due to its vast ecosystem of products and services. Customers appreciate its user-friendly interfaces and robust features, while suppliers value its market influence and potential for collaboration and growth.

Challenges and Opportunities

Basic Prompt

How did Google change or disrupt the industry? How does competitors or the government or customers react? Limit your response to 100 words.

Google changed the industry by **revolutionizing Internet search with its PageRank** algorithm, offering more relevant results. Acquisitions like YouTube and Android expanded its reach. Competitors respond with innovations to challenge Google's dominance.

Discussion and Lessons Learned

Your Advanced Question for Starting Prompt Engineering

Explain the actions taken to address the challenge or capitalize on the opportunity. This could involve strategies implemented, decisions made, or interventions undertaken. What happened recently? Limit your response to 100 words.

Google has **diversified its revenue streams beyond advertising by expanding into hardware** with products like Pixel phones and Nest devices. It emphasizes privacy features and transparency to address concerns. Recent actions include **investing in renewable energy projects** and committing to carbon neutrality to address environmental challenges. In response to regulatory scrutiny, Google has implemented changes to its search and advertising practices. Additionally, it continues to **invest in artificial intelligence and cloud computing** to stay competitive and capitalize on emerging opportunities in these fields.

12.5.2 Bing

Bing	Bing is the search engine of Microsoft
Founder(s)	Bill Gates and Paul Allen
Revenue 2023	245 billion USD (Microsoft)
Employees	221k employees (Microsoft)
Year of foundation	1975 (Bing 2009)
Business idea or how the company earn money	Bing earns **revenue primarily through advertising** on its search engine platform, including **pay-per-click ads, sponsored content, and partnerships**. Additionally, it may generate income from data analytics services and search syndication agreements

Figure 12.14 illustrates the interaction between Bing, OpenAI, and the Prometheus model, highlighting a process where inputs are tested, analyzed, and improved. Bing leverages OpenAI to analyze test data, which feeds back into the Prometheus model for iterative improvements, creating a feedback loop to enhance performance.

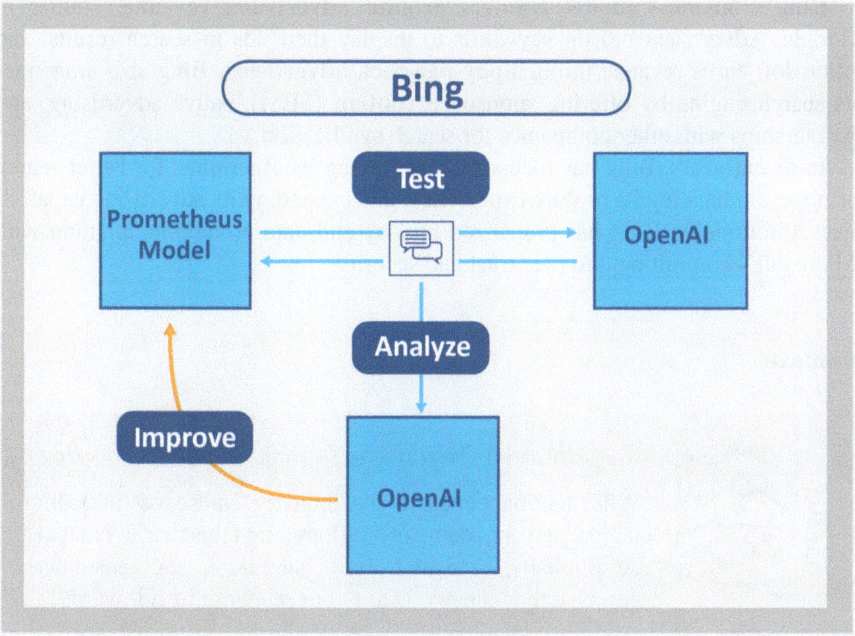

Fig. 12.14 Integration of Bing Copilot. (Powered by OpenAI)

About Bing

Basic Prompt

Describe the history, products, and business model of the company in 200 words.

Bing, launched by Microsoft in 2009, aimed to provide **a competitive alternative to other search engines, particularly Google.** Initially conceived as a replacement for Microsoft's Live Search, Bing quickly gained attention for its visually appealing homepage, daily background images, and intuitive user interface. It introduced features like instant answers, image search with hover preview, and integrated social media results, enhancing the search experience.

Bing's product portfolio expanded beyond Web search to include services like Bing **Maps**, Bing **Ads** (formerly Microsoft Advertising), and Bing **Places** for Business, catering to both consumers and advertisers.

Bing's business model revolves around advertising revenue, similar to Google. Advertisers bid on keywords to display their ads in search results, and Microsoft earns revenue through **pay-per-click advertising**. Bing also monetizes its search engine by offering **sponsored content** (SEM), native advertising, and partnerships with other companies for search syndication.

In recent years, Bing has focused on improving its algorithms for better search accuracy, enhancing its **mobile experience**, and expanding its advertising capabilities. Additionally, Bing has prioritized privacy and data protection, aligning with Microsoft's commitment to user trust and security.

Context

Your Advanced Question for Starting Prompt Engineering

What has happened to the industry landscape, including major players, company culture, and historical context? Additionally, consider how suppliers and customers perceive the industry. Limit your response to 100 words.

In the search engine industry, Bing competes with major players like Google, which dominates the market. **Bing's company culture emphasizes innovation, user experience, and data privacy.** Suppliers and customers view Bing as a viable alternative to Google, particularly in regions where Microsoft has a strong presence.

Challenges and Opportunities

Basic Prompt

How did the company change or disrupt the industry? How do competitors or the government or customers react? Limit your response to 100 words.

Competitors responded with their own enhancements, while governments scrutinized Bing's market practices less intensely than Google's. Customers welcomed Bing's diverse features but often defaulted to Google due to habit or brand loyalty. **While Bing hasn't achieved the market dominance of Google, it remains a significant player**, providing users with an alternative search experience and contributing to healthy competition in the industry.

Discussion and Lessons Learned

Your Advanced Question for Starting Prompt Engineering

Explain the actions taken to address the challenge or capitalize on the opportunity. This could involve strategies implemented, decisions made, or interventions undertaken. What happened recently? Limit your response to 100 words.

To address competition, Bing has focused on partnerships and innovation. It powers search for Microsoft products like Windows and Office, securing a user base. **Investments in artificial intelligence (MS-Copilot) enhance search relevance** and user experience. Bing also explores **niche markets like voice search and augmented reality.** Recently, it integrated with Microsoft's Edge browser, improving accessibility. Additionally, Bing launched new features such as visual search and intelligent answers, aiming to differentiate itself. These actions underscore Bing's commitment to innovation and user satisfaction, helping it maintain relevance in the competitive search engine landscape.

12.5.3 MetaGer

MetaGer	
Founder(s)	Wolfgang Sander-Beuermann
Revenue 2023	German-based metasearch engine operated by the non-profit organization (SUMA-EV)
Employees	Small team (compare SUMA-EV)
Year of foundation	1996
Business idea or how the company earn money	MetaGer generates **revenue primarily through donations**, grants, and partnerships. It ensures user privacy by not tracking or storing personal data, appealing to privacy-conscious users and organizations

MetaGer (Fig. 12.15) is a privacy-focused search engine that **aggregates results from multiple sources** while **ensuring anonymity by not tracking users** or storing search data. Its primary purpose is to provide secure, unbiased search results without personalized advertising or data collection.

About MetaGers

Basic Prompt

Describe the history, products, and business model of the company with 200 words.

MetaGer, founded in 1996 by Wolfgang Sander-Beuermann, stands as **a pioneer in the realm of privacy-focused metasearch engines**. Its journey began with a mission to **provide users with a search alternative that respects their privacy and doesn't track their online activities.**

MetaGer's primary product is its metasearch engine, which **aggregates results from various search engines while prioritizing user privacy.** This unique approach resonates with individuals who value data protection and seek alternatives to mainstream search engines that often collect and monetize user data. The business model of MetaGer revolves around several key pillars. Firstly, it relies on **donations** from users who appreciate its commitment to privacy and want to support its operations. These donations help cover the costs of maintaining the platform and furthering its development. Secondly, MetaGer may receive **grants from organizations** that share its vision of promoting privacy and free access to knowledge. These grants enable the organization to expand its reach, improve its technology, and explore new avenues for innovation.

Fig. 12.15 MetaGer

Context

Your Advanced Question for Starting Prompt Engineering

Describe the situation or environment surrounding the industry. This might include other (big) industry players, company culture, or historical context depending on the subject, how do suppliers or customers think about that? 100 words.

In the realm of online search, MetaGer operates within a competitive landscape dominated by industry giants like Google, Bing, and Yahoo. Suppliers and customers view MetaGer **favorably for its commitment to transparency and ethical practices,** fostering a culture of trust and integrity.

Challenges and Opportunities

Basic Prompt

How did MetaGer change or disrupt the industry? How does competitors or the government or customers react? 100 words.

MetaGer is **prioritizing user privacy,** challenging the dominance of search engines that heavily track and monetize user data. Competitors initially dismissed MetaGer, but its focus on privacy gained attention as users increasingly sought alternatives. Government regulators, recognizing the importance of data privacy, have supported MetaGer's mission. Customers, particularly those concerned about online privacy, have embraced MetaGer's platform, driving its growth and establishing it as a notable player in the search engine market. Overall, MetaGer's disruptive approach has shifted industry norms toward greater transparency and respect for user privacy.

Discussion and Lessons Learned

Your Advanced Question for Starting Prompt Engineering

Explain the actions taken to address the challenge or capitalize on the opportunity. This could involve strategies implemented, decisions made, or interventions undertaken. What happened recently? 100 words

To address the challenge of competition and capitalize on the opportunity presented by growing privacy concerns, MetaGer has focused on several key strategies. They've continuously improved their **search algorithms to deliver relevant results** while **maintaining user anonymity.** Additionally, they've emphasized transparency in their operations and engaged in outreach efforts to educate users about online privacy.

12.5.4 Review: Problems and Challenges of the Search Engine Market

General problems in the search engine market include data privacy concerns, monopolistic practices, algorithmic bias, misinformation proliferation, limited competition, ad-driven revenue models, and user data exploitation. Common findings in the search engine market include:

- Dominance of Google: Google maintains a significant market share, overshadowing competitors like Bing, MetaGer, and Startpage.
- Algorithmic Complexity: Search engines use intricate algorithms to index and rank Web content, influencing search results and user experience.
- Advertising Revenue: Primary income for search engines is generated through advertising, with Google's AdWords program being particularly lucrative.
- Competition: Despite Google's dominance, competition exists in specialized search engines, vertical search, and emerging technologies like voice search and AI-driven assistants.
- User Privacy Concerns: There's a growing awareness and concern regarding user privacy, leading to the popularity of privacy-focused search engines like Startpage and MetaGer.
- Technological Advancements: Search engines continually evolve, integrating new technologies such as AI, machine learning, and natural language processing to improve search accuracy and relevance.

The main problem, besides search quality, for search engine companies is **balancing monetization with user trust and privacy.**

Side Bar:How Does PageRank Works

PageRank, Google's algorithm, quantifies the importance of web pages based on links, assessing both the quantity and authority of incoming links. Websites with numerous incoming links from authoritative sources (qualitative) gain higher rankings, reflecting credibility and relevance. To prevent cyclic link structures, Google employs random page access. Key to PageRank is semantic analysis, considering keywords, content relevance, and user intent. It prioritizes pages with optimal performance and mobile-friendliness, enhancing user experience. Easy navigation and internal linking contribute to PageRank by facilitating access to valuable content. Thus, PageRank shapes search results by evaluating link quantity, authority, semantics, performance, and user experience.

Further Readings

Alphabet (2024) https://abc.xyz/investor/
Microsoft (2024) https://www.microsoft.com/en-us/investor/default

Questions

1. Use OpenAI/ChatGPT and investigate the dominance of the PageRank Algorithm and assess whether Microsoft's CoPilot (generative AI) presents a transformative alternative.
2. In the past, it was expected that Social Search would break the dominance of Google, but this has not happened. Does this mean social search is no longer interesting, or how could it further develop, perhaps with the help of AI bots? Start a prompt discussion.

12.6 Social Networks

Meta/Facebook, Microsoft/LinkedINn, X/Twitter

Basic Prompt

Describe the primary functions and purposes of social networks in modern society

Social networks are **digital platforms designed to connect individuals,** enabling communication, sharing of information, and building communities. They **facilitate interactions between friends, family, colleagues, and strangers**, allowing users to share updates, photos, videos, and thoughts in real time. Social networks serve various purposes, from maintaining personal relationships and networking professionally to staying informed about current events and engaging in discussions on diverse topics. Overall, they play a vital role in modern society by **bridging distances, fostering connections, and facilitating the exchange of ideas**.

12.6.1 Meta/Facebook

Meta/Facebook	
Founder(s)	Mark Zuckerberg, Eduardo Saverin, Dustin Moskovitz, and Chris Hughes
Revenue 2023	134 billion USD
Employees	67k employees
Year of foundation	2004 (Facebook has been a brand under the Meta name until 2021)
Business idea or how the company earn money	Facebook **earns money primarily through advertising revenue**. Businesses pay to display ads on the platform, targeting users based on their demographics, interests, and behavior. Additionally, **Facebook offers businesses advertising tools,** sponsored content, and paid promotional features to reach a wider audience and increase engagement

Figure 12.16 illustrates the small-world phenomenon, based on Stanley Milgram's "six degrees of separation" experiment, demonstrating that individuals in large global networks are connected through an average of six intermediaries. Figure 12.16 features the connections in a small world.

About Meta/Facebook

Basic Prompt

Describe the history, products, and business model of the company in 200 words.

Facebook, founded by Mark Zuckerberg along with his college roommates Eduardo Saverin, Andrew McCollum, Dustin Moskovitz, and Chris Hughes in 2004, **began as a social networking platform exclusively for Harvard University students**. It quickly expanded to other universities, then to the general public, **becoming the world's largest social media platform.** Initially,

Facebook's primary product was its **social networking website, allowing users to create profiles, connect with friends, and share updates, photos, and videos.** Over time, Facebook has diversified its product offerings through acquisitions, **including Instagram, WhatsApp**, and Oculus VR. Facebook's business model centers around **advertising revenue**, where businesses pay to display ads targeted to users based on demographics, interests, and behaviors. It also **generates revenue from payments, such as fees for virtual goods in games, and from its hardware products** like Oculus VR headsets. Despite its success, Facebook has faced challenges related to privacy concerns, misinformation, and regulatory scrutiny. In response, the company has implemented measures to improve user privacy controls, combat misinformation, and comply with regulations. Additionally, Facebook has expanded its focus on E-Commerce and digital payments to diversify its revenue streams and mitigate risks associated with overreliance on advertising.

Context

Your Advanced Question for Starting Prompt Engineering

How has the industry ecosystem surrounding social media changed? Consider factors such as major competitors, the prevailing company culture, and relevant historical context. Additionally, explore the perspectives of suppliers and customers on the industry and its key players. Limit your response to 100 words.

The social media industry operates within a dynamic landscape shaped by technological advancements, **regulatory pressures, and evolving user preferences.** Besides major players like Facebook, Google, and Twitter, emerging platforms continually challenge market dominance. Company cultures often prioritize innovation, user engagement, and monetization strategies, sometimes at the expense of user privacy concerns. Suppliers typically view Facebook as a **lucrative advertising platform,** while customers value its connectivity and content-sharing capabilities. However, increasing scrutiny over data practices has led to growing skepticism among both users and regulators, prompting Facebook to navigate a delicate **balance between profitability and public trust.**

Fig. 12.16 The small-world phenomenon

Challenges and Opportunities

Basic Prompt

Describe the history, products, and business model of the company in 200 words.

Facebook pioneers online social networking, **reshaping communication,** and **advertising.** Competitors adapted by mimicking features or innovating new platforms. Governments reacted with heightened regulatory scrutiny, especially regarding **privacy and antitrust issues**. Customers initially embraced Facebook's connectivity but grew wary amid privacy scandals. Overall, Facebook transformed how people interact online, sparking a shift in communication and advertising paradigms.

Discussion and Lessons Learned

Your Advanced Question for Starting Prompt Engineering

Explain the actions taken to address the challenge or capitalize on the opportunity. This could involve strategies implemented, decisions made, or interventions undertaken. What happened recently? Limit your response to 100 words.

To address **privacy concerns** and capitalize on opportunities, Facebook implemented various strategies. They enhanced **user privacy controls, introduced transparency measures, and invested in AI for content moderation.** Additionally, they diversified revenue streams beyond advertising, **focusing on E-Commerce and digital payments.** Recently, Facebook rebranded as Meta, emphasizing its focus on the metaverse, a virtual reality space. This move signals a strategic pivot toward immersive experiences and decentralized technologies. However, challenges persist, with ongoing regulatory scrutiny and user skepticism necessitating continued efforts to balance innovation with accountability and trust.

12.6.2 Microsoft/LinkedIn

Microsoft/LinkedIn	LinkedIn is part of Microsoft Corporation
Founder(s)	Reid Hoffman, Allen Blue, Konstantin Guericke, Eric Ly, and Jean-Luc Vaillant
Revenue 2023	245 billion USD (Microsoft)
Employees	221k employees (Microsoft)
Year of foundation	2002 (acquired by Microsoft in 2016)
Business idea or how the company earn money	LinkedIn earns money primarily through its **premium subscription services, advertising solutions, and talent solutions** for recruiters and companies. Premium subscriptions offer enhanced features for professionals while advertising solutions enable businesses to target users with sponsored content. Talent solutions provide recruitment tools for employers to find and hire qualified candidates

The Fig. 12.17 displays global membership distribution by region, with the United States having the highest number at 202+ million members, followed by India with 105+ million members. It highlights significant memberships across regions such as Europe, Asia, and South America, showcasing wide geographical coverage with notable numbers in countries like Brazil (65M+), Indonesia (23M+), and the United Kingdom (35M+).

About Microsoft/LinkedIn

Basic Prompt

Describe the history, products, and business model of the company in 300 words.

LinkedIn, founded in 2002 and launched in 2003 by Reid Hoffman and others, has evolved **from a professional networking platform into a comprehensive ecosystem for professionals worldwide**. Initially focused on connecting individuals for **networking and job-seeking** purposes, LinkedIn has expanded its offerings to include a range of products and services.

LinkedIn is a **leading professional networking platform** with over 990 million members worldwide. It enables users to **connect with colleagues, discover job opportunities, and share industry insights.** LinkedIn also offers tools for skills assessment, professional development, and business networking. Its robust analytics help businesses target potential hires and customers. **Owned by** Microsoft since 2016 for approximately $26.2 billion, the reason was to combine LinkedIn with Office 365 and enhance the professional network by gaining more data insights. New AI features and functionalities, especially for premium accounts, have been introduced. It also supports (Helpguide) people in overcoming workplace challenges.

There was a scandal about Expose data 2021 (misuse of data. LinkedIn, using the data in a non-consent way. LinkedIn's flagship product is its networking platform, where users create professional profiles, connect with colleagues and peers, and engage in professional discussions. Over time, LinkedIn has introduced **features like news feed updates**, groups, and messaging to enhance user engagement. LinkedIn's business model revolves around monetizing its vast user base through various channels. Its **premium subscription service offers additional features such as advanced search filters, InMail messaging,** and insights into profile views. Advertising solutions allow businesses to target LinkedIn users with sponsored content, display ads, and sponsored InMail messages. Additionally, LinkedIn's talent solutions provide tools for recruiters and employers to find, attract, and hire talent through job postings, recruitment advertising, and applicant tracking systems. Through acquisitions like Lynda.com (now LinkedIn Learning) and partnerships with companies like Microsoft, LinkedIn has diversified its offerings to include professional training and development resources, further solidifying its position as the go-to platform for professionals seeking networking, career advancement, and skill enhancement opportunities.

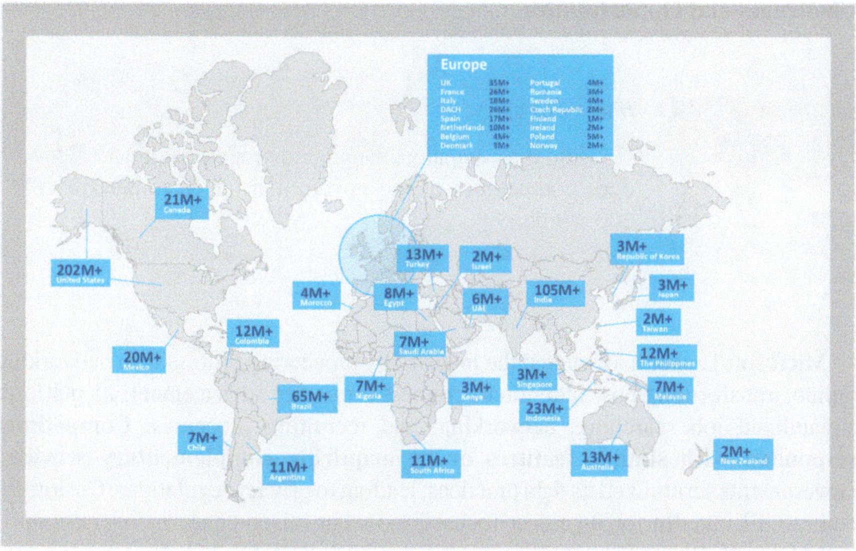

Fig. 12.17 LinkedIn—more than 990 million users in over 200 countries (2024)

Context

Your Advanced Question For starting Prompt Engineering

Describe the situation or environment surrounding the industry. This might include other (big) industry players, company culture, or historical context depending on the subject, how do suppliers or customers think or react? What happened recently? Limit your response to 100 words.

LinkedIn operates within a competitive landscape alongside other major players in the social networking and professional services sectors, including Facebook, Twitter, and Microsoft (which acquired LinkedIn in 2016). Its company culture emphasizes **professional networking, career development,** and fostering meaningful connections. Customers perceive LinkedIn as a valuable **platform for networking, job seeking, and skill development, while suppliers may view it as a lucrative advertising channel or recruitment platform.** Historical context includes LinkedIn's evolution from a networking site to a comprehensive professional ecosystem, reflecting changing trends in digital communication and career management.

Challenges and Opportunities

Basic Prompt

How did the company change or disrupt the industry? How does competitors or the government or customers react? 100 words

Microsoft/LinkedIn disrupted the industry by pioneering professional networking online, transforming how individuals connect for career advancement. Its platform streamlined job searching, networking, and recruiting processes. **Competitors responded with similar features or by acquiring complementary services.** Governments scrutinized its data practices, leading to privacy regulations. Customers embraced LinkedIn for its career-focused tools but raised concerns over data privacy. Overall, **LinkedIn catalyzed a shift toward digital networking and career management,** prompting both innovation and regulation within the industry.

Discussion and Lessons Learned

Your Advanced Question for Starting Prompt Engineering

Explain the actions taken to address the challenge or capitalize on the opportunity. This could involve strategies implemented, decisions made, or interventions undertaken. What happened recently? Limit your response to 100 words.

To address privacy concerns and capitalize on opportunities, LinkedIn has implemented robust data protection measures, enhanced user privacy controls, and increased transparency regarding data usage. They've also focused on diversifying revenue streams beyond advertising by investing in premium subscription services and expanding their talent solutions offerings. Recently, LinkedIn has introduced new features such as LinkedIn Stories and improved analytics tools for businesses. Additionally, they continue to refine their algorithms to provide more relevant content and job recommendations to users. These efforts aim to enhance user experience, drive engagement, and maintain LinkedIn's position as a leading professional networking platform.

12.6.3 X/Twitter

X/Twitter	
Founder(s)	Jack Dorsey, Noah Glass, Biz Stone, and Evan Williams
Revenue 2023	3 billion USD (estimated ;delisted from stock exchange)
Employees	3k employees (estimated, privately owned by Elon Musk)
Year of foundation	2006
Business Idea or how the company earn money	X (former Twitter) **earns money primarily through advertising**, where businesses pay to promote tweets, accounts, or trends. Additionally, it generates **revenue from data licensing services for analytics and research purposes.** Recently, Twitter has explored subscription-based features like Twitter Blue to diversify its revenue streams

Figure 12.18 indicates that X is losing market share in the advertising market. The chart illustrates a consistent upward trend in the values from 2011 to 2021, peaking at 4,505.69 units in 2021. However, there is a slight decline in 2022, dropping to 4,000 units, indicating a modest reduction following a period of growth.

About X/Twitter

Basic Prompt

Describe the history, products, and business model of the company in 300 words.

Twitter, founded in March 2006 by Jack Dorsey, Noah Glass, Biz Stone, and Evan Williams, emerged as a **microblogging platform allowing users to share short, real-time updates called tweets (broadcasting).** It quickly gained popularity for its simplicity and immediacy. Twitter's core product revolves around its platform, where users can post tweets, follow accounts, and engage in public conversations. Over the years, Twitter **introduced features like hashtags, retweets, and multimedia content**, expanding its utility and appeal. The company's business model centers on advertising, with promoted tweets, accounts, and trends serving as primary revenue streams. Advertisers leverage Twitter's vast user base and targeting capabilities to reach specific audiences. Twitter also earns revenue through data licensing agreements, providing access to its real-time and historical data for analytics and research purposes. Despite its success, Twitter has faced challenges such as user growth stagnation and profitability concerns. To address this, the company has explored various initiatives, including product enhancements, acquisitions (e.g., Periscope), and diversification into live streaming and subscription-based services like Twitter Blue, aiming to sustain growth and profitability in the competitive social media landscape.

In 2022, Elon Musk acquired Twitter and rebranded it to X, aiming to **create a superapp** by integrating streaming services, payments, and shopping features. With 245 million daily active users globally in 2023, **X focuses on posting and sharing real-time information, retweeting, liking, direct messaging, and hosting live audio chat rooms** (Twitter Spaces). Previously available only for verified business accounts, analytics features now require subscriptions. Verification has shifted from stringent criteria to a paid model. This change, alongside more lenient content moderation, has led to an increase in hate speech. Unlike Twitter, X remains inaccessible in China.

Context

Your Advanced Question for Starting Prompt Engineering

Describe the industry environment, including major players, company culture, and historical context. How do suppliers and customers perceive the industry? Limit your response to 100 words.

Twitter operates within a dynamic social media landscape alongside major players like Facebook, Instagram, and LinkedIn. Its company culture emphasizes open communication, real-time updates, and fostering public discourse. Customers perceive Twitter as a **valuable platform for news, information, and public engagement,** while advertisers leverage its reach and targeting capabilities for marketing purposes. Suppliers may view X/Twitter as an essential advertising channel, providing opportunities to reach a diverse user base. Historical context includes Twitter's role in shaping online communication and facilitating movements like Arab Spring and Black Lives Matter, highlighting its societal impact and relevance.

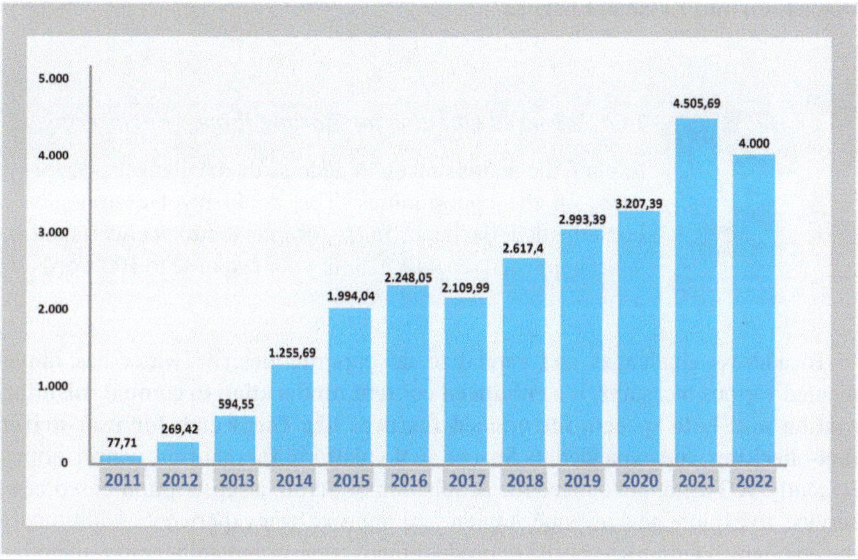

Fig. 12.18 X is losing revenue in the advertising market (in billion dollars)

Challenges and Opportunities

Basis Prompt

How did the company change or disrupt the industry? How do competitors or the government or customers react? 100 words

X/Twitter disrupted the industry by popularizing microblogging, enabling real-time public conversation and **breaking news dissemination.** Competitors responded with similar features, acquisitions, or platform enhancements. Governments scrutinized X/Twitter for its role in disseminating misinformation and regulating user content. **Customers embraced X/Twitter for its immediacy and engagement but raised concerns over harassment and moderation policies.** Overall, X/Twitter's impact revolutionized online communication, reshaping how individuals and organizations interact, consume news, and engage with content while also prompting discussions on digital ethics and governance.

Discussion and Lessons Learned

Your Advanced Question for Starting Prompt Engineering

Explain the actions taken to address the challenges or capitalize on the opportunities. This could involve strategies implemented, decisions made, or interventions undertaken. What happened recently? Limit your response to 100 words.

To address challenges and capitalize on opportunities, X/Twitter has implemented various measures. It's **enhanced content moderation to combat misinformation and hate speech, introduced features like Birdwatch for user-driven fact-checking**, and expanded its Spaces audio platform for real-time conversations. Recently, X/Twitter announced the acquisition of Scroll, a subscription-based news service, to explore new revenue streams and improve user experience. Additionally, the company continues to invest in product innovation, community engagement initiatives, and partnerships to foster a healthier and more inclusive platform while navigating regulatory scrutiny and evolving user expectations.

12.6.4 Review: Problems and Challenges of Social Networks

Common findings and challenges in social networks include **privacy concerns, misinformation, content moderation issues, algorithmic bias, mental health impacts, and regulatory challenges.** Users demand greater privacy protection and transparency. Misinformation dissemination remains a significant issue, affecting public opinion and elections. **Content moderation struggles to balance free speech with harmful content removal.** Algorithmic biases perpetuate discrimination. **Excessive social media use correlates with mental health issues.** Regulatory scrutiny increases, focusing on antitrust, data privacy, and content moderation. Addressing these challenges requires collaboration among social media companies, governments, and users to prioritize safety, privacy, and well-being while navigating regulatory complexities.

The social media industry encompasses platforms like Facebook, Twitter, Instagram, LinkedIn, and TikTok. These players compete by offering unique features, user experiences, and **advertising solutions to attract and retain users.**

They primarily earn **money through advertising, sponsored content, and premium features**. However, a significant challenge across the industry is managing user privacy concerns and data protection, especially in the wake of increased scrutiny and regulations such as General Data Protection Regulation (GDPR) and California Consumer Privacy Act (CCPA). **Balancing monetization strategies with user trust and satisfaction** remains a critical challenge for social media companies.

The **trend toward building superapps like WeChat (China)** aims to create lock-in effects by offering a wide range of services within one platform. Due to the "Great Firewall," platforms like Facebook (banned in China since 2009), LinkedIn, and X (formerly Twitter) are inaccessible in several countries, including China, North Korea, and Iran, due to government restrictions. Users often rely on Virtual Private Networks (VPNs) to bypass these blocks. In China, Weibo serves a similar function to X. These countries often have region-specific social networks catering to various demographics and interests, such as Russian government platforms or those targeting specific age groups.

Further Readings

Meta (2024) https://abc.xyz/investor/
Microsoft (2024) https://www.microsoft.com/en-us/investor/default
X/Twitter (2024) https://fortune.com/2024/08/22/elon-musk-x-twitter-owner-list/

Questions

1. Why did Microsoft acquire LinkedIn (2016), and what was the strategic move behind it?
2. Examine the ethical and political complexities of free speech and censorship. How can content moderation effectively reconcile these competing interests?
3. Users are increasingly concerned about data privacy, especially after scandals like Cambridge Analytica, which highlight how platforms collect and use their data. Please find arguments and discuss.

12.7 Generative AI (OpenAI/ChatGPT and Google/Gemini)

OpenAI/ChatGPT and Google/Gemini

OpenAI chatGPT

Gemini

Basic Prompt

Describe generative AI companies in 80 words.

Generative AI companies **utilize machine learning to produce diverse, original content across multiple domains**. By leveraging algorithms and neural networks, they **create art, video, music, text,** and beyond, often blurring the line between human and machine creations. These firms drive innovation in entertainment, marketing, and design, offering customizable solutions for creative expression and problem-solving. As pioneers in artificial creativity, they **shape the future of content production**, ushering in new forms of expression and redefining the boundaries of imagination and possibility.

12.7.1 OpenAI/ChatGPT

OpenAI	
Founder(s)	Elon Musk, Sam Altman, Greg Brockman, Ilya Sutskever, Wojciech Zaremba, John Schulman
Revenue 2023	4 billion USD
Employees	800 employees
Year of foundation	2015 (Microsoft is a dominant investor)
Business idea or how the company earn money 50 words max	OpenAI/ChatGPT could offer **premium subscription tiers** with advanced features like **personalized responses, extended conversation limits, or ad-free usage**. Additionally, it could monetize through partnerships with businesses for AI-powered customer support or data analysis services. Another avenue is licensing its technology for integration into various applications, generating revenue through royalties

Figure 12.19 indicates in a very simplified way how OpenAI/ChatGPT generates automated content. The chart outlines a three-step process for training a model using reinforcement learning techniques. Step 1 involves collecting demonstration data and training a supervised policy through human-labeled examples, which helps fine-tune the initial model. In Step 2, comparison data is gathered, and a reward model is trained by ranking outputs, followed by Step 3, where the policy is optimized using the proximal policy optimization (PPO) algorithm, refining the model based on the reward signals from the reward model.

About OpenAI/ChatGPT

Basic Prompt

Describe the history, products, and business model of OpenAI/ChatGPT in 200 words.

OpenAI, founded in 2015, emerged as a **pioneer in artificial intelligence** research and development. **Initially established as a nonprofit organization**, it later transitioned into a for-profit entity with a mission to ensure that **artificial general intelligence (AGI) benefits all of humanity.** One of its notable products is OpenAI/ChatGPT, an AI-driven conversational agent that utilizes natural language processing (NLP) to generate human-like text responses.

OpenAI/ChatGPT's evolution traces back to OpenAI's research in **deep learning and language modeling.** It builds upon advancements in neural network architectures, particularly transformer models, to understand and generate coherent text across various topics and contexts. With multiple iterations and improvements, OpenAI/ChatGPT has become increasingly proficient at mimicking human-like conversations, answering questions, providing recommendations, and even generating creative content like stories or poems.

OpenAI's business model revolves around leveraging its AI technologies to offer innovative solutions to individuals and businesses. While specific details may vary, potential revenue streams for OpenAI/ChatGPT and similar products could **include subscription services, licensing agreements, and enterprise solutions.** For instance, OpenAI might offer premium subscription tiers with advanced features for individual users while also providing enterprise-level solutions for businesses seeking AI-powered customer support or content generation services.

Moreover, OpenAI might explore partnerships with companies across various industries to **integrate** OpenAI/**ChatGPT into their platforms, enhancing user experiences and driving revenue through licensing fees or royalties**. Additionally, OpenAI could offer consulting services or custom solutions tailored to specific business needs, leveraging its expertise in AI research and development.

Context

Your Advanced Question for Starting Prompt Engineering

Describe the environment of the generative AI industry, including major players, company culture, and historical context. How do suppliers and customers perceive this industry? Limit your response to 100 words.

The generative AI industry is characterized by intense competition and rapid innovation, with **major players like OpenAI, Google, and Microsoft leading** the charge. Company cultures prioritize collaboration, creativity, and ethical AI development. Historical context includes breakthroughs in deep learning and neural networks, driving advancements in generative models. **Suppliers focus on providing high-quality data and computing resources, while customers anticipate cutting-edge solutions for content creation, personalization, and automation**. There's a

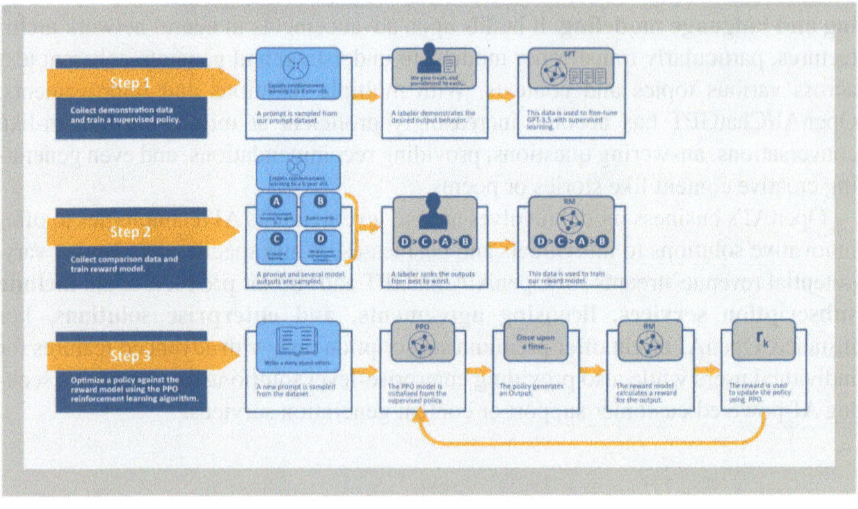

Fig. 12.19 OpenAI/ChatGPT—how to generate automated content

growing awareness of the societal implications of AI, prompting both suppliers and customers to prioritize responsible and ethical AI practices in their engagements.

Challenges and Opportunities

Basic Prompt

How did OpenAI/ChatGPT change or disrupt the industry? How do competitors or the government or customers react? Limit your response to 100 words.

OpenAI disrupted the industry by **democratizing access to advanced natural language processing (NLP) capabilities.** Its ChatGPT product transformed how individuals and businesses engage with AI-driven conversational agents, setting **new standards for human-like text generation.** Competitors may respond by investing in their own NLP technologies or forming partnerships to remain competitive. Governments may enact regulations to ensure responsible AI deployment and mitigate potential risks. Customers, intrigued by Chat OpenAI's innovation, may demand more personalized, efficient, and context-aware AI interactions across various sectors, influencing the evolution of customer service, content creation, and digital experiences.

Discussion and Lessons Learned

Your Advanced Question for Starting Prompt Engineering

Explain the actions taken to address the challenge or capitalize on the opportunity. This could involve strategies implemented, decisions made, or interventions undertaken. What happened recently? Limit your response to 100 words

To address challenges and capitalize on opportunities in generative AI, companies have intensified research efforts, focusing on refining algorithms, improving model capabilities, and enhancing ethical frameworks. Recent actions include investing in AI safety research, promoting transparency in AI development, and collaborating with industry partners to establish standards and best practices. Additionally, there's a growing emphasis on educating the public about AI's capabilities and limitations. Recently, companies have also expanded their product offerings, introducing new applications of generative models in areas like healthcare, finance, and entertainment, further cementing generative AI's role in shaping the future of technology and society.

OpenAI/ChatGPT has faced criticism for bias, data privacy violations, and generating inappropriate content, highlighting challenges in ensuring ethical and reliable AI outputs.

12.7.2 Google/Gemini

Google	Gemini is a Google/Alphabet initiative
Founder(s)	Google
Revenue 2023	307 billion USD (Alphabet)
Employees	183k employees (Alphabet)
Year of foundation	2021
Business idea or how the company earn money	Google Gemini **monetize through various revenues such as licensing its advanced AI model to businesses for data analysis,** natural language processing applications, and personalized user experiences. Additionally, it could offer **premium subscription** services with enhanced features or partner with companies for AI-powered customer support solutions, generating revenue through service contracts and royalties

Figure 12.20 indicates how the quality of content generated by LLMs varies. The chart compares different language models, with GPT-4.0 leading at a score of 100, followed by GPT-4 Turbo and Claude 3 Opus at 94. Other models like Llama 3 (70B) and Mistral 8x22B rank at 88, while models like GPT-3.5 Turbo and Mistral 8x7B have lower scores at 65, showing a wide range of performance levels across various models.

About Google/Gemini

Basic Prompt

Describe the history, products, and business model of Google/Gemini in 300 words.

Google/Gemini emerged as a **groundbreaking project within Google**, aiming to advance the capabilities of artificial intelligence (AI) models for natural language understanding and generation. It represents a significant evolution beyond previous models like GPT-3, with enhanced features and capabilities (note: see Alphabet, also Waymo and Google metaverse, Chap. 10).

The project likely began in response to the growing demand for more sophisticated AI models capable of understanding and generating natural language at a deeper level. Drawing on Google's vast resources in AI research and development, Gemini likely originated from a team of experts dedicated to pushing the boundaries of AI technology.

Google Gemini's **primary product is its advanced AI model,** which excels in natural language understanding and generation. It can comprehend complex language patterns, context, and nuances, enabling it to generate more accurate and contextually relevant responses. **This model can be integrated into various applications and services, including chatbots, virtual assistants, content creation tools,** and more.

Additionally, Google Gemini might offer developer tools and APIs that allow businesses and developers to **leverage its AI capabilities within their own products and services.** These tools could include APIs for text analysis, language translation, sentiment analysis, and other natural language processing tasks. Google Gemini likely adopts a multifaceted business model to monetize its products and services:

- **Licensing and Partnerships:** Google Gemini may license its advanced AI model to businesses, allowing them to integrate it into their applications and services. This licensing model could involve one-time fees or recurring royalties based on usage.
- **Subscription Services:** Google Gemini might offer premium subscription tiers with access to advanced features and capabilities. Businesses and developers could subscribe to these services to access enhanced AI models, developer tools, and support.
- **Enterprise Solutions:** Google Gemini could provide customized AI solutions and services to enterprise clients, including AI-powered customer support, data analysis, and personalized user experiences. These solutions would be tailored to meet the specific needs of each client and could be offered as part of long-term service contracts.

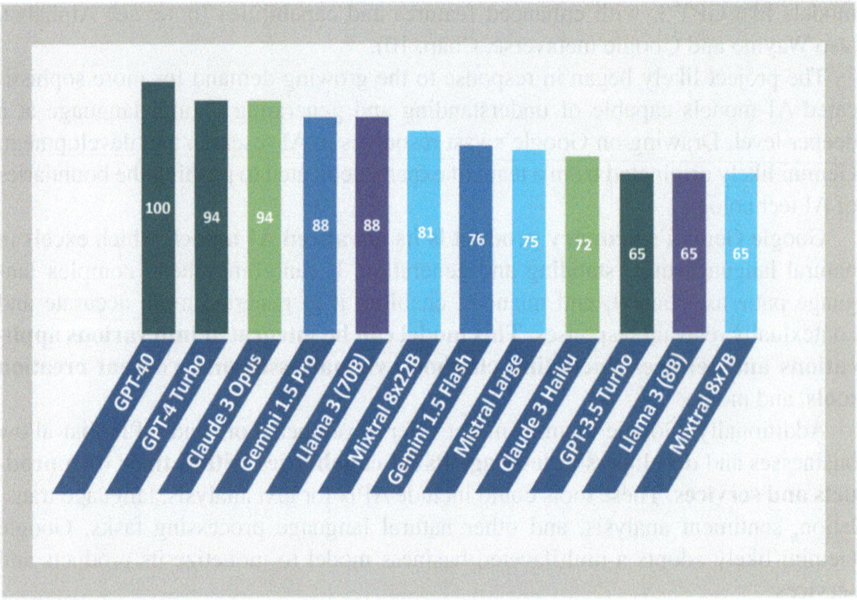

Fig. 12.20 Quality of content generated by LLMs varies

Context

Your Advanced Question for Starting Prompt Engineering

Describe the situation or environment surrounding the industry. This might include other (big) industry players, company culture, or historical context depending on the subject. How do suppliers or customers react? Limit your response to 100 words.

In the field of AI and natural language processing, Google Gemini operates within a competitive landscape alongside **major industry players such as OpenAI,** Microsoft**, and IBM (Watson).** Customers view Google's expertise and resources favorably, expecting innovative solutions and reliable support. Suppliers are eager to collaborate, recognizing the potential for mutual growth and technological advancement. Google's culture of innovation and collaboration fosters a dynamic environment where employees are empowered to push boundaries and drive progress. However, **there may be concerns about data privacy and ethical considerations surrounding AI** development, prompting stakeholders to prioritize responsible practices.

Challenges and Opportunities

Basic Prompt

How did Google Gemini change or disrupt the industry? How do competitors or the government or customers react? Limit your response to 100 words.

Google Gemini significantly changed the industry by advancing AI capabilities in natural language understanding and generation. Its integration of **advanced machine learning techniques enabled more accurate and context-aware responses,** enhancing user experience and business applications. Competitors responded by accelerating their own AI development efforts, increasing investment in research, and forming strategic partnerships. Governments scrutinized Gemini's impact on data privacy and market competition, leading to potential regulatory actions. Customers benefitted from improved AI services but **raised concerns about data security and ethical use, prompting debates on responsible AI** deployment and usage policies.

Discussion and Lessons Learned

Your Advanced Question for Starting Prompt Engineering

Explain the actions taken to address the challenge or capitalize on the opportunity. This could involve strategies implemented, decisions made, or interventions undertaken. What happened recently? Limit your response to 100 words.

To address challenges and capitalize on opportunities in generative AI, companies have intensified research efforts, focusing on refining algorithms, improving model capabilities, and enhancing ethical frameworks. Recent actions include investing in AI safety research, promoting transparency in AI development, and collaborating with industry partners to establish standards and best practices. Additionally, there's a growing emphasis on educating the public about AI's capabilities and limitations. Recently, companies have also expanded their product offerings, introducing new applications of generative models in areas like healthcare, finance, and entertainment, further cementing generative AI's role in shaping the future of technology and society.

OpenAI/ChatGPT has faced criticism for bias, data privacy violations, and generating inappropriate content, highlighting challenges in ensuring ethical and reliable AI outputs.

Your Advanced Question for Starting Prompt Engineering

Explain the actions taken to address the challenge or capitalize on the opportunity. This could involve strategies implemented, decisions made, or interventions undertaken. What happened recently? Limit your response to 100 words.

To address the challenges posed by Google Gemini's advancements, **competitors ramped up their R&D efforts,** focusing on developing their own cutting-edge AI models. They invested in talent acquisition, strategic partnerships, and innovation labs to accelerate progress. Additionally, they **diversified their product offerings and focused on enhancing user experiences** to remain competitive in the market. Recently, there has been increased collaboration between industry players and academic institutions to drive collective innovation and address common challenges in AI development. This collaborative approach aims to foster greater advancements and ensure responsible AI deployment in various domains.

12.7.3 Review: Problems and Challenges of Generative AI Service Companies

General findings and problems that affect the entire case study are described here. Several common problems and challenges affect generative AI service companies:

- **Data Quality and Bias:** Generative AI models heavily rely on training data, which may be biased or incomplete, leading to biased outputs or inaccurate predictions.
- **Ethical Concerns:** There are ethical implications surrounding the use of generative AI, including the potential for misuse, manipulation, or generating harmful content.

- **Lack of Control:** Generative AI models may produce unpredictable or undesirable outputs, leading to challenges in controlling the quality and relevance of generated content.
- **Intellectual Property:** Issues regarding ownership and copyright arise when using generative AI to create content, raising questions about the originality and ownership of generated works.
- **Scalability and Efficiency:** Generating high-quality content at scale can be resource-intensive and time-consuming, posing challenges in scaling up operations and meeting demand efficiently.
- **Regulatory Compliance:** Compliance with regulations and standards regarding data privacy, content moderation, and ethical AI usage presents significant challenges for generative AI service providers.
- **Security Risks:** Generative AI models may be vulnerable to adversarial attacks or exploitation, posing risks to data security and integrity.
- **User Acceptance and Trust:** Building trust and acceptance among users for generated content is crucial but challenging, especially when users are skeptical of AI-generated content's authenticity and reliability.

Addressing these challenges requires a multifaceted approach involving technological advancements, ethical considerations, regulatory frameworks, and industry collaboration to ensure the responsible development and deployment of generative AI services.

Further Readings

Alphabet (2024) https://abc.xyz/investor/
Open AI (2024) https://app.dealroom.co/companies/openai

Questions

1. How are generative large language models (LLMs) trained and how do they operate? Please include details on the types of data used, the architecture of the models, the steps involved in training, how these models generate text, and the challenges faced during their development.
2. Please discuss what the quality of large language models (LLMs) depends on and why the ranking of the best LLMs frequently changes?

12.8 B2B E-Commerce Case

Shopify, eBay, Salesforce, and SAP

Basic Prompt

Describe B2B retail business in the context of Digital Business management in 100 words.

A B2B retail business, such as a wholesale electronics supplier, provides products to other businesses like retail stores and online marketplaces. The company offers bulk purchasing options, competitive pricing, and personalized account management. By leveraging a robust CRM system, it tracks customer preferences, manages inventory efficiently, and provides tailored marketing campaigns. This enhances customer relationships, increases sales, and ensures timely deliveries. The business also utilizes data analytics to predict trends and adjust offerings, maintaining a competitive edge in the market.

The following companies are examples of those involved in various aspects of digital business: Shopify for creating online marketplaces, eBay for using marketplaces, SAP for building supply chain management, and Salesforce for customer relationship management.

12.8.1 Shopify

Shopify	
Founder(s)	Tobias Lütke, Daniel Weinand, and Scott Lake
Revenue 2024	7 billion USD
Employees	8k employees
Year of foundation	2006
Business Idea or how the company earn money	Shopify provides a platform for businesses **to create online stores, earn money by offering subscription plans, transaction fees, and additional services like Shopify Payments** and Shopify Shipping

Figure 12.21 displays Shopify's financial performance and its growth trajectory. The chart displays significant growth over the years from 2012 to 2023, with a sharp increase after 2017. By 2023, the value surpasses $8 billion, indicating a major acceleration in financial performance or revenue growth.

About Shopify

Basic Prompt

Describe the history, products, and business model of Spotify in 200 words.

Founded in 2006 by Tobias Lütke, Daniel Weinand, and Scott Lake, Shopify arose from Lütke's frustration with available E-Commerce platforms while setting up a snowboard shop. Initially a solution for his own needs, it pivoted into a platform for other merchants. **Today, Shopify is a leading E-Commerce solution, offering a suite of products and services for businesses of all sizes. Its flagship product is its user-friendly E-Commerce platform,** enabling merchants to **create**

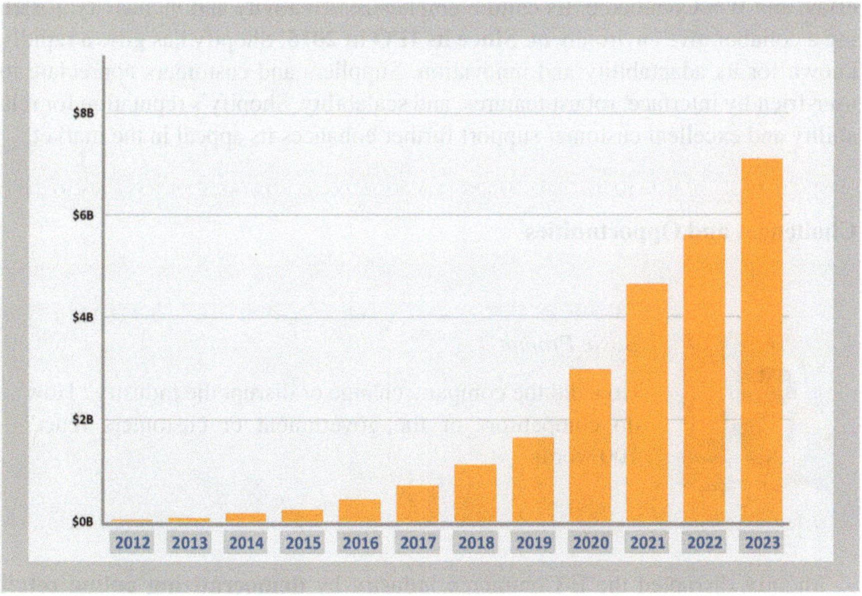

Fig. 12.21 Shopify's financial performance and its growth trajectory

customizable online stores without technical expertise. Shopify also provides complementary services such as payment processing, shipping management, and point-of-sale solutions. **Operating on a subscription-based model,** merchants pay monthly fees for access to the platform, supplemented by transaction fees and additional service charges. Shopify's success lies in its adaptability and continuous innovation, expanding its ecosystem with a marketplace of apps, themes, and educational resources. With a global presence and diverse user base, **Shopify remains committed to supporting entrepreneurship** and sustainability initiatives. Its history is characterized by a dedication to empowering merchants, making it a pivotal player in the ever-evolving landscape of E-Commerce.

Context

Your Advanced Question for Starting Prompt Engineering

Describe the situation or environment surrounding the industry. This might include other (big) industry players, company culture, or historical context depending on the subject. How do suppliers or customers react? Limit your response to 100 words.

In the E-Commerce industry, Shopify competes with major players like Amazon, eBay, and WooCommerce. Its culture emphasizes creativity and inclusivity, fostering a collaborative environment. **Since its IPO in 2015**, Shopify has grown rapidly, known for its adaptability and innovation. Suppliers and customers appreciate its user-friendly interface, robust features, and scalability. Shopify's reputation for reliability and excellent customer support further enhances its appeal in the market.

Challenges and Opportunities

Basic Prompt

How did the company change or disrupt the industry? How do competitors or the government or customers react? 100 words

Shopify disrupted the E-Commerce industry by **democratizing online retail, offering an accessible platform for businesses of all sizes.** Its user-friendly interface and customizable solutions challenged traditional E-Commerce platforms. Competitors responded with innovations and pricing adjustments to remain competitive. Government regulations regarding online commerce and data privacy influenced Shopify's operations, leading to compliance measures and adjustments. **Customers welcomed Shopify's ease of use and flexibility, leading to a loyal user base and positive market reception.** Overall, Shopify's disruptive impact reshaped the E-Commerce landscape, prompting adaptation and innovation across the industry.

Discussion and Lessons Learned

Your Advanced Question for Starting Prompt Engineering

Explain the actions taken to address the challenge or capitalize on the opportunity. This could involve strategies implemented, decisions made, or interventions undertaken. What happened recently? Limit your response to 100 words.

To address challenges and capitalize on opportunities, Shopify continually enhances its platform with **new features and services.** Recent initiatives include expanding its fulfillment network to improve order processing and delivery times, enhancing **integrations with social media** platforms for seamless selling, and investing in AI technology to personalize customer experiences. Additionally, Shopify has focused on **international** expansion to tap into new markets and diversify revenue streams. These actions reflect Shopify's commitment to innovation and its efforts to stay ahead in the competitive E-Commerce landscape.

12.8.2 eBay

eBay	
Founder(s)	Pierre Omidyar
Revenue 2024	12 billion USD
Employees	127k employees
Year of foundation	1995
Business idea or how the company earn money	eBay **operates as an online marketplace,** facilitating consumer-to-consumer and business-to-consumer sales. The company **earns money through listing fees, final value fees,** and optional seller services such as promoted listings and store subscriptions

Figure 12.22 on eBay's revenue and profit development highlights significant shifts in the company's financial performance over time.

About eBay

Basic Prompt

Describe the history, products, and business model of the company in 200 words.

eBay, founded in 1995 by Pierre Omidyar, revolutionized online commerce by **creating a platform for individuals to buy and sell goods through auctions or fixed-price listings**. Originally conceived as an online marketplace for collectibles, eBay quickly expanded to include a wide range of products, from electronics and fashion to automotive parts and home goods.

The company's core product is its E-Commerce platform, which connects buyers and sellers globally, enabling transactions across various categories. eBay generates revenue primarily through listing fees, final value fees, and optional seller services such as promoted listings and store subscriptions.

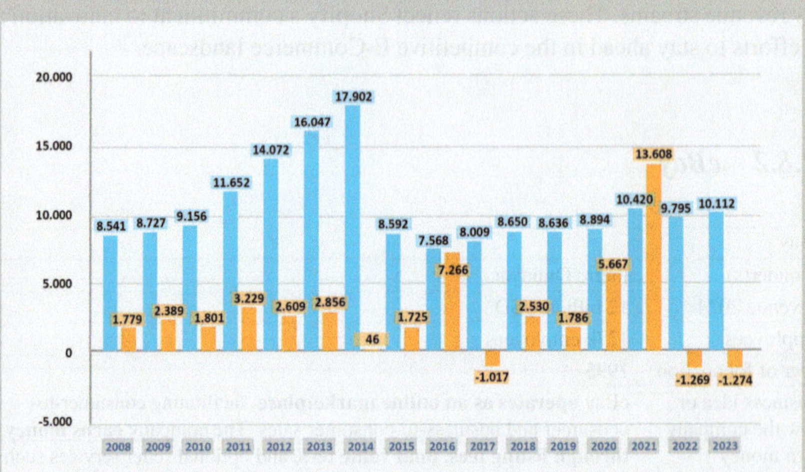

Fig. 12.22 eBay's revenue (blue) and profit (orange) development (in billion dollars)

Over the years, eBay **has evolved its business model to adapt to changing market dynamics. It has introduced features like Buy It Now, allowing users to purchase items immediately at a set price, and eBay Motors, specializing in automotive sales.** Additionally, eBay has expanded into new markets through acquisitions, such as StubHub for event ticketing and PayPal for online payments.

Despite facing competition from E-Commerce giants like Amazon, eBay remains a significant player in the online retail space, known for its diverse product selection, user-friendly interface, and global reach. Its history is characterized by innovation, adaptability, and a commitment to connecting buyers and sellers worldwide.

Context

Your Advanced Question for Starting Prompt Engineering

Describe the situation or environment surrounding the industry. This might include other (big) industry players, company culture, or historical context depending on the subject, how do suppliers or customers think about that? Limit your response to 100 words.

In the E-Commerce industry, eBay competes with major players like Amazon, Alibaba, and Walmart. Its culture values entrepreneurship and innovation, **fostering a dynamic work environment**. Historically, eBay has been **known for its community-driven approach, with users actively participating in auctions and discussions. However, in recent years, the company has faced challenges from competitors and changes in consumer behavior.** Suppliers appreciate eBay's platform for reaching a global audience, while customers value its diverse product selection and competitive pricing. Overall, eBay operates within a dynamic and competitive landscape, continually evolving to meet the needs of both buyers and sellers.

Challenges and Opportunities

Basic Prompt

How did the company change or disrupt the industry? How do competitors or the government or customers react? Limit your response to 100 words.

eBay **disrupted the retail industry by democratizing online commerce, empowering individuals to buy and sell goods globally.** Its **auction-style** format and diverse product range challenged traditional retail models. Competitors responded with similar platforms and strategies, while governments-imposed regulations to ensure fair trade practices. Customers embraced eBay for its convenience, selection, and potential bargains, driving its success. However, increased competition and changes in consumer preferences have prompted eBay to adapt its business model over time to remain relevant in the evolving E-Commerce landscape. eBay's revenue and profit/loss from 2008 to 2023, showing trends in Fig. 12.23 in both revenue growth and fluctuations in profitability. This includes years of positive profit and periods with losses, reflecting eBay's variable financial performance over this period.

Discussion and Lessons Learned

Your Advanced Question for Starting Prompt Engineering

Explain the actions taken to address the challenge or capitalize on the opportunity. This could involve strategies implemented, decisions made, or interventions undertaken. What happened recently? Limit your response to 100 words.

To address challenges and capitalize on opportunities, eBay has implemented several strategic initiatives. It has **focused on enhancing user experience through platform improvements and personalized recommendations.** eBay also expanded its product offerings, such as launching authentication services for high-end goods and integrating augmented reality for virtual try-ons. Recently, eBay has prioritized seller support and streamlined seller tools to improve efficiency. Additionally, the company has invested in marketing campaigns to attract new customers and retain existing ones. These efforts demonstrate eBay's commitment to staying competitive and relevant in the ever-changing E-Commerce landscape.

eBay, in addition to traditional online sales—which feature fewer auctions and increasingly more new items from professional sellers—has **opened a separate classifieds marketplace for auctions of used goods**.

12.8.3 Salesforce

Salesforce	
Founder(s)	Marc Benioff, Parker Harris, Dave Moellenhoff, Frank Dominguez
Revenue 2023	31 billion USD
Employees	79k employees
Year of foundation	1999
Business idea or how the company earn money	Salesforce is a **cloud-based software company that provides customer relationship management (CRM)** solutions to businesses. The company earns money through **subscription fees for its cloud-based software services**, which include sales management, marketing automation, customer service, and analytics tools. Additionally, Salesforce offers various add-on services, training programs, and consulting services to help businesses maximize the value of its CRM platform

Figure 12.23 shows Salesforce's historic revenue growth. The chart shows a significant and steady increase from 2001 to 2024, with growth accelerating sharply after 2015. By 2024, the value approaches 40,000 units, indicating rapid expansion or accumulation over the last decade.

About Salesforce

Basic Prompt

Describe the history, products, and business model of the company in 200 words.

Salesforce, founded in 1999 by Marc Benioff, Parker Harris, Dave Moellenhoff, and Frank Dominguez, is a trailblazer in **cloud-based software solutions, primarily focusing on customer relationship management (CRM).** The company began with a vision to revolutionize CRM by moving it to the cloud, making it more accessible and scalable for businesses of all sizes.

Salesforce's flagship product is its CRM platform, which offers a suite of tools and services to help businesses manage their sales, marketing, customer service, and analytics processes. These cloud-based solutions enable companies to streamline operations, improve customer engagement, and drive growth.

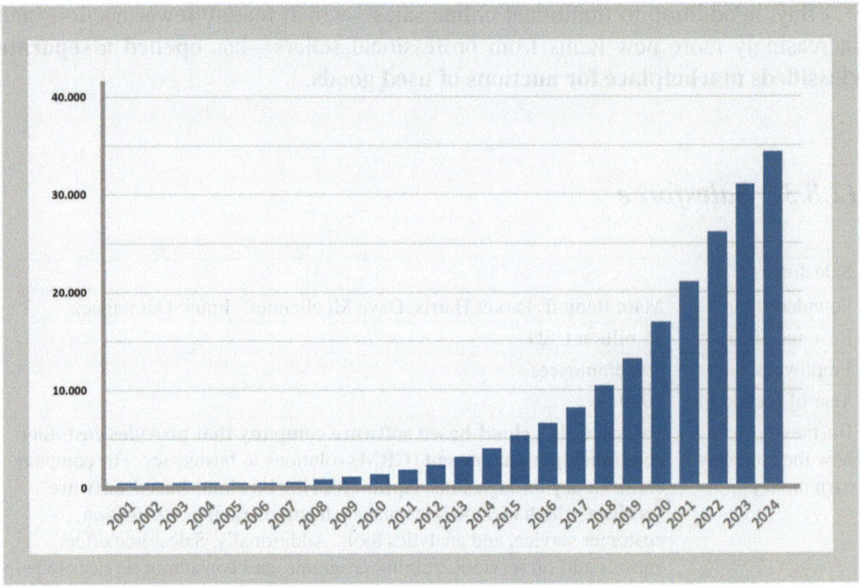

Fig. 12.23 Salesforce's revenue development (in billion dollars)

The company operates on a subscription-based business model, where customers **pay recurring fees for access to its CRM platform and related services.** This model provides predictable revenue streams for Salesforce while offering flexibility and scalability for its customers. Over the years, Salesforce has expanded its product portfolio through acquisitions and strategic partnerships, offering a wide range of solutions beyond CRM. These include **Salesforce Marketing Cloud, Service Cloud, Commerce Cloud, and Salesforce Platform,** among others. Salesforce's history is characterized by innovation, with a strong focus on leveraging emerging technologies such as artificial intelligence and machine learning to enhance its offerings. As a pioneer in cloud computing and CRM, Salesforce continues to lead the industry, empowering businesses to connect with their customers in new and meaningful ways.

Context

Your Advanced Question for Starting Prompt Engineering

Explain the actions taken to address the challenge or capitalize on the opportunity. This could involve strategies implemented, decisions made, or interventions undertaken. What happened recently? Limit your response to 100 words.

Describe the environment of the industry and Salesforce, including major players, company culture, and historical context. How do suppliers and customers perceive this industry? Limit your response to 100 words.

The industry surrounding Salesforce is characterized by intense competition among **major players like Microsoft Dynamics, Oracle,** and SAP. Salesforce, known for its innovative cloud-based CRM solutions, emphasizes a **customer-centric company culture, focusing on continuous innovation** and user-friendly platforms. Historically, Salesforce has disrupted the traditional **software market by pioneering the SaaS model,** influencing how businesses manage customer relationships. **Suppliers appreciate Salesforce's robust ecosystem and integration capabilities,** while customers value its scalability and comprehensive analytics. However, concerns about data privacy and the need for constant updates and training are prevalent among users, reflecting the dynamic nature of the industry.

Challenges and Opportunities

Basic Prompt

How did the company change or disrupt the industry? How do competitors or the government or customers react? 100 words

Salesforce **disrupted the industry by pioneering cloud-based CRM solutions,** challenging traditional on-premise software models. Its scalable, subscription-based platform democratized access to advanced CRM tools, empowering businesses of all sizes. Competitors responded with similar cloud offerings, fueling innovation and market growth. Governments have scrutinized Salesforce's data handling practices, leading to compliance measures like GDPR. Customers embraced Salesforce for its user-friendly interface, flexibility, and continuous innovation, driving its widespread adoption. Overall, Salesforce's disruptive impact reshaped the CRM industry, fostering competition, innovation, and a heightened focus on customer-centric solutions.

Discussion and Lessons Learned

Your Advanced Question for Starting Prompt Engineering

Explain the actions taken to address the challenges or capitalize on the opportunities. This could involve strategies implemented, decisions made, or interventions undertaken. What happened recently? Limit your response to 100 words.

Salesforce has implemented several strategic initiatives. The company continuously invests in research and development to innovate its CRM platform, **integrating emerging technologies like artificial intelligence and machine learning to enhance user experiences** and drive business outcomes. Salesforce also focuses on **expanding its product portfolio through strategic acquisitions and partnerships,** broadening its capabilities beyond traditional CRM. Recent efforts include the acquisition of Slack, aimed at enhancing collaboration and communication within its platform. Additionally, Salesforce prioritizes customer success, offering comprehensive training programs, support services, and a vibrant community to empower users. These actions underscore Salesforce's commitment to innovation, customer-centricity, and market leadership in the dynamic landscape of cloud-based CRM solutions.

12.8.4 SAP

SAP	
Founder(s)	Dietmar Hopp, Hasso Plattner, Claus Wellenreuther, Klaus Tschira, and Hans-Werner Hector
Revenue 2023	33billion USD
Employees 2023	107k employees
Year of foundation	1972
Business idea or how the company earn money	SAP **provides enterprise software solutions for businesses, including ERP (enterprise resource planning), CRM (customer relationship management), and analytics.** The company earns money through **software licensing, maintenance fees,** and cloud subscriptions

Figure 12.24 illustrates the SAP product portfolio. The chart highlights SAP's key business solutions, including ERP, financials, CRM, supply chain, human capital, spend management, and a business technology platform.

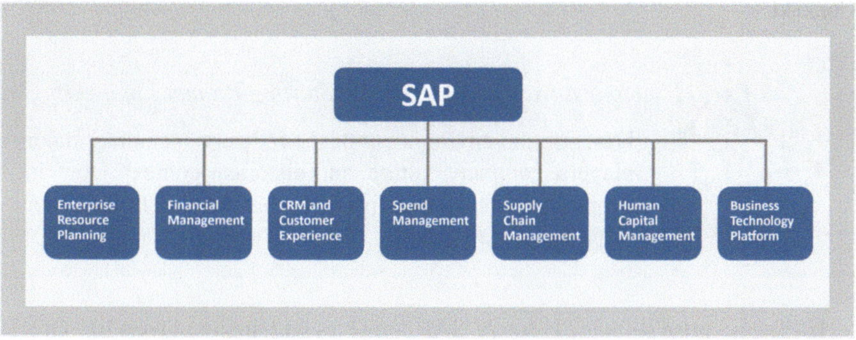

Fig. 12.24 SAP product portfolio

About SAP

Basic Prompt

Describe the history, products, and business model of the company in 200 words.

SAP, founded in 1972 by Dietmar Hopp, Hasso Plattner, Claus Wellenreuther, Klaus Tschira, and Hans-Werner Hector, is a **global leader in enterprise software solutions.** Initially **focused on developing standard software for real-time data processing, SAP revolutionized business operations with its ERP (enterprise resource planning) systems.** These systems integrated various business functions, such as finance, HR, supply chain, and manufacturing, into a single, cohesive platform, streamlining processes and improving efficiency.

Over the years, **SAP expanded its product portfolio** to include a wide range of enterprise software solutions, including CRM (customer relationship management), SCM (supply chain management), BI (business intelligence), and HCM (human capital management). These solutions cater to businesses of all sizes and industries, empowering them to manage their operations effectively and drive growth. SAP **operates on a business model based on software licensing, maintenance fees, and cloud subscriptions**. Customers pay for access to SAP's software solutions, which are continuously updated and enhanced to meet evolving business needs. Additionally, **SAP offers consulting, training, and support services to help customers maximize the value of its software.**

Context

Your Advanced Question for Starting Prompt Engineering

Describe the environment of the industry including major players, company culture, and historical context. How do suppliers and customers perceive this industry? Limit your response to 100 words.

In the enterprise software industry, SAP competes with major players like Oracle, Microsoft, and Salesforce. Its culture emphasizes innovation and customer-centricity, fostering a collaborative environment. Historically, **SAP has been known for its robust ERP solutions and strong focus on industry-specific functionality.** Suppliers appreciate SAP's global reach and reputation for reliability, while customers value its comprehensive suite of enterprise software solutions. However, **some customers may find SAP's solutions complex and expensive to implement**, leading to considerations of alternatives or customization options. Overall, SAP operates within a competitive landscape, continually evolving to meet the evolving needs of businesses worldwide.

Challenges and Opportunities

Basic Prompt

How did the company change or disrupt the industry? How do competitors or the government or customers react? Limit answer to 100 words.

SAP changed the industry by pioneering comprehensive ERP solutions, revolutionizing how businesses manage their operations. Its **integrated approach streamlined processes, enhancing efficiency and decision-making.** Competitors responded by diversifying their offerings and investing in cloud-based solutions. Governments imposed regulations to ensure data security and privacy compliance. Customers embraced SAP for its industry-specific functionality and scalability, driving widespread adoption. However, some customers faced challenges with complex implementations and high costs, prompting demand for more flexible solutions. Overall, **SAP's disruptive impact reshaped the enterprise software landscape,** spurring innovation and driving digital transformation across industries.

Discussion and Lessons Learned

Your Advanced Question for Starting Prompt Engineering

Explain the actions taken to address the challenge or capitalize on the opportunity. This could involve strategies implemented, decisions made, or interventions undertaken. What happened recently? Limit your response to 100 words.

SAP has implemented several strategic initiatives. The company has focused on enhancing user experience and simplifying its product offerings through initiatives like the SAP Business Technology Platform. Additionally, S**AP has invested in cloud-based solutions, expanding its SAP S/4HANA** Cloud offerings to provide customers with more flexible deployment options. Recent acquisitions, such as the **acquisition of Signavio,** have further strengthened SAP's position in the market by enhancing its process mining and business process intelligence capabilities. These efforts demonstrate SAP's commitment to innovation and customer-centricity in the dynamic enterprise software landscape.

12.8.5 Review: Problems and Challenges of B2B E-Commerce

In the realm of B2B retail, several common challenges tend to emerge, impacting the efficiency and profitability of businesses. **Complex supply chains often pose logistical hurdles,** requiring meticulous coordination among various suppliers and partners. Inventory management presents another significant challenge, as businesses strive to **balance stock levels with fluctuating demand while minimizing costs.** Building and maintaining strong customer relationships is paramount, demanding personalized attention and exceptional service to meet the unique needs of B2B clients. Additionally, integrating and optimizing technology solutions, such as E-Commerce platforms and CRM systems, can be daunting tasks, requiring substantial investment and expertise. Competitive pricing pressures further compound the challenge, necessitating strategic pricing strategies to remain competitive in the market. Regulatory compliance adds another layer of complexity, particularly in highly regulated industries. Lastly, **market volatility and economic uncertainty demand agility and adaptability from B2B retailers** to navigate changing conditions effectively. Addressing these challenges requires a holistic approach, encompassing strategic planning, investment in technology and infrastructure, and a strong focus on customer relationships and market dynamics.

Further Readings

Ebay (2024) https://investors.ebayinc.com/overview/default.aspx
Salesforce (2024) https://investor.salesforce.com/overview/default.aspx
SAP (2024) https://www.sap.com/investors/en.html
Shopify (2024) https://investors.shopify.com/home/default.aspx

Questions

1. Why did Microsoft acquire LinkedIn in 2016, and what was the strategic move behind it?
2. What are the key differences between B2B and B2C E-Commerce models, and how do these differences impact the sales and marketing strategies of businesses?
3. How has the adoption of B2B E-Commerce platforms transformed traditional supply chain management and customer relationship management practices?

12.9 Transformation in the Media Industry

Netflix, Sony PlayStation, Spotify

NETFLIX PlayStation Spotify

Basic Prompt

Describe the media industry with a focus on Movies, Games and Music in 100 words

The media industry, encompassing movies, games, and music, is a dynamic and rapidly evolving sector. Movies captivate audiences with compelling storytelling and visual effects, with platforms like Netflix revolutionizing how we consume films through streaming and original content production. The gaming industry, led by giants like Sony PlayStation, offers immersive experiences through advanced graphics and interactive gameplay, integrating entertainment services such as Netflix and Spotify. Music, integral to both films and games, has been transformed by platforms like Spotify, which provide extensive libraries and personalized playlists, reshaping how we discover and enjoy music. Technological advancements, such as virtual reality and artificial intelligence, continue to drive innovation, enhancing user experiences and creating new opportunities for content creation and distribution across all three segments. This interconnected ecosystem highlights the media industry's adaptability and its significant impact on global entertainment consumption.

12.9.1 Netflix

Netflix	
Founder(s)	Reed Hastings and Marc Randolph
Revenue 2023	33 billion USD
Employees	13k employees
Year of foundation	1997
Business idea or how the company earn money	Netflix revolutionized entertainment by **offering a subscription-based streaming service, initially focusing on DVD rentals** before transitioning to digital content. Through a vast library of TV shows, movies, and original productions, it provides on-demand viewing, enabling users to **enjoy entertainment anytime, anywhere, without ads, via various devices**

Figure 12.25 indicates the number of US streaming subscribers in millions. The chart highlights Netflix's leading position in the streaming market, significantly ahead of Disney+, Hulu, and BBOnow.

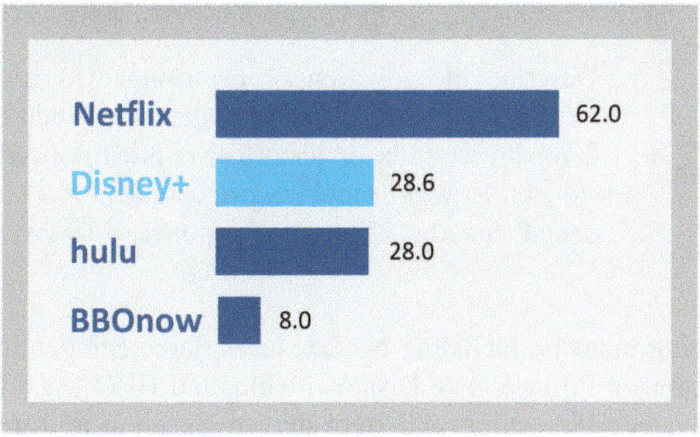

Fig. 12.25 Netflix leads—US streaming subscribers in millions

About the Company

Basic Prompt

Describe the history, products, and business model of Netflix in 200 words.

Netflix, founded in 1997 by Reed Hastings and Marc Randolph, initially **offered DVD rentals by mail**, revolutionizing the home entertainment industry with its subscription-based model. In **2007, it launched its streaming service, providing on-demand access** to a vast library of movies and TV shows. The company operates on a **subscription-based business model,** offering tiered pricing plans based on video quality and the number of simultaneous streams. This approach eliminates ads and provides uninterrupted viewing experiences for subscribers.

Netflix's success is also attributed to its **investment in original content production,** starting with "House of Cards" in 2013. By creating exclusive, high-quality shows and films, Netflix distinguishes itself from competitors and retains subscribers.

Utilizing data analytics, Netflix personalizes recommendations (recommendation engines) for users, enhancing their viewing experiences and driving engagement, using collaborative filtering for **predicting user preferences by analyzing similar users' past** behavior. This helps recommend items users might enjoy. This data-driven approach enables the company to adapt to changing consumer preferences and maintain its position as a leader in the global streaming market.

Context

Your Advanced Question for Starting Prompt Engineering

Describe the situation or environment surrounding the industry. This might include other (big) industry players, company culture, or historical context depending on the subject. How do suppliers or customers react? What happened recently? Limit your response to 100 words.

The streaming industry, including Netflix, faces fierce competition from major players like Amazon Prime Video, Disney+, Hulu, and HBO Max. Netflix's company culture values innovation and **data-driven decision-making,** fostering a creative environment. Its history of **disrupting traditional entertainment models has reshaped consumer behavior.** Content creators see NETFLIX as a valuable distribution partner, but negotiations can be intricate. Customers appreciate Netflix's user-friendly interface, vast content library, and ad-free viewing experience, though subscription fatigue is a concern amidst growing competition. To maintain its market position, Netflix continues to invest in original content and adapt to evolving consumer preferences.

Netflix disrupted the market with **dynamic pricing**, tiered content quality (high-end and budget-friendly), and **a shift from relying on competitors' content (surpassing HBO in 2017)** to producing their own originals. By 2018, with over 130 million subscribers globally, they offered tiered subscription models with and without ads, making cable TV a less appealing option. Streaming services, while disrupting the entertainment industry, face challenges in profitability compared to traditional models like DVD rentals and cable television. Established players in these older models struggle to adapt to the changing landscape, leading to issues like subscriber churn and pressure to keep up with content creation.

Netflix **didn't invent binge-watching, but their on-demand model made it a mainstream habit**. Traditional products and services are merging into comprehensive solutions for customer needs.

Generative AI's potential is threatened by copyright. Training on copyrighted data and creating outputs too similar to existing works could lead to legal trouble.

Challenges and Opportunities

Basic Prompt

How did Netflix change or disrupt the industry? How do competitors or the government or customers react? 100 words

Netflix **disrupted the entertainment industry by pioneering DVD rental-by-mail and later transitioning to streaming, reshaping how people consume media.** Competitors responded by launching their own streaming platforms, intensifying competition. Government scrutiny over content regulation and antitrust concerns has grown. Customers embraced the convenience of on-demand streaming but face subscription fatigue with the proliferation of platforms. Overall, Netflix's innovation catalyzed a paradigm shift in media consumption habits, prompting both adaptation and regulatory scrutiny from competitors, government, and customers alike.

Discussion and Lessons Learned

Your Advanced Question for Starting Prompt Engineering

Explain the actions taken to address the challenges or capitalize on the opportunities. This could involve strategies implemented, decisions made, or interventions undertaken. What happened recently? Limit your response to 100 words.

To address challenges and capitalize on opportunities, Netflix continues to **invest heavily in original content production**, securing exclusive deals with top talent and studios. They focus on **global expansion, tailoring content to regional preferences.** Recently, Netflix has doubled down on diversifying its content library, expanding into new genres and formats, including documentaries, reality shows, and international productions. Additionally, they have experimented with **interactive content,** gaming, and merchandising tie-ins to enhance user engagement. These strategies aim to retain subscribers amidst increasing competition while positioning Netflix as a leader in the evolving landscape of digital entertainment.

Increased competition and peak subscriptions during COVID have impacted Netflix. Despite global revenue rising by 5% due to streaming, cash flow is negative due to self-produced content. The industry faces challenges from streaming services, while US revenue decreased in 2017. Studios collaborate with streamers, offer lower prices with ads, and enhance user experience with AI.

12.9.2 Sony PlayStation

Sony PlayStation	Sony PlayStation is part of Sony Corporation
Founder(s)	Masaru Ibuka and Akio Morita
Revenue 2023	87 billion USD (SONY Corporation)
Employees 2023	113k employees (SONY Corporation)
Founded year	1946
Business idea or how the company earn money	Sony PlayStation, part of Sony Corporation, is a renowned gaming brand launched in 1994. It revolutionized home entertainment with cutting-edge graphics, immersive gameplay, and a vast library of exclusive titles. PlayStation consoles, including PS5, continue to set industry standards, captivating millions of gamers worldwide

Figure 12.26 indicates the market size of the global games market. Sony PlayStation is part of the console games market.

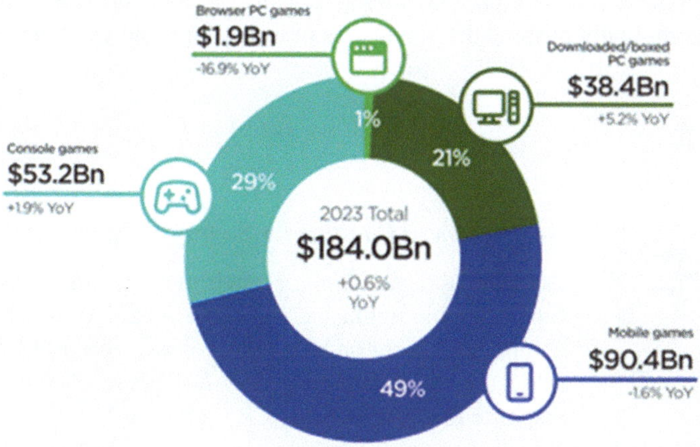

Fig. 12.26 Sony PlayStation is part of the console games market. (Adapted from Newzoo)

About Sony PlayStation

Basic Prompt

Describe the history, products, and business model of Sony PlayStation in 200 words.

Sony PlayStation, introduced in 1994, transformed the gaming industry with its innovative technology and extensive game library. The original PlayStation set new standards with its CD-ROM format and 3D graphics. Its successor, the PlayStation 2 (PS2), released in 2000, became the best-selling console of all time, thanks to its DVD playback and backward compatibility. The PlayStation 3 (PS3), launched in 2006, introduced Blu-ray technology and online gaming. In 2013, the PlayStation 4 (PS4) continued the trend with enhanced graphics and virtual reality (VR) support. The latest, PlayStation 5 (PS5), released in 2020, features an ultra-fast SSD, ray tracing, and 3D audio, offering an immersive gaming experience. PlayStation's business model has evolved significantly. Initially focused on hardware sales, it now includes digital downloads, subscriptions like PlayStation Plus, and exclusive game titles. This diversification has helped Sony adapt to changing consumer demands and maintain a strong market presence. The PlayStation Network (PSN) further enhances the ecosystem, providing a platform for online multiplayer gaming, digital media, and social interaction. Overall, PlayStation remains a dominant force in the gaming industry, continually pushing the boundaries of technology and entertainment.

Context

Your Advanced Question for Starting Prompt Engineering

Describe the situation or environment surrounding the Industry. This might include other (big) industry players, company culture, or historical context depending on the subject. How do suppliers or customers react? Limit your response to 100 words.

The games industry is highly competitive, with major players like Sony, Microsoft, and Nintendo driving innovation. The rise of mobile gaming and platforms like Steam and Epic Games Store has diversified the market. Company cultures emphasize creativity and rapid adaptation to tech trends. Suppliers focus on cutting-edge hardware, while customers demand immersive experiences and seamless online services. Historical context shows a shift from physical to digital, with increasing emphasis on community and social interaction in gaming.

Challenges and Opportunities

Basic Prompt

How did Sony PlayStation change or disrupt the industry? How do competitors or the government or customers react? Limit response to 100 words.

Sony PlayStation revolutionized the games industry by introducing 3D graphics and CD-ROM technology, making games more immersive and affordable. Competitors like Nintendo and Sega had to innovate rapidly to keep up. Customers embraced the enhanced gaming experience, leading to massive sales. Governments generally supported the industry's growth, recognizing its economic impact

Discussion and Lessons Learned

Your Advanced Question for Starting Prompt Engineering

Explain the actions taken to address the challenges of the games industry or capitalize on the opportunities. This could involve strategies implemented, decisions made, or interventions undertaken. What happened recently? Limit your response to 200 words.

The gaming industry, a dynamic and rapidly evolving sector, faces significant challenges while presenting vast opportunities. The COVID-19 pandemic disrupted supply chains, leading to shortages of gaming hardware. Companies like Sony and Microsoft struggled to meet the high demand for their latest consoles. To address this, they diversified supply chains and shifted toward digital distribution.

Another challenge is increasing government scrutiny over loot boxes, microtransactions, and gaming addiction. Companies have implemented measures to promote responsible gaming, such as spending limits. Technological advancements like cloud gaming and AI offer both challenges and opportunities. Cloud gaming services like Microsoft's Xbox Cloud Gaming democratize access to gaming but require significant infrastructure investment. AI is being used to create more realistic and adaptive game environments.

The rise of esports and competitive gaming has opened up new revenue streams through sponsorships and live event ticket sales. Companies are investing in esports infrastructure to capitalize on this growing market. In conclusion, the gaming industry must navigate a complex landscape of challenges and opportunities. By addressing supply chain issues, adapting to regulatory changes, embracing technological advancements, and capitalizing on the esports market, gaming companies can position themselves for continued growth and success.

12.9.3 Spotify

Spotify	
Founder(s)	Daniel Ek and Martin Lorentzon
Revenue 2023	14 billion USD
Employees 2023	9k employees
Year of foundation	2006
Business idea or how the company earn money	Spotify's business model is based on a freemium model, offering a basic service for free and a premium subscription with additional features for a fee. The company generates revenue through advertising and premium subscriptions

In 2022, Spotify reported having 489 million monthly active users. Figure 12.27 illustrates the growth of Spotify's premium subscribers. The chart shows a steady increase from Q1 2020 to Q4 2022, peaking at 164.2 million user followed by a gradual decline in 2023, reaching 149.6 million user by Q1 2024.

About Spotify

Basic Prompt

Describe the history, products, and business model of Spotify in 200 words.

Spotify revolutionized the music industry by offering on-demand streaming. Initially launched in Sweden, it quickly expanded globally. Spotify offers two main subscription tiers: free, with ads and limited features, and premium, with ad-free listening, higher audio quality, offline playback, and exclusive content. Beyond these core offerings, Spotify has introduced features like Spotify Connect, Spotify Family, Spotify Duo, Spotify for Students, Spotify for Artists, and podcasts. Spotify's business model revolves around a freemium strategy, generating revenue

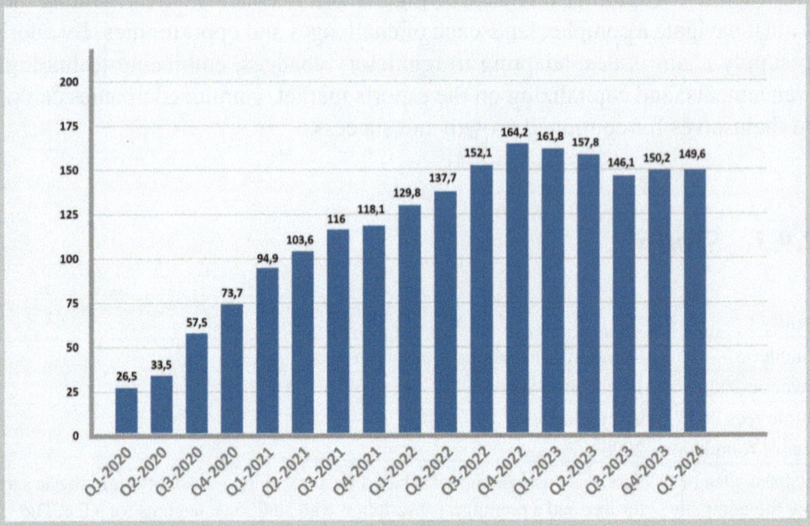

Fig. 12.27 Development of Spotify's premium subscriber (in million user)

through premium subscriptions and advertising. By leveraging its extensive music library, user-friendly interface, and innovative features, Spotify has established itself as a dominant force in the music streaming industry.

Context

Your Advanced Question for Starting Prompt Engineering

Describe the situation or environment surrounding the industry. This might include other (big) industry players, company culture, or historical context depending on the subject. How do suppliers or customers react? Limit your response to 100 words.

The music streaming industry is highly competitive, with major players like Apple Music, Amazon Music, and Spotify vying for market share. The industry culture is fast-paced, driven by innovation and consumer trends. Historical context includes the disruption caused by digital streaming and the decline of physical music sales. Suppliers, such as record labels and artists, often have complex relationships with streaming platforms, negotiating licensing deals and revenue sharing. Customers generally value convenience, affordability, and a vast music library, but concerns about artist compensation and platform dominance persist.

Challenges and Opportunities

Basic Prompt

How did Spotify or disrupt the industry? How do competitors or the government or customers react? Limit your response to 100 words.

Spotify disrupted the music industry by offering a convenient, on-demand streaming service at a time when physical music sales were declining. This disrupted the traditional business model of the music industry, leading to challenges for record labels and artists. Competitors responded by launching their own streaming services, intensifying competition. Governments have grappled with issues like fair compensation for artists and the impact of streaming on cultural diversity. Customers have largely embraced streaming, but concerns about pricing, artist royalties, and platform dominance persist.

Discussion and Lessons Learned

Your Advanced Question for Starting Prompt Engineering

Explain the actions taken to address the challenges of the music streaming industry or capitalize on the opportunities. This could involve strategies implemented, decisions made, or interventions undertaken. What happened recently? Limit your response to 200 words.

The music streaming industry has faced several challenges and opportunities in recent years. To address these, industry players have implemented various strategies. For instance, platforms like Spotify have expanded their offerings beyond music, including podcasts and audiobooks, to diversify revenue streams. They've also invested in personalized recommendations and curated playlists to enhance user experience.

To address concerns about artist compensation, some platforms have introduced transparency tools and negotiated fairer deals with labels. Additionally, there's been a growing focus on copyright protection and combating music piracy.

Recent developments include the rise of AI-generated music and the potential for blockchain technology to revolutionize music distribution. However, challenges such as competition from free, ad-supported services and concerns about data privacy persist.

Overall, the music streaming industry continues to evolve, with players adapting to changing consumer preferences and technological advancements while navigating regulatory challenges and ethical considerations.

12.9.4 Review: Problems and Challenges of the Media industry

General findings and problems that affect the entire case study are described here. What are the common findings?

The rise of powerful **new streaming services has disrupted the industry's value chain.** Established players previously held more control over content distribution and pricing. However, with this new landscape, they've **lost some of that control, facing intense price pressure** as these well-funded competitors fight for market share. Netflix's stock price plummeted in 2022 after experiencing its first subscriber decline in a decade, raising concerns about the streaming giant's profitability.

The media industry, including streaming services, faces several challenges, some of which are:

Content Discovery: With an abundance of content available, helping users discover content they'll enjoy becomes crucial. Algorithms play a significant role here, but balancing personalized recommendations with diverse content discovery can be challenging.

- **Content Costs:** Creating original content or licensing existing content can be expensive. Streaming services often engage in bidding wars for popular shows and movies, driving up costs.
- **Subscriber Acquisition and Retention:** Competition among streaming services is fierce. Acquiring and retaining subscribers requires offering compelling content, competitive pricing, and a smooth user experience.
- **Monetization:** Balancing subscription fees, ads (if applicable), and other revenue streams while keeping users satisfied can be tricky. Finding the right balance between profitability and user experience is crucial.
- **Quality of Service:** Streaming services must ensure a high-quality streaming experience across various devices and network conditions. Issues like buffering, poor video quality, or service outages can lead to user frustration and churn.
- **Content Licensing and Rights:** Negotiating content licensing agreements and navigating complex rights issues, especially on a global scale, poses challenges for streaming services. Exclusive deals and regional restrictions can complicate content availability.
- **Regulatory Challenges:** Regulatory requirements vary by region and can impact content availability, censorship, and data privacy. Compliance with regulations while maintaining a seamless user experience is essential.
- **Technological Advancements:** Keeping up with evolving technology, such as advancements in video codecs, streaming protocols, and device compatibility, is necessary to remain competitive and provide an optimal user experience.
- **Piracy and Copyright Infringement:** Protecting content from piracy and enforcing copyright laws is an ongoing challenge for the media industry, especially in the digital age where content can be easily copied and distributed.
- **User Data Privacy:** Collecting and utilizing user data to personalize experiences while respecting user privacy rights and complying with regulations like GDPR or CCPA requires careful navigation.

These challenges are not exhaustive and can vary based on factors like market dynamics, technological advancements, and regulatory environments. The competition for users' attention and time (**attention economy**) with games, YouTube, podcasts, and other media adds further challenges. However, addressing these challenges effectively is essential for the sustained success of streaming services and the media industry as a whole.

Further Readings

Netflix (2024) https://ir.netflix.net/financials/quarterly-earnings/default.aspx
Newzoo (2024) https://newzoo.com
Sony (2024) https://www.sony.com/en/SonyInfo/IR/
Spotify (2024) https://investors.spotify.com/home/default.aspx

Questions

1. Given the increasing competition in the streaming market, how is Netflix attempting to differentiate itself and overcome the challenges of content acquisition, user retention, and profitability?
2. What are the primary challenges facing the digital products industry, including issues related to piracy, revenue models, consumer behavior, and technological advancements?
3. How can Spotify utilize AI to personalize recommendations, improve content discovery, enhance user interfaces, and address potential privacy concerns and biases in its algorithms?

12.10 Potential of Digital Worlds (Metaverse)

Meta, Google, and Apple

Meta Alphabet Google

Basic Prompt

Describe the potential of Digital Worlds in 160 words

The term "Omniverse" is used as an extension of the "metaverse" (sometimes both terms are used interchangeably). Although there have been successful forms of the metaverse, such as online games and Second Life since 2003, sustainable business models remain rare, and the technology, especially hardware devices, is still in its early stages. Nevertheless, tech giants are investing immense sums in an augmented three-dimensional Internet. These approaches will be discussed below.

The potential of the digital world is vast, **encompassing enhanced virtual and augmented realities, immersive experiences,** and innovative business models. It offers unprecedented opportunities for remote collaboration, education, and entertainment. By leveraging advanced technologies like AI, blockchain, and IoT, the digital world can **revolutionize industries, streamline processes, and foster global connectivity.** Additionally, it enables personalized and interactive consumer experiences, driving economic growth and societal advancements while breaking down geographical barriers.

12.10.1 Meta (Metaverse)

Meta's metaverse	
Founder(s)	Mark Zuckerberg, Eduardo Saverin, Andrew McCollum, Dustin Moskovitz, Chris Hughes
Revenue 2024	134 billion USD
Employees	67k employees
Year of foundation	2004 (Facebook rebranded into Meta 2021)
Business idea or how the company earn money	A metaverse development company creates **virtual environments and experiences for users.** Revenue streams include virtual real estate sales, in-app purchases for virtual goods and services, advertising within the metaverse, **subscription models for premium features**, and partnerships with brands for virtual events and experiences, fostering a thriving digital ecosystem

Figure 12.28 metaverse outlines how the metaverse could work. The chart outlines key components of virtual environments, including spatialized audio, avatars, social interaction, and networking, which enhance immersive experiences. It also highlights cross-platform access, monetization, content creation tools, and interoperable standards, showing how virtual worlds integrate various aspects for user engagement and interaction.

About Meta (Metaverse)

Basic Prompt

Describe the history, products, and business model of the company in 200 words.

Meta's metaverse emerged from Zuckerberg's vision to create the **next-gen Internet.** Key steps included **acquiring Oculus, rebranding Facebook to META,** and heavily investing in VR/AR technologies. This led to the development of Horizon Worlds and a scalable ecosystem, supported by advanced infrastructure and strategic partnerships, fostering immersive digital experiences.

Meta's products include Oculus VR headsets for **immersive experiences** and Horizon Worlds, a social VR platform. Their **business model revolves around hardware sales, software/services like in-app purchases and subscriptions, advertising, virtual real estate** sales, and partnerships with brands for branded experiences.

This metaverse vision marks a fundamental shift in digital interaction, **blurring the lines between reality and imagination**. It offers new avenues for socialization, entertainment, commerce, and creativity in a **virtual world seamlessly integrated with the physical one.** Expanding AI data centers for designing AI solutions, including hardware and software in mixed reality, involves addressing corporate social responsibility and other ethical considerations. This includes supporting responsible data handling practices and safeguarding the integrity of elections.

Context

Your Advanced Question for Starting Prompt Engineering

Describe the environment of the industry, including major players, company culture, and historical context. How do suppliers and customers perceive this industry? Limit your response to 100 words.

The metaverse industry is dynamic, with Meta (formerly Facebook) leading amidst fierce **competition from tech giants like** Google**,** Microsoft**,** and **Apple**. Company cultures prioritize innovation and collaboration, drawing on diverse talent

to push virtual reality boundaries. Historically rooted in sci-fi and early VR, metaverse concepts gained traction in the 2000s with platforms like Second Life, **evolving with advancements in VR, AR, and blockchain.** Suppliers offer essential components, viewing the industry as a lucrative frontier for growth. Customers are intrigued by immersive experiences but wary of privacy and addiction concerns, driving companies to address these issues proactively.

Challenges and Opportunities

Basic Prompt

How did Meta change or disrupt the industry? How do competitors, the government, or customers react? (100 words)

Brands like Honda, Walmart, and Audi pioneer this digital frontier, **from virtual showrooms to telehealth consultations.** The Metaverse presents unparalleled opportunities for market expansion, personalized engagement, and operational efficiency. **AI and the Metaverse are transforming industries and jobs**. Embracing it, businesses cultivate brand loyalty, optimize marketing strategies, and drive revenue growth. As this dynamic ecosystem evolves, companies must navigate its complexities strategically, harnessing its transformative potential to stay ahead in the ever-changing landscape of digital commerce.

Discussion and Lessons Learned

Your Advanced Question for Starting Prompt Engineering

Explain the actions taken to address the challenge or capitalize on the opportunity. This could involve strategies implemented, decisions made, or interventions undertaken. What happened recently? Limit your response to 100 words.

Meta addressed the challenge of building the metaverse through **several strategic actions.** They **rebranded to Meta in October 2021,** shifting their focus to the metaverse. Meta acquired Oculus in 2014 to gain VR expertise and invested heavily in VR/AR technologies, developing the Oculus Rift, Quest headsets, and AR glasses. They **launched Horizon Worlds to create and explore virtual**

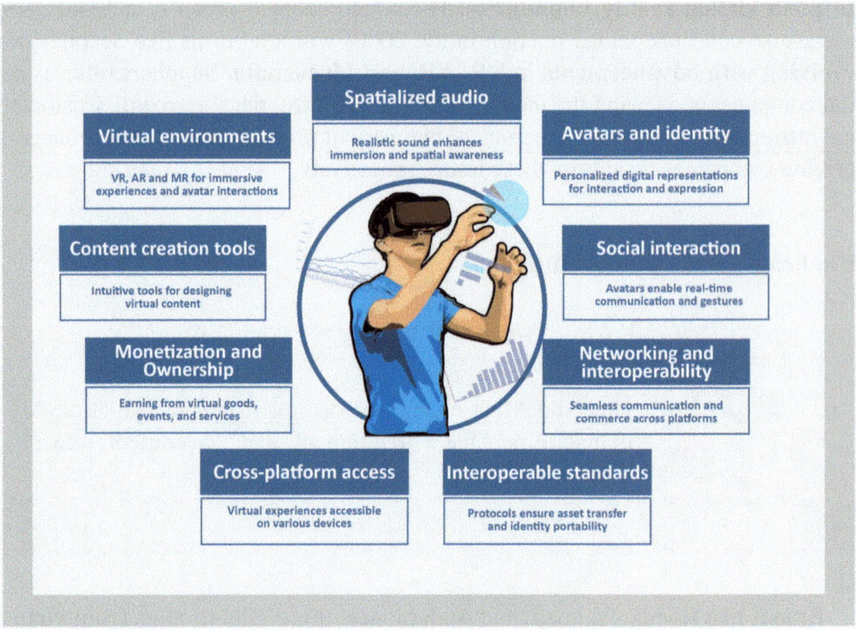

Fig. 12.28 Metaverse—how it could work

environments and built a scalable ecosystem with cloud computing, AI, and networking. Additionally, Meta formed strategic partnerships to foster diverse applications. Recent developments include enhancing user safety, expanding Horizon Worlds, and introducing Quest Pro for better immersive experiences. It might be **too early to deploy such solutions**, as the use cases are **not fully developed**, and users may **not yet be ready or willing to pay** for them.

12.10.2 Alphabet (Google's Metaverse Initiative)

Google 's metaverse	
Founders	Larry Page, Sergey Brin
Revenue	307 billion USD (Alphabet)
Employee	183k (Alphabet)
Year of foundation	1998 (rebranded from Google to Alphabet 2015)
Business idea and how the company earn money	Google generates **revenue primarily through advertising via its search engine, display network, and YouTube.** Additionally, it offers cloud computing services (Google Cloud Platform), hardware products (Pixel phones, Nest devices), and software subscriptions (Google Workspace). Data analytics and AI-driven services also contribute to its diverse revenue streams. Many of **these initiatives can be used to create a metaverse**

Alphabet has not announced a dedicated metaverse strategy but invests significantly in AR and immersive computing. Their AR efforts include projects like Google Lens and Google Maps' AR features. Google invest in AR and VR and space transportation (SpaceX), also Google Earth, Google Maps, Picasa, etc. **could be a part of building a future** Google **metaverse.**

Figure 12.29 shows some visuals that could be featured in Google's potential metaverse portfolio. The image showcases elements that could be part of Google's potential metaverse portfolio, featuring tools like Google Maps, Street View, 360-degree photography, and Google Earth. These technologies emphasize immersive mapping experiences, virtual exploration, and integration of spatial data, which could serve as foundations for a virtual or augmented reality environment within the metaverse.

About Alphabet (Google's Metaverse Initiative)

Basic Prompt

Describe the history, products, and business model of Google in the metaverse in 200 words.

Google, founded in 1998 by Larry Page and Sergey Brin, initially gained prominence through its search engine. Over the years, it **expanded into various technological domains** including cloud computing, software, hardware, and advertising. In 2015, Google reorganized under the parent company Alphabet Inc., allowing it to diversify its ventures.

In the context of the metaverse, Google's involvement is more **focused on augmented reality (AR) and immersive computing rather than a fully fledged metaverse strategy.** Sundar Pichai, CEO of Google, has emphasized AR as a significant area of development. Google's notable products in this realm include **Google Glass**, an AR headset first released in 2013, and Google Lens, a visual search tool that integrates AR functionalities. Moreover, Google has launched Project Starline, aiming to create immersive, lifelike video conferencing experiences without the need for specialized glasses. They also continue to **develop AR features in Google Maps and integrate AR into various services,** enhancing real-world navigation and interaction with digital content.

Google's business model in the metaverse-related space leverages its strengths in data analytics, AI, and cloud computing. Their partnership with MultiversX highlights their interest in supporting Web 3 and metaverse infrastructure. Google Cloud provides scalable, high-performance tools for decentralized applications, showcasing Google's **strategic investments in emerging technologies that could underpin future metaverse** experiences.

Context

Your Advanced Question for Starting Prompt Engineering

Describe the environment of the metaverse industry, including major players, company culture, and historical context. How do suppliers and customers perceive this industry? Limit your response to 100 words.

The metaverse industry is rapidly evolving, driven by major tech players like Meta, Google, Microsoft, and Apple. These companies are investing heavily in AR, VR, and AI technologies to build immersive digital environments. The company culture in these firms emphasizes innovation, collaboration, and the development of cutting-edge technologies. **Suppliers are focusing on advanced hardware and software components,** while **customers are showing increasing interest in immersive experiences for gaming, social interaction, and remote work**. Historical context includes the evolution from basic online virtual worlds to sophisticated, interconnected digital ecosystems, reflecting a broader trend toward digital transformation across industries.

Yet, concerns over data privacy and market dominance persist, drawing regulatory scrutiny. Despite challenges, Google's influence and innovation continue to shape the tech industry, driving advancements and setting standards for digital services and products.

Challenges and Opportunities

Basic Prompt

How did Google 's metaverse change or disrupt the industry? How do competitors or the government or customers react? Limit response to 100 words.

Google's involvement in the metaverse has advanced AR and immersive computing, significantly influencing the industry. Project Starline, Google Lens, and AR features in Maps have set new standards for immersive experiences. Competitors like Meta and Microsoft have accelerated their own metaverse initiatives, focusing on VR and AR technologies. Governments are scrutinizing these developments for regulatory compliance and privacy concerns. Customers show growing interest, driven by enhanced user experiences and practical applications in remote work, education, and social interaction. Google's approach has pushed the industry toward more integrated and user-friendly AR solutions, encouraging broader adoption and innovation.

Discussion and Lessons Learned

Your Advanced Question for Starting Prompt Engineering

Explain the actions taken to address the challenge or capitalize on the opportunity. This could involve strategies implemented, decisions made, or interventions undertaken. What happened recently? Limit your response to 100 words.

To address the challenges and opportunities in the metaverse, Google has **focused on advancing its AR and immersive computing technologies**. Recent actions involve forming Google Labs to oversee AR projects and leveraging its expertise in smart glasses through acquisitions like North. These initiatives aim to create more immersive, interactive experiences, pushing the boundaries of digital interaction and positioning Google as a key player in the evolving metaverse landscape.

12.10.3 Apple (Apple's Metaverse Initiative)

Apple	The metaverse initiative is part of Apple
Founders	Steve Jobs, Steve Wozniak, and Ronald Wayne
Revenue 2023	383 billion USD
Employee 2023	161 k employees
Year of foundation	1976 (started with initiatives in VR and AR in the mid-2010s)
Business idea and how the company earn money	Apple's business model focuses on **premium hardware sales, software services,** and digital content. The company earns money from selling devices like iPhones, iPads, and Macs, alongside revenue from services like the App Store, Apple Music, iCloud, and AppleCare. **Apple created its own ecosystem**

Figure 12.30 indicates how APPLE could generate an Eco-System for the Metaverse. Apple's approach to the metaverse focuses on augmented and mixed reality through devices like the Apple Vision Pro headset, powered by the new VisionOS operating system. While Apple avoids using the term "metaverse" explicitly, it aims to offer immersive experiences for collaboration, entertainment, and productivity

About Apple (Apple's Metaverse Initiative)

Basic Prompt

Describe the history, products, and business model of Apple in the context of the metaverse in 200 words.

Apple, founded in 1976 by Steve Jobs, Steve Wozniak, and Ronald Wayne, **disrupted technology with products like the iPhone,** iPad, and Mac. Its ecosystem encompasses software (iOS, macOS), services (Apple Music, iCloud), and accessories, driving revenue through product sales and subscriptions.

Apple's journey into the metaverse realm **began with its investments in augmented reality (AR) and virtual reality (VR) technologies.** The company has been developing AR capabilities since the mid-2010s, launching ARKit in 2017, a platform for creating AR experiences on iOS devices (Decrypt) (XR Today). In 2023, Apple unveiled its **first mixed reality headset, the Vision Pro**, which integrates both AR and VR functionalities. This device, priced at $3,499, emphasizes "spatial computing" and aims to enhance the immersive experience by allowing users to interact with digital content as if it were physically present in their space. Apple's Vision Pro operates on **visionOS, a dedicated operating system** designed for mixed reality. This system supports a range of applications, including **work, entertainment, gaming, and communication,** aiming to create a seamless blend of digital and physical worlds (Decrypt) (XR Today). The headset features advanced technologies such as hand-tracking, eye-tracking, and high-resolution displays to provide a more intuitive and immersive user experience (CoinTelegraph).

Apple's **business model in the metaverse area focuses on selling premium hardware integrated with sophisticated software and services.** By leveraging its ecosystem, Apple aims to provide a cohesive and high-quality user experience, differentiating itself from competitors like Meta and Microsoft.

Context

Your Advanced Question for Starting Prompt Engineering

Describe the environment of the industry, including major players, company culture, and historical context. How do suppliers and customers perceive this industry? Limit your response to 100 words.

Apple operates within a dynamic tech ecosystem alongside industry giants such as Google, Microsoft, Amazon, and Facebook. Renowned for its commitment to innovation and design excellence, **Apple has pioneered consumer electronics, software, and services.** Its vertically integrated approach ensures seamless user experiences across devices and platforms. Suppliers value Apple's brand and scale, while customers laud its premium products and privacy measures. However, the company faces ongoing scrutiny regarding market dominance and app store policies. Despite challenges, Apple's influence permeates the tech landscape, driving trends and setting benchmarks for quality and innovation in consumer technology.

Challenges and Opportunities

Basic Prompt

How did Apple change or disrupt the metaverse industry? How do competitors, the government, or customers react? 100 words

Fig. 12.29 Google's potential metaverse portfolio

Apple faces the challenge of maintaining its position as a leader in consumer technology and invented the smartphone 2010. Apple disrupted the metaverse industry by launching the Vision Pro headset, which integrates advanced AR and VR functionalities. This device, with its high-quality design and user-friendly interface, raised industry standards for mixed reality experiences. Competitors like Meta and Microsoft accelerated their innovation efforts in response, striving to keep pace with Apple's advancements. Governments are scrutinizing these developments for regulatory and privacy implications. Customers have shown significant interest, appreciating Apple's seamless integration of hardware and software, although some concerns remain about the high cost.

Discussion and Lessons Learned

Your Advanced Question for Starting Prompt Engineering

Explain the actions taken to address the challenge or capitalize on the opportunity. This could involve strategies implemented, decisions made, or interventions undertaken. What happened recently? Limit your response to 100 words.

Fig. 12.30 Eco-system

Apple navigates challenges by prioritizing innovation, investing in R&D, and diversifying revenue streams. Recent initiatives include expanding services like Apple Music and Apple TV+ and advancing privacy features across its product lineup. To address challenges and capitalize on opportunities in the metaverse, Apple introduced the Vision Pro headset, emphasizing advanced AR and VR capabilities with a seamless user experience. The strategy includes developing visionOS, a dedicated operating system, and integrating it with existing Apple ecosystems like iOS and macOS. This approach positions Apple as a leader in mixed reality, prompting competitors to innovate and governments to examine regulatory implications.

12.10.4 Review: Problems and Challenges of the Metaverse

User and businesses has concerns about privacy and data security. How to ensure user data is protected in immersive environments is critical. All three companies **face scrutiny over data handling and privacy concerns.** Each company develops **proprietary technologies and try to lock in the user**. **Interoperability** can enhance the creation of seamless experiences across different platforms and devices. However, the investment required is immense. **High costs are driven by advanced hardware** like Apple's Vision Pro, which is expensive and limits accessibility for many users.

Governments are increasingly monitoring these technologies for compliance with antitrust laws, data protection regulations, and consumer rights. These challenges require continuous innovation and collaboration with regulators and stakeholders to ensure a safe, inclusive, and accessible metaverse. **The three most important risks regarding competition in the metaverse for Google, Microsoft,**

Meta, and Apple are market saturation, consumer adoption, and regulatory challenges. While there are already some innovative application cases, widely demanded (mass market) or well-accepted business models are still not available.

Further Readings

Alphabet (2024) https://abc.xyz/investor/
Apple (2024) https://investor.apple.com/investor-relations/default.aspx
Meta (2024) https://investor.fb.com/home/default.aspx

Questions

1. How did Apple reshape the technology market?
2. How will the development of the metaverse impact social interactions and the way people connect with each other?
3. What are the potential economic opportunities and challenges that businesses might face as they integrate into the metaverse?

Appendix: Applied Prompt Engineering

In this chapter, you can try out Prompt Engineering with an example. An AI-philosophical application of Prompt Engineering should take place here, in which you conduct a discussion with the use of AI with your friends and family. Please consider this as a starting prompt to initiate the discussion. Please take the following contents and transform them into the AI Prompt schema.

Philosophical conversation with and about AI
Niklas Luhmann (well-known German sociologist) argued that **complexity can only be reduced by adding more complexity.** In the context of AI, this means that in a complex Internet—full of fake news and security risks—humans alone can't accurately assess information. Advanced AI algorithms are needed to categorize and evaluate content, potentially through trust mechanisms or by separating the Internet into anonymous and personalized spaces, where individuals are accountable for their interactions. The question then arises: How can complexity for humans be reduced and fake news effectively addressed?
Plato, in around 380 BCE, already explored in his *Allegory of the Cave* that humans do not perceive the real world but only see it as shadows. This is also confirmed by more recent research, which shows that everyone perceives reality subjectively and therefore differently. How will we perceive the new world of the omniverse, and can we handle different avatars in different worlds and personalities at the same time?
The philosopher **Descartes** recognized for his insight **Cogito, ergo sum** ("I think, therefore I am"). Will IT systems also be classified as an "I" if they continue to become smarter and potentially develop consciousness? How can we determine, when communicating over the Internet, whether we are interacting with a human or a machine (Turing test of AI)?
Kant, the great thinker, posed three key questions: **What can I know?** What should I do? What may I hope for? This leads to the question of what defines a human being. Can these questions also apply to AI? Will AI develop its own consciousness. And why should students learn for written exams when everything can be accessed via ChatGPT?

S. Schneider, L. Anderie, *Digital Business Management*,
https://doi.org/10.1007/978-3-031-83177-5

Many philosophers, like **Hume and Schopenhauer,** explored free will, with Schopenhauer arguing it's shaped by environmental factors. In the age of Big Data, some argue we are losing **free will** as behavior becomes more predictable, influenced by algorithms and social pressure to conform. However, others believe human agency remains intact. Self-reflection and decision-making complexity resist complete prediction, and access to data can enhance informed choices. The debate continues, balancing technological determinism with the persistence of human autonomy.
Do we have a fate, or can we determine our own lives? AI is increasingly presenting us with suggestions for our decisions, and we tend to accept these more and more (algorithmic authority). **Friedrich Nietzsche** believed that humans should accept and affirm their fate, a concept he called "Amor fati." - this means "love of fate". It refers to the concept of embracing everything that happens in life, including suffering loss and happiness, as necessary and meaningful. However, isn't it also possible for us to influence our fate?
In the 1990s, chess grandmasters were defeated by AI systems (e.g. IBM's Deep Blue) that were trained by humans and fed with a limited set of chess rules. Conversely, in the more complicated game of Go, a grandmaster was defeated by a Google system called AlphaGo that was trained by another AI. These systems were not provided with the rules; instead, two AI systems played against each other and improved continuously. **Will AI systems become more intelligent than humans**, and will there be a point where they develop into superintelligence, beyond which this development becomes irreversible?

Copyrights and Legal Information

Pictures in the chapter 'B2C E-Commerce Online Shops' generated with ChatGPT and DALL-E.

Airbnb: © Airbnb. Airbnb is a registered trademark of Airbnb, Inc.
Alphabet: © Alphabet. Alphabet is a registered trademark of Alphabet Inc.
Alibaba: © Alibaba. Alibaba is a registered trademark of Alibaba Group Holding Limited.
Amazon: © Amazon. Amazon is a registered trademark of Amazon.com, Inc.
Amazon Web Services (AWS): © Amazon. Amazon Web Services is a registered trademark of Amazon.com, Inc.
Apple: © Apple. Apple is a registered trademark of Apple Inc.
Bing: © Microsoft. Bing is a registered trademark of Microsoft Corporation.
ChatGPT: © OpenAI. ChatGPT is a registered trademark of OpenAI LP.
eBay: © eBay Inc. eBay is a registered trademark of eBay Inc.
Facebook (Meta): © Meta Platforms, Inc. Facebook is a registered trademark of Meta Platforms, Inc.
Google / Alphabet: © Google LLC. Google is a registered trademark of Google LLC.
Gemini: © Google LLC. Gemini is a registered trademark of Google LLC.
LinkedIn (Microsoft): © Microsoft Corporation. LinkedIn is a registered trademark of Microsoft Corporation.
Meta (Metaverse): © Meta Platforms, Inc. Meta is a registered trademark of Meta Platforms, Inc.
LinkedIn (Microsoft): © Microsoft Corporation. LinkedIn is a registered trademark of Microsoft Corporation.
Microsoft / LinkedIn: © Microsoft Corporation. Microsoft is a registered trademark of Microsoft Corporation.
Microsoft Azure: © Microsoft Corporation. Microsoft Azure is a registered trademark of Microsoft Corporation.
Netflix: © Netflix, Inc. Netflix is a registered trademark of Netflix, Inc.
OpenAI/Chat GPT: © OpenAI. OpenAI is a registered trademark of OpenAI LP.

S. Schneider, L. Anderie, *Digital Business Management*,
https://doi.org/10.1007/978-3-031-83177-5

Index

S. Schneider, L. Anderie, *Digital Business Management*,
https://doi.org/10.1007/978-3-031-83177-5